EFFECTIVE PROTOTYPING WITH EXCEL

A Practical Handbook for
Developers and Designers

Nevin Berger

Michael Arent

Jonathan Arnowitz

Fred Sampson

ELSEVIER

The Morgan Kaufmann Series in Interactive Technologies
AMSTERDAM · BOSTON · HEIDELBERG · LONDON
NEW YORK · OXFORD · PARIS · SAN DIEGO
SAN FRANCISCO · SINGAPORE · SYDNEY · TOKYO
Morgan Kaufmann is an imprint of Elsevier

MORGAN KAUFMANN PUBLISHERS

Morgan Kaufmann Publishers is an imprint of Elsevier.
30 Corporate Drive, Suite 400, Burlington, MA 01803, USA

This book is printed on acid-free paper.

© 2009 by Elsevier Inc. All rights reserved.

Library of Congress Cataloging-in-Publication Data
Application Submitted

ISBN: 978-0-12-088582-4

For information on all Morgan Kaufmann publications,
visit our Web site at www.mkp.com or www.elsevierdirect.com

Printed and bound by CPI Group (UK) Ltd, Croydon, CR0 4YY

Transferred to Digital Print 2012

EFFECTIVE PROTOTYPING
WITH EXCEL

The Morgan Kaufmann Series in Interactive Technologies

Series Editors: Stuart Card, PARC; Jonathan Grudin, Microsoft; Jakob Nielsen, Nielsen Norman Group

CONTENTS

DEDICATIONS

In memory of Gene Berger and Sam Norman.
-NB

To my loving and supportive wife, Jacqueline, and children, Nick and Vanessa.
-MA

I gratefully acknowledge the love and support of my children, Warren, Willy, Ariel, and Miranda Sampson, without whom there would be no point; the inspiration of music by Philip Glass, Frank Zappa, David Byrne, Moby, and Blondie; and the unyielding persistence of the lovely yet talented Spanky Kushner, my lead critic, who keeps me honest.

I dedicate this volume to the memory of James Julius Sampson, whose mission in life was to teach compassion: *May the long-time sun shine upon you, all love surround you, and the pure light within you guide you all the way on.*
-FS

I dedicate this book for my life-partner and spouse Minne Fekkes.
-JA

ACKNOWLEDGMENTS

The authors thank our reviewers, who contributed so much to this book: John Armitage, Deborah Mayhew, and Dirk-Jan Hoets. With their thoughtful comments and attention to detail, we are confident the only errors that remain are our own.

Lastly, we would like to make special mention of an essential figure in the creation of this book: Diane Cerra. Diane was the guiding force behind this book, and the series of which it is a part. She helped to guide this work to its present shape more than anyone else. We are especially grateful, and thank Diane from the bottom of our hearts. Diane, the next Timpano is in your honor.

PART 1

TURNING EXCEL INTO A PROTOTYPING TOOL

You might be an experienced interaction designer who never dreamed of using Microsoft Excel as a prototyping tool, or you might be new to prototyping and looking to use a tool you already have for your first prototyping exercise. Either way, in Part 1 of *Effective Prototyping With Excel* you will learn how easy it is to adapt Excel as a prototyping tool.

- In Chapter 1 you will consider the challenge faced by one software developer.
- In Chapter 2 you will create your first Excel prototype and learn how easy it really is to do so.
- In Chapter 3 you will set up an Excel prototyping canvas, the basis for all Excel prototypes.
- In Chapter 4 you will set up an Excel prototyping template to help you become a prototyping power user.

CHAPTER 1

A DEVELOPER'S DILEMMA

In this chapter you will learn

- A case study
- The benefits of using Excel® for prototyping
- The productivity and collaboration opportunities
- Our goal in creating this book

Note

If you are eager to dive immediately into Excel prototyping, skip ahead to the "How to create your first Excel prototype" section of Chapter 2, on page 16.

A Case Study

In an unnamed software company, long ago and far away, a developer learned that his product was going to have little access to the company's user interface design resources. This meant that he received no help with the design—only random, ad hoc advice from product stakeholders. The developer was concerned about his product's usability. He did not want to see his efficient coding wasted on a less than optimal user interface design. He heard that some user interface designers had set up a stealth prototyping service to assist developers who needed some unscheduled and unbudgeted help. How such a thing was possible he didn't know or care; he needed their help.

In desperation the developer went to the designers' Friday office hours. He thought he would need a whole day to mock up a prototype based on the functional requirements he had received. He was disappointed to hear that he would have only an hour of the designers' time and could not imagine that he might walk away with anything that resembled a codeable prototype.

At the prototyping office, the two designers explained that they would develop the prototype together; he would get enough direction so that he could do the rest himself. He could not believe it, but what could he do? He did not know any prototyping tools, nor did he have the skills to use such tools.

Much to his surprise, the designers opened Microsoft Excel and used a template file to implement his designs. The file looked like nothing he had ever seen in Excel before. The spreadsheet grid was changed into a layout grid, and the worksheets resembled software window layouts rather than spreadsheets. He learned in the session how, by using only copy and paste commands, the designers could quickly create his basic window layout. In fact, within the hour the two designers finished the work he needed and gave him an Excel file with his designs.

Back at his own office, the developer was satisfied with the results until he realized that there were some functions that had been neglected. At first he thought he had to wait until the next Friday for another appointment with the designers. But when he opened the Excel file and realized that, because he had used Excel before to create spreadsheets, he was very familiar with the software's features. With no more training than that short session with the designers, he started to add the missing functionality.

Within the Excel file he found worksheets with the widgets and buttons he needed and even a worksheet of instructions. He found it easy to copy buttons and to add fields and text. He made a few mistakes, but **CTRL-Z** always undid them. In fact, he learned, as with normal Excel use, that **CTRL-Z** undid and **CTRL-Y** redid multiple steps. This allowed him to make changes, back up, and go forward to compare his changes before committing to them. No one taught him this prototyping technique; he stumbled on it by exploring the skills he had already learned with Excel for creating spreadsheets.

After what he thought of as playing around, he realized that he had put the finishing touches on his prototype and had something to show product management. Without thinking about it, the developer became an Excel prototyper and had produced a good enough prototype of his application screens within an hour.

This book will share with you this developer's experience with the simplicity and ease of Excel prototyping. Having worked in many companies and seen how using Excel as a prototyping tool helped designers, developers, and product managers better express their requirements, we feel that we have the experience with Excel prototyping to empower you as well.

Introduction

This book is about how to prototype with Excel (or another spreadsheet application with similar functionality).

This book will also touch lightly on the larger topic of prototyping. Although the book does not attempt to completely cover the topic of prototyping, it will discuss prototyping as it relates to prototyping with Excel. For a comprehensive discussion on prototyping, we refer the reader to our first book, *Effective Prototyping for Software Makers*.

Excel is an amazing prototyping tool. It is amazing because it is the only tool we know that combines these advantages into a single tool:

- Prototyping flexibility
- Efficiency and ease of use
- Professional results
- No special skills required
- Readily available

Excel Prototyping

"Using Excel for prototyping? I don't get it!"

This is a common reaction from people when we first try to describe prototyping with Excel. The concept is far from what you use Excel for in your daily work. For some it is like claiming that their washing machine can mow the lawn. People cannot visualize how it can be done until they see it.

When you look at Excel, you probably just see a spreadsheet; you just can't think outside the table cell. To understand Excel as a prototyping tool, you will have to step out of the mental model that says Excel is only a spreadsheet application. This book will show you how.

Prototyping Flexibility

As a prototyping tool, Excel is not only easy to use, it is quite flexible for the various methods of prototyping. You can create static screen wireframes, screens with click-through interaction and navigation, and even prototypes that can be optimized for different types of usability testing.

To illustrate what we mean, the following images are prototypes created in Excel. You can experience these prototypes for yourself by visiting the book's Website and downloading each of these examples as native Excel files: www.effectiveprototyping.com/ep_excel/.

An interaction flow diagram in Excel, which might be the most basic visualization of a software concept, is illustrated in Figure 1.1.

Storyboard Prototypes

A *storyboard* is a narrative prototype, usually created in the early stages of the software-making process, to articulate business and marketing requirements in the form of a usage scenario or story. These stories narrate the user actions needed to perform tasks as specified by marketplace, customer, and user requirements. These requirements are interpreted into a scenario before the storyboarding process begins. Because requirements drive the storyboarding process, they provide early insight into what users, the software, and the system are meant to do in conjunction with each other. The primary goal of a storyboard is to align the design team's thinking to the goals and behaviors of the software, regardless of the screen design.

Figure 1.2 is an example of a storyboard in which an interactive narrative is shown through text and images. The user interface design embodied in an Excel prototype reflects this narrative as you click from one screen to another, with each screen contained in a worksheet.

Figure 1.1.
Interaction flow diagram in Excel.

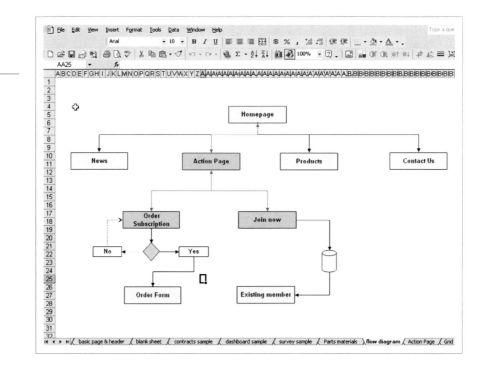

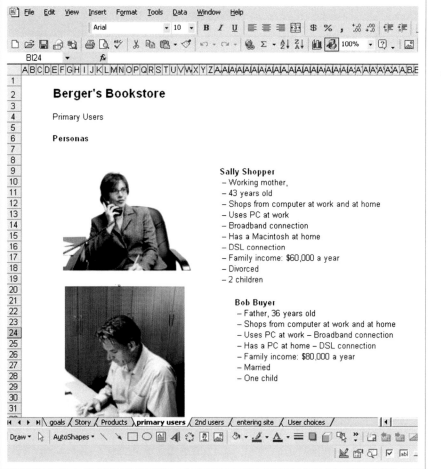

Figure 1.2.

A storyboard portraying envisioned software interaction.

Wireframe Prototypes

A *wireframe* is a narrative prototype, usually created in the beginning of the design process. The narration is usually derived from a use case or scenario, often the same scenario used in a storyboard. This prototype shows *flowcharts*, high-level sketches visualizing conceptual assumptions about the product structure and general inter-action. The primary goal of this method is to get a design team to agree on basic concepts.

Figure 1.3 shows a rough wireframe of a Website that was created in minutes. This tool allows functional and rough conceptual issues to be separated from the detailed, more precise designs that should come later.

Figure 1.4 shows a medium-fidelity wireframe that evolved from the rough wireframe shown in Figure 1.3. The design of a medium-fidelity wireframe can help establish a visual design direction. It can also show a more evolved concept that includes interaction. As a result, stakeholders get a better idea of the design commitment without your prototyping a finished product.

Figure 1.5 shows a similar design to the previous two figures but with higher visual and content fidelity, to serve as the specification.

Paper Prototypes

A *paper prototype* is an interactive prototype that consists of a paper mockup of the user interface. The interface represents a fully functional interface that allows you to

Figure 1.3.

A screen from a rough wireframe of a Website.

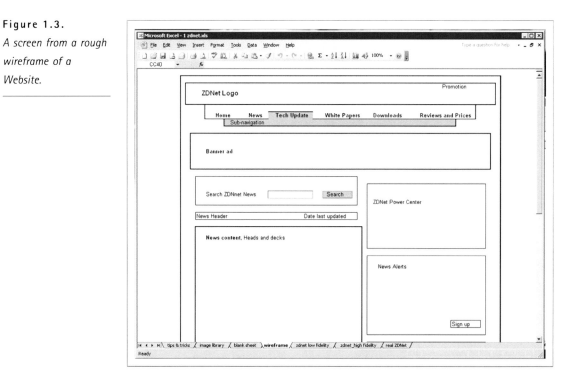

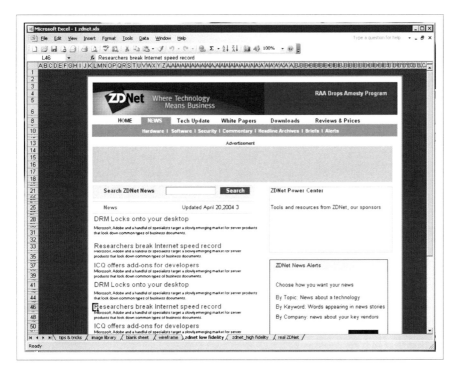

Figure 1.4.
A screen from a medium-fidelity prototype of a Website.

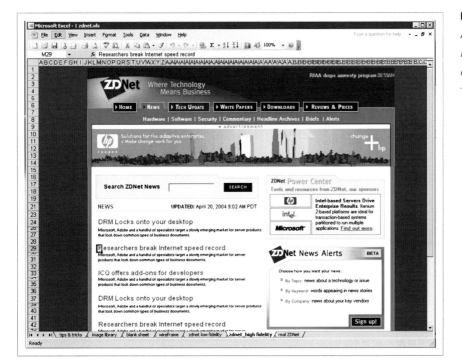

Figure 1.5.
A screen from a high-fidelity prototype of a Website.

usability-test a design. The intended audiences are targeted users who test the design and the software makers who use the prototype as a means to implement the software.

Digital Interactive Prototypes

A *digital interactive prototype* is a digital version of a paper prototype. Interactive prototyping shares the same objectives as paper prototyping; that is, they can both be used to

- Understand task flow and context of use
- Validate assumptions in scenarios, requirements, and user profiles
- Shape task sequencing and interaction design direction
- Evolve prototypes from early rough sketches to the next level of detail
- Validate a visual design direction

Figure 1.6 shows that Excel can also be used to create interactive prototypes of list-driven products such as email clients.

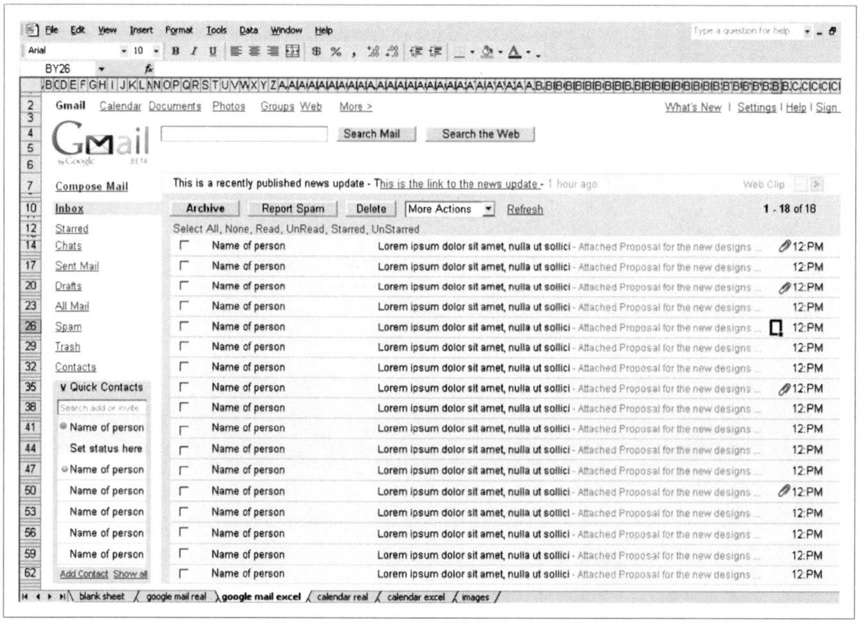

Figure 1.6.

Screen from a prototype of a list-driven product—an email client.

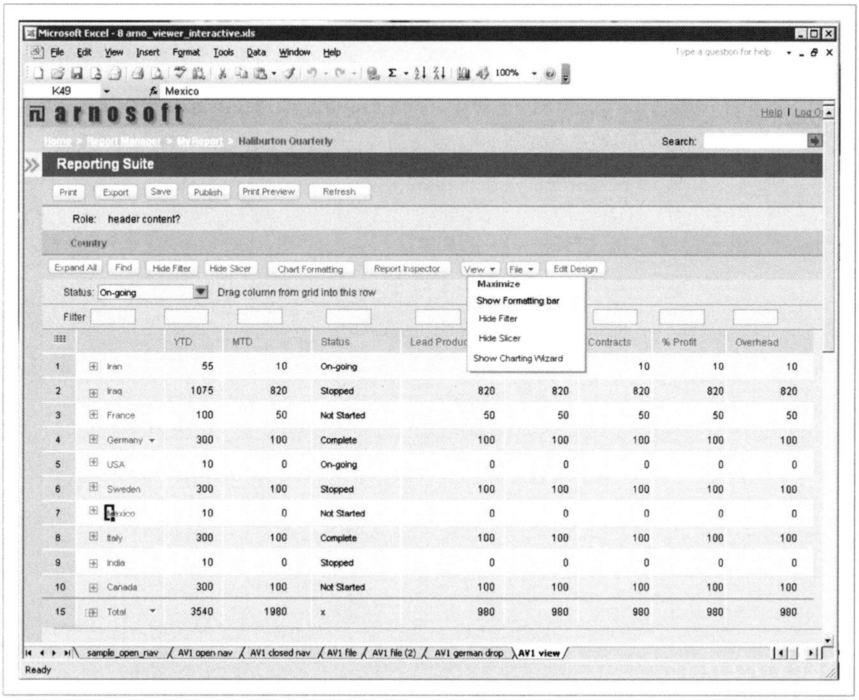

Figure 1.7.
Screen from a prototype of interactive business software.

Figure 1.7 shows that Excel can also be used to prototype interactive business software. Notice the drop-down list, which was activated by a user clicking on the menu button.

Excel can also be used to prototype a range of designs, from Windows applications to AJAX-enabled Websites. Figure 1.8 (page 14) shows an example of a Windows application prototyped in Excel.

Efficient and Easy

By using Excel, the user can quickly and easily create user interface prototypes. The results are both quick and professional looking. We know of few other tools that offer this level of quality for a minimum of effort. Nearly all the effort involves using features that you probably already know: cut, copy, paste, cell formatting, and so on.

Professional Results

Regardless of the level of prototyping, Excel's adapted layout grid ensures that you get professional-looking layouts. Field alignment and spatial distribution have never

Figure 1.8.

Screen from a prototype of a Windows application. Prototype courtesy of Dirk-Jan Hoets.

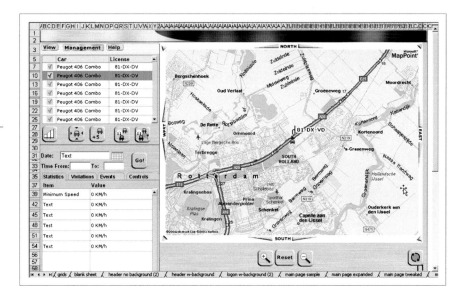

been easier. Applying company colors and graphics can also be automated, allowing you to leverage the work of professional designers in your company to achieve professional-looking results.

No Special Skills Required

Prototyping in Excel requires only the use of basic desktop and Excel functionality. You can create forms, tabs, and tables using simple cell formatting. You can create 3-D borders for buttons or input fields simply by using cell borders. Field length can be changed via drag and drop or copy and paste. The only mental shift required is to stop thinking of the Excel grid as a spreadsheet, instead thinking of it as a graphics layout grid.

Readily Available

If you want your prototyping process to empower your software makers, you need a tool that everyone can use. Excel is a readily available tool; it is frequently included on business computers. For the few of you who don't have Excel, there are alternatives such as OpenOffice, available for free, that put 90 percent of the techniques from this book to use, although some commands will differ.

Still Not Convinced?

As we start to explain the process of prototyping with Excel, you will eventually understand how it is done. The figures in this chapter help, but you might need some quick, hands-on experience, which we cover in the next chapter.

At our tutorials and seminars at PeopleSoft, Ziff Davis Media, Google, and SAP Labs, we encountered the same doubt. After our demonstrations, the results were the same at all these venues: Excel became an important tool in the audience's proto- typing toolbox. This is not to say that Excel is *the* essential tool; Excel does not fulfill all prototyping needs. But for basic wireframes and digital interactive prototypes, Excel is an efficient tool you will not want to be without.

Who Should Consider Using Excel?

This book is for anyone who needs to prototype an interface for desktop software or the Web. It is intended not only for designers but for anyone who is part of the software- making process. Software makers include the full range of participants, from people with extensive graphics experience to those with little or no graphics background.

Some of the professionals we have seen using Excel for prototyping include

- Developers and programmers
- Web designers
- Product managers
- Information architects
- User experience professionals
- Usability engineers
- Graphic designers

In short, any stakeholder who needs to express a software idea or requirement visu- ally or interactively can use Excel. We want to emphasize that this book is about how to prototype with Excel, not how to prototype in general.

Prototyping Productivity

Simply knowing the features that Excel offers is not enough to make use of the power of this tool. We have developed a methodology to ensure that Excel becomes a highly productive tool for you. In this book, you will learn the concept of the *Excel template*. A template can contain all the elements you need to make a prototype, with worksheets that are already built to your site specifications and layout grid for such things as

- Font styles
- Colors
- Graphics
- Icons
- Web widgets
- Input boxes

This all might sound too easy; it is if you think that you don't have to spend time creating these things yourself. With the methods you will learn from this book, setting up the template becomes simple. As a bonus, you can download templates already created for you to help you get started. Visit our Website at www.effective-prototyping.com/ep_excel to get some ideas of what's available.

Our Goal

Our goal in writing this book is for you to discover that Excel is as easy, productive, and flexible a prototyping tool as any that's available. So that you can try it yourself and see its potential, we show you how to use the features in Excel by beginning with a quick demonstration. Then we provide more detail to give you a working knowledge of all the features that you will need to build a prototype using Excel.

CHAPTER 2

GETTING STARTED: YOUR FIRST EXCEL PROTOTYPE

In this chapter you will learn

- Examples of Excel prototypes
- How to create your first Excel prototype
- About this book
- How to use this book
- How to use the associated files

Examples of Excel Prototypes

You need a quick and easy way to create prototypes. The prototyping tool should make credible-looking prototypes in variable degrees of fidelity. The tool should allow varying degrees of interactivity appropriate to your prototyping goals but not require you to code extensively. The ideal tool would also leverage skills that you already have so that you do not need to learn anything new. And the truly ideal tool would already be on your computer—for example, Microsoft Excel.

Look at the examples that follow (Figures 2.1–2.4, pages 20–21). These prototypes look as though they were made in a graphics tool, not a spreadsheet application. These prototypes were made possible by users learning to think of Excel as a graphics-based design tool rather than an application for spreadsheet calculations. After you make that mental leap, you will use styles, copy and paste, and drag and drop to unlock a new, very powerful prototyping tool.

How to Create Your First Excel Prototype

Let's assume that you are in a deadline situation. You have only 30 minutes in which to create a digital prototype to demonstrate a software concept at a design meeting with a couple of software engineers. The Excel prototype is based on a rough paper sketch that you have worked out with the product manager (Figure 2.5, page 22).

Figure 2.1.

A Google calendar interface built in Excel.

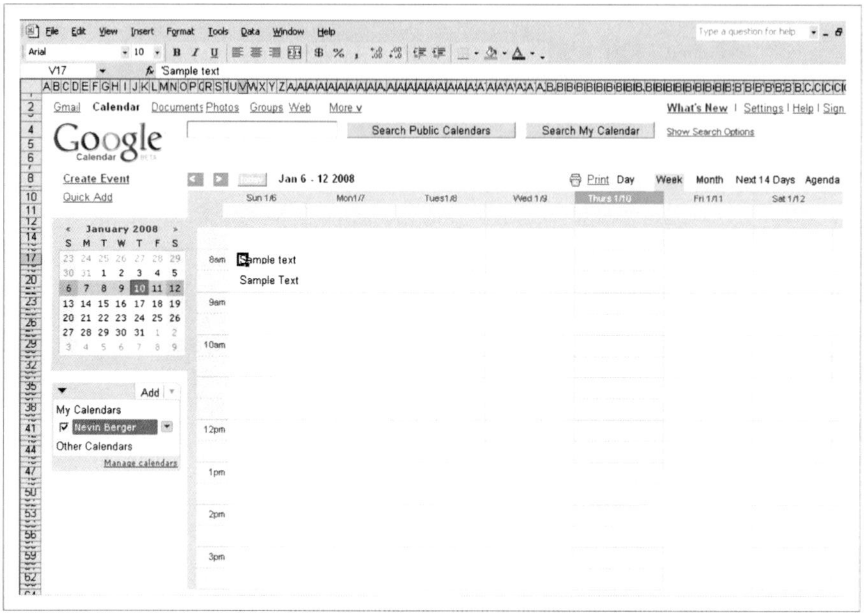

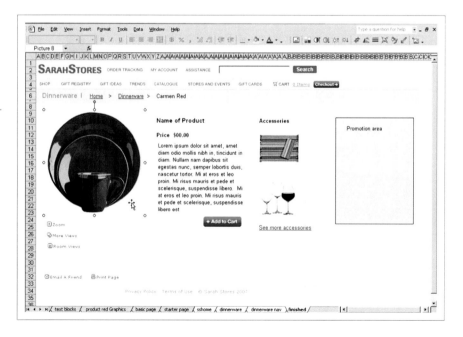

Figure 2.2.

A prototype for a housewares e-commerce site built in Excel.

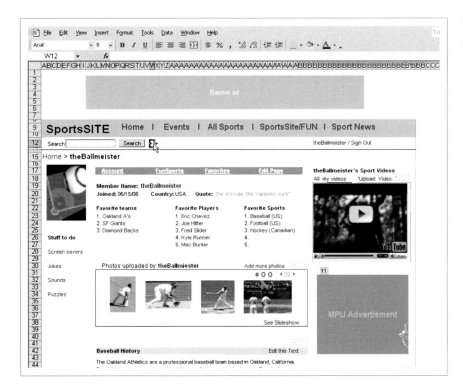

Figure 2.3.

An Excel interactive wireframe prototype of a sports Website.

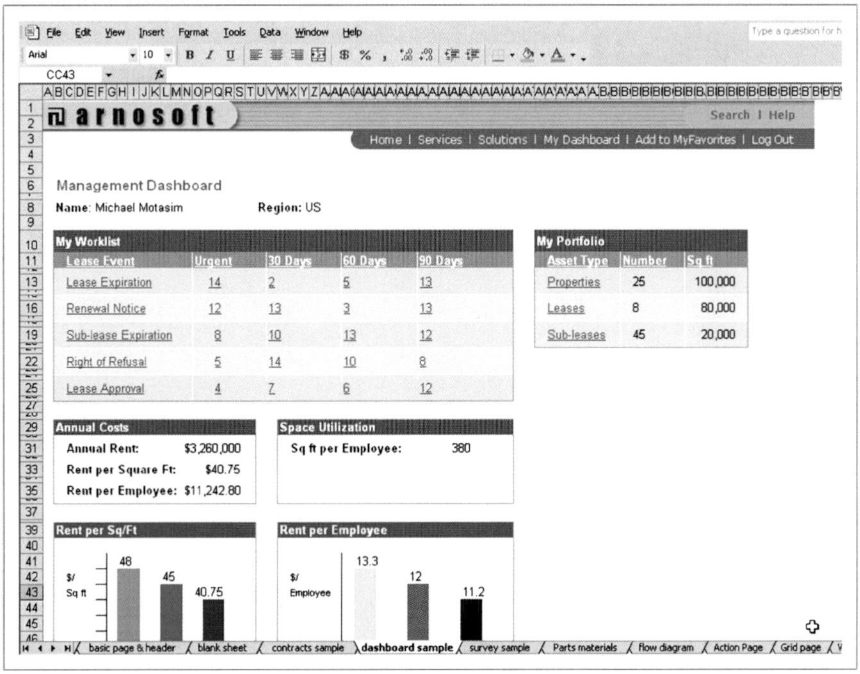

Figure 2.4.

An Excel dashboard prototype for a business software user interface.

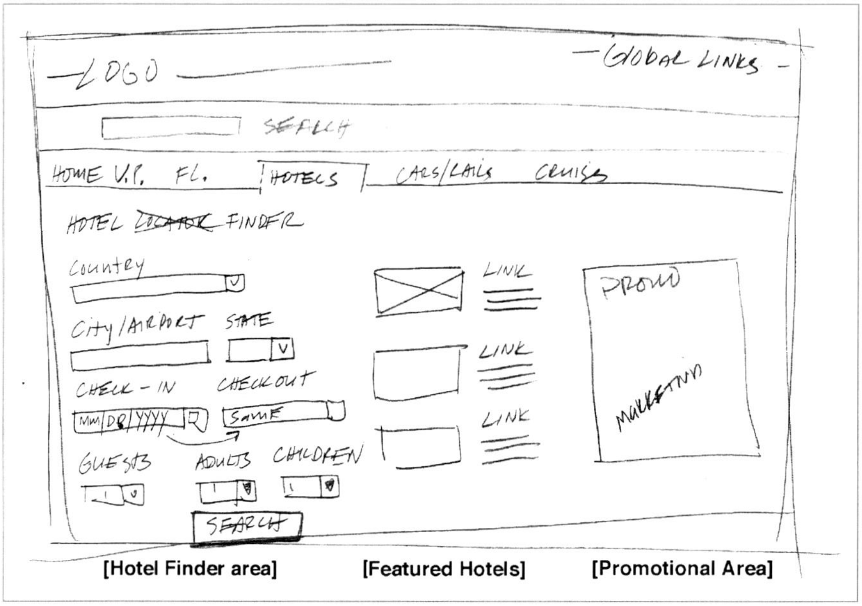

Figure 2.5.

The paper prototype sketch that serves as a basis for the ensuing Excel prototype building exercise.

Note

As with all the samples shown in this book, you can download a convenient ready-to-use template from the authors' Effective Prototyping Website: www.effectiveprototyping.com/ep_excel/.

To Adapt the Template:

Right-click the worksheet tab named **canvas**, choose **Rename** (Figure 2.6), and type in a new text label, Hotel Page (Figure 2.7).

Tip

You can also double-click the tab and type in the new name.

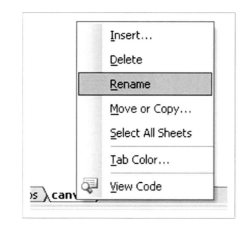

Figure 2.6.
The Rename function selected.

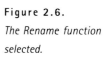

Figure 2.7.
The canvas worksheet tab renamed to Hotel Page.

To Add a Header:

1. Click the tab named **image library**, which includes premade graphics that you can use and reuse.

2. Select the graphic that includes the site logo and header, TravelGenie, by clicking it (Figure 2.8).

3. Copy the graphic by pressing **CTRL-C**.

4. Return to the **Hotel Page** tab; then press **CTRL-V** to paste in the header graphic.

5. With the graphic still selected, drag it to the upper-left corner of the worksheet.

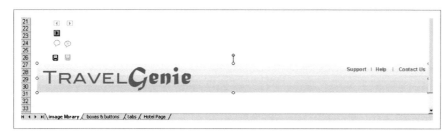

Figure 2.8.
The header graphic, TravelGenie, selected in the Image Library.

Note

The graphic should fill the entire width of the worksheet.

Hint

Place the cursor in cell A1 and then paste the graphic in the correct position (Figure 2.9).

6. Select the three rows below the header (rows 5, 6, and 7).

7. While the rows are still selected, right-click within the selected area and choose **Format Cells** from the menu.

8. In the Format Cells dialog box, click the **Patterns** tab; then select the gray box located two squares above the white box in the color palette (Figure 2.10).

Figure 2.9.

The header graphic, TravelGenie, pasted into the prototype screen.

Figure 2.10.

Applying a gray color to the three rows selected.

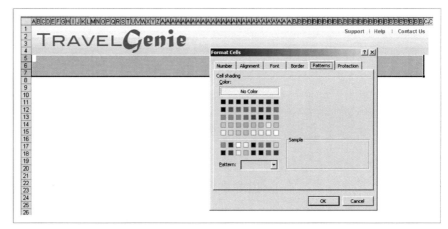

9. Click **OK**.

10. In cell B6, type in the name of the site: `TravelGenie`.

11. With the cell selected, click the **Bold** button (Figure 2.11).

To Add a Search Text Entry Box and Accompanying Search Button:

1. Click the **boxes and buttons** worksheet tab.

2. Select the entire text entry box (1) in row 17 (Figure 2.12).

3. With the box still selected, copy the box.

4. Return to the Hotel Page tab and select the cell that is two cells to the right of the TravelGenie text that you have just entered.

5. Paste the text entry box into position (Figure 2.13, page 26).

6. Return to the **boxes and buttons** worksheet and select the **Search** button.

7. Copy the **Search** button; then paste it to the right of the text entry box (Figure 2.14, page 26).

Figure 2.11.
Bolding the label Travel-Genie.

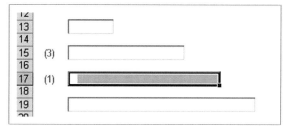

Figure 2.12.
The text entry box (1) selected for copying.

Figure 2.13.

The search text entry box pasted into position.

Figure 2.14.

The Search button pasted into position.

To Add Page Navigation:

1. Go to the **tabs** worksheet and find the navigation bar of tabs with **Hotel** selected.

2. Select the entire bar and copy it (Figure 2.15).

3. Return to the **Hotel Page** worksheet, select cell 8A, and paste the entire navigation bar into position (Figure 2.16).

Figure 2.15.

Navigation bar selected for copying.

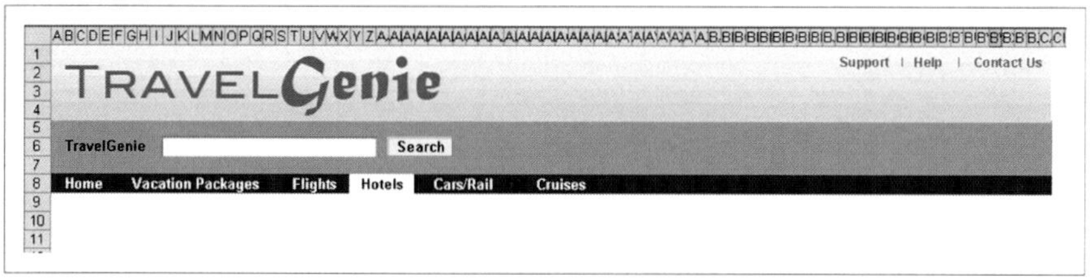

Figure 2.16.

The navigation bar pasted into the prototype worksheet.

To Build the Hotel Finder Area:

1. Select cell B10 and type in the text Hotel Finder; then make the text bold (Figure 2.17).

2. Go to the **boxes and buttons** worksheet; then select and copy the combo box graphic (3).

3. Be sure to copy the box as well as the graphic of the down arrow at the right end of the box (Figure 2.18).

4. Return to the **Hotel Page** worksheet and select cell C14.

Figure 2.17.
The text Hotel Finder added and bolded.

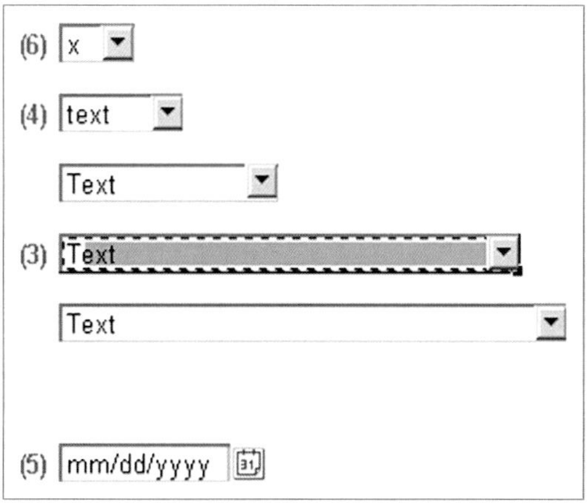

Figure 2.18.
The combo box and arrow graphic selected for copying.

5. Paste the combo box into position (Figure 2.19).

6. Select the cell at the far left of the combo box entry field; then type United States to replace the placeholder Text (Figure 2.20).

Figure 2.19.

Combo box graphic pasted into position.

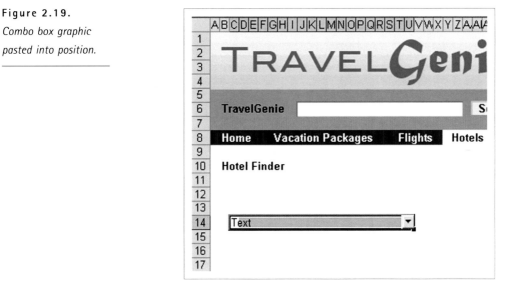

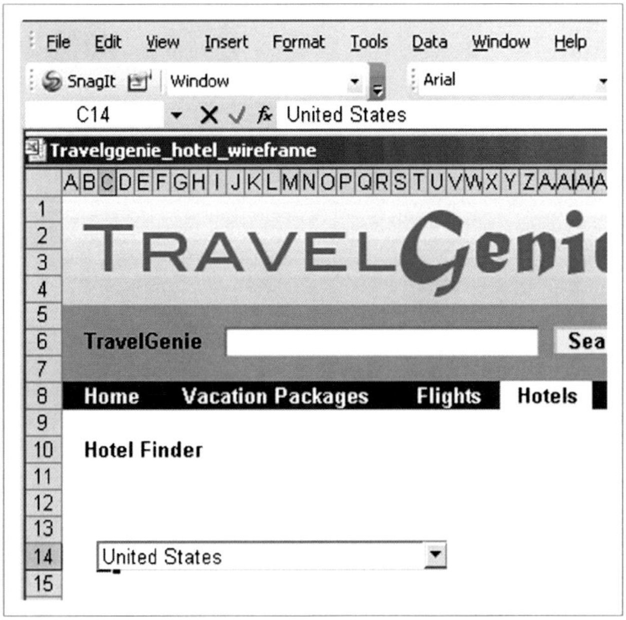

Figure 2.20.

Text added into combo box.

7. In the cell directly above the finished combo box, type in the label `Country`; then make the text bold (Figure 2.21).

8. Referring to Figure 2.5, use the same method to create the remainder of the text entry and combo boxes, labels, and entered text (boxes 3–6).

Note

Be sure to leave space for the text labels above each input box.

9. Copy the **Search Hotels** button (7) and paste it into position (see Figure 2.22, page 30).

To Create a Grouping Box Around the Hotel Finder Area:

1. Select all the cells that encompass the Hotel Finder area.

2. Right-click in the selected area and choose **Format Cells** from the menu.

3. In the Format Cells dialog box, click the **Border** tab.

4. Select the one-point black line style, and click the **Outline** icon (Figure 2.23, page 30).

An outline appears around the **Hotel Finder** grouping box (Figure 2.24, page 31).

Figure 2.21.
Combo box label text added above the combo box.

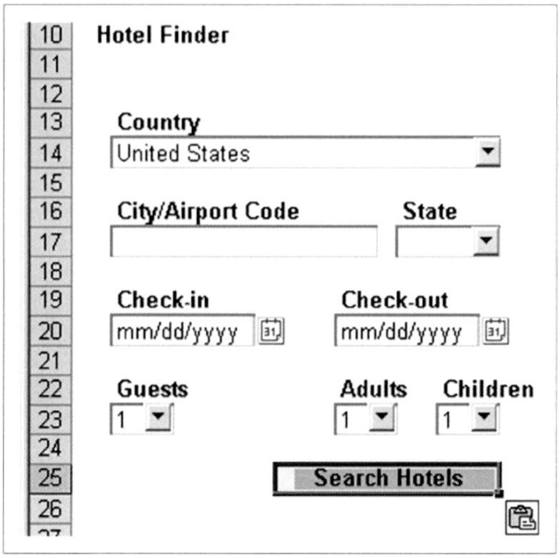

Figure 2.22.

The Search Hotels button added to the Hotel Finder area.

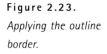

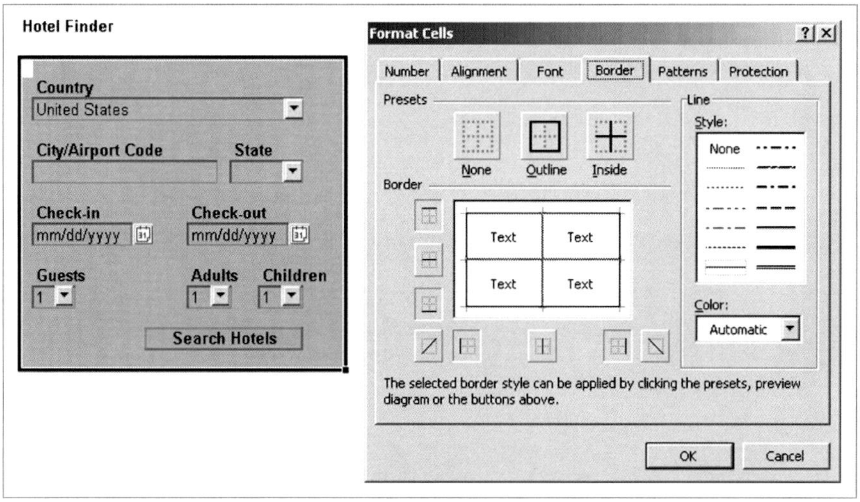

Figure 2.23.

Applying the outline border.

To the right of the Hotel Finder, you'll create and position placeholders for three images and accompanying descriptive text for the Featured Hotels area.

To Create the Placeholder, the Images, and Descriptive Text for the Featured Hotels Area:

1. To create the first placeholder image, select the **Rectangle** function in the **Drawing** menu.

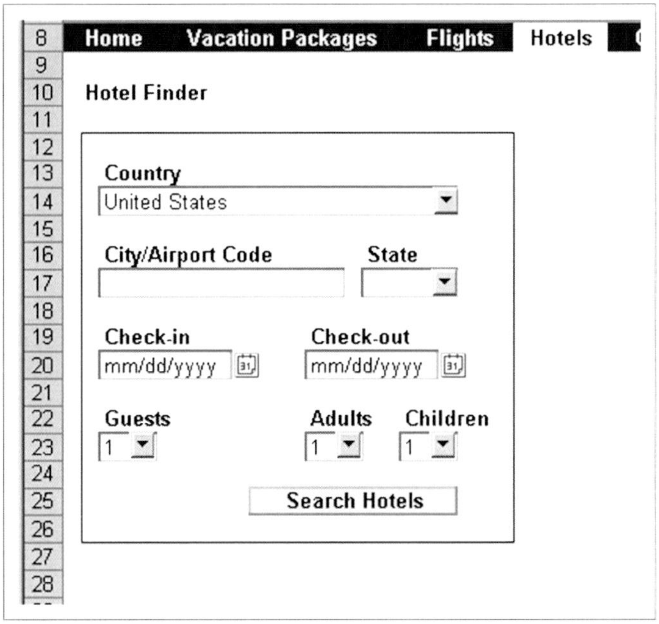

Figure 2.24.

A surrounding border added to the Hotel Finder area.

2. Click in the worksheet to the right of the Hotel Finder area and drag a rectangle shape (Figure 2.25, page 32).

3. Right-click the border of the rectangle that you just created and select **Format AutoShape** from the menu.

4. In the dialog box that appears, select a fill color of gray; then select the **No Line** color attribute (Figure 2.26, page 32).

5. To make the remaining image boxes, copy the one you just created; then paste it two times so that the boxes align vertically (Figure 2.27, page 33).

To Create the Placeholder Descriptive Text:

1. In the **image library** worksheet, copy the desired preformatted text and paste it in place to the right of the top placeholder box.

2. Paste two more copies of the text aligned vertically under the top placeholder text and aligned horizontally to the right of the placeholder images they are associated with (Figure 2.28, page 33).

To Create the Placeholder Promotional Information Area:

1. Select the Rectangle drawing tool again and draw a box for the promotional information area to the right of the Featured Hotels area.

Figure 2.25.

A placeholder rectangle positioned to the right of the Hotel Finder area.

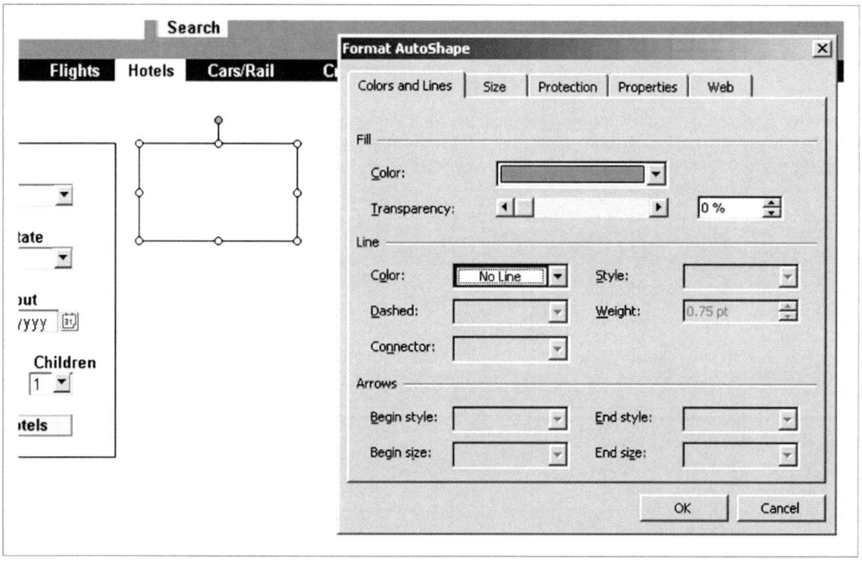

Figure 2.26.

The Format AutoShape dialog box.

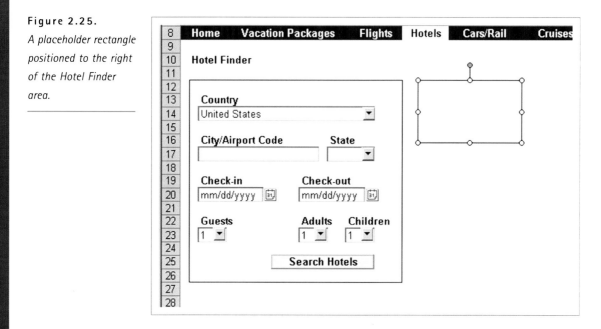

2. Right-click the rectangle, choose **Add Text** from the menu that appears (Figure 2.29), then type in the text `Promo`.

All the elements you need in your initial prototype are now assembled and arranged in the prototype worksheet (Figure 2.30, page 34). Save the file and send it to everyone on your team; the design meeting can begin on time!

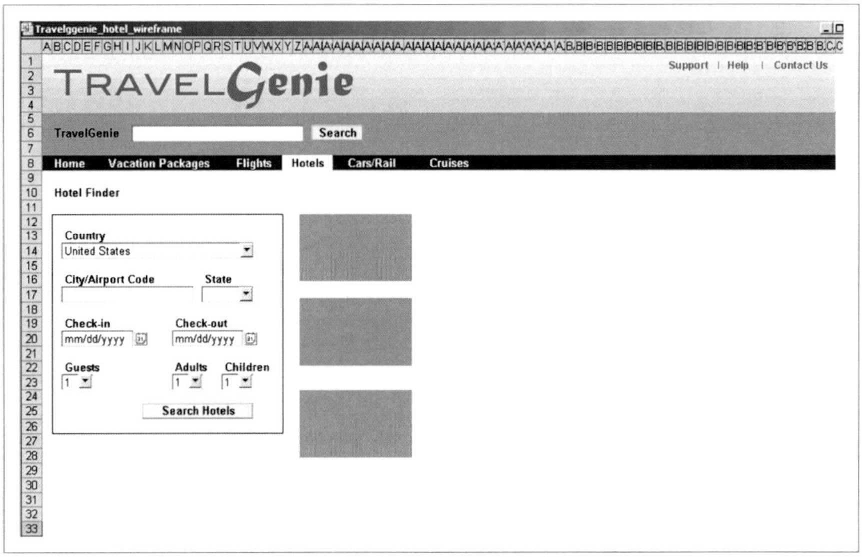

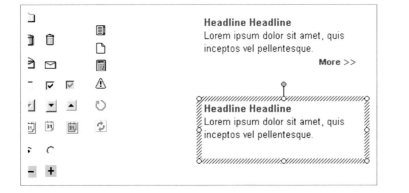

Figure 2.27.

Image boxes placed in vertical alignment.

Figure 2.28.

Preformatted text selected in the image library worksheet.

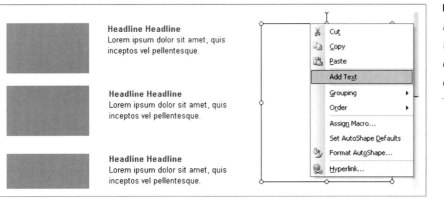

Figure 2.29.

Placeholder descriptive text added to the right of the Featured Hotels area.

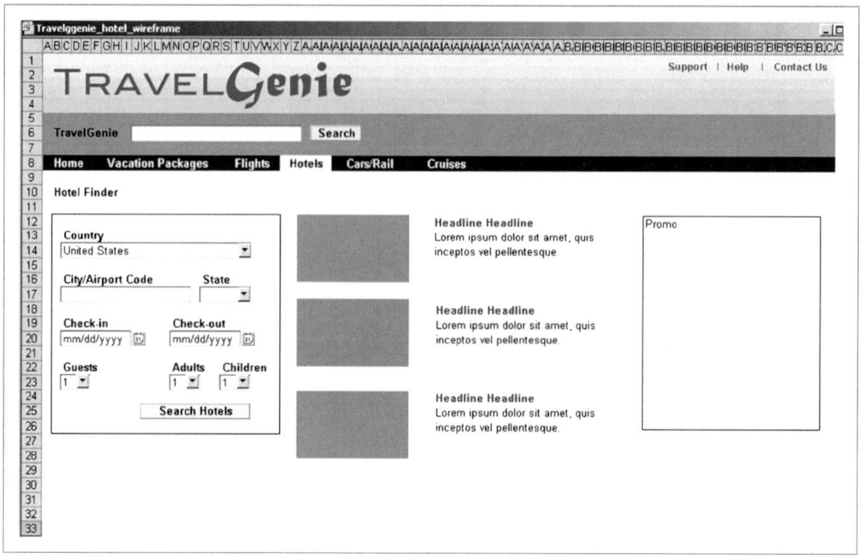

Figure 2.30.

A finished Excel prototype design.

Figure 2.30.
A finished Excel prototype design.

Summary

You have learned the first steps to becoming a successful Excel prototyper. Following similar steps in subsequent chapters will make you an even more accomplished Excel prototyper. You can start with a template, follow the step-by-step instructions, and learn both basic and advanced techniques of prototyping.

A Note About Excel

There are many spreadsheet applications now available in the marketplace. Aside from the dominant application, Microsoft Excel, other similar spreadsheet applications are now available for prototyping: Apple's Numbers, OpenOffice's Spreadsheet, and Google's Trixely. All these programs can do much the same thing in varying degrees; you only need to learn the different command structures and functions. Although we chose Excel due to its current pervasiveness, we do not necessarily recommend or endorse Excel to the exclusion of another spreadsheet application that you might already know. To use another product to achieve the same results, you might need to make a table that translates the Excel commands and functions portrayed in this book to those of your spreadsheet program. If you do make a translation table, we invite you to share it within the Effective Prototyping community by posting it to our book's Website: www.effectiveprototyping.com.

About This Book

This *how-to* style instructional book was inspired by our experience using Microsoft Excel as a rapid prototyping tool, a technique that was pioneered by former People-Soft engineer Mark Miller. (See Appendix B for more about our story on the discovery of Excel prototyping.) All the authors worked at PeopleSoft, in varying capacities, during the period from 2003–2005. We quickly saw the value of this unique use of Excel and proceeded to evolve the techniques from a simple tool to the robust rapid prototyping environment discussed in upcoming chapters. We were so excited about our discovery that we wanted to evangelize it by offering tutorials and writing this book. We decided that the best way to demonstrate how to use Excel is through practical examples of prototyping methods.

Each chapter will follow roughly this organization: what you will learn, introduction, how-to exercises, and summary. Each chapter begins with a brief list of what you will learn in the chapter, followed by a short introduction to the prototyping principles covered which will serve as the framework for the how-to examples. After the brief introduction, the body of the chapter focuses on a procedural, step-by-step instruction on how to perform the prototyping activity with Excel. The procedures are based on a case study scenario illustrated with supporting visual examples. Each chapter closes with a summary that is meant to wrap up the chapter as well as give you a hint of what to expect in the next chapter.

Excel has many redundant commands and ways to accomplish the various prototyping procedures. If there is an alternative way we know about, we will call it out in tips and notes, each clearly marked in a shaded box.

How to Use This Book

This book is structured and paced to guide you from an initial overview of Excel prototyping to presentations of more and more specific techniques of Excel prototyping. Accompanying each chapter are relevant principles of Excel prototyping that will become the structure from which we will describe the how-to techniques. Three different prototyping methods are used to demonstrate Excel prototyping through how-to procedures: storyboards, wireframes, and digital interactive prototypes.

You'll find that the procedures build on each other as you progress through the book. However, if you are already an Excel expert and familiar with many of its functions and techniques, you can skip through many of the procedures you already know and concentrate on the new parts that make prototyping in Excel come alive for you.

The examples and procedures in this book are based on Excel in Microsoft Office 2002 on Windows XP. You might need to adapt to the version of Excel on your computer.

How to Use the Associated Files

Although this book is a standalone how-to guide, it is accompanied by a set of templates and sample content, which can be found on our Website: www.effectiveprototyping.com.

You can download all the files in a single compressed archive from www.effective-prototyping.com/ep_excel/prototypes.zip. Enter the user name **excel** and the password **elsevier**.

We suggest that you download the files now so that they're available as you work through the book. As you begin each chapter, you might find it convenient to open the associated files for easy reference.

CHAPTER 3

BASICS: THE EXCEL PROTOTYPING CANVAS

In this chapter you will learn how to create a prototyping canvas.

Creating a Prototyping Canvas

To use Excel for prototyping, you will fundamentally change the way you use Excel. When you first open Excel, you see an empty traditional spreadsheet ready for you to begin entering data. To create prototypes, you will transform the traditional spreadsheet of delineated rows and columns into a blank canvas.

The metaphor of the painter's canvas is useful here because it has a great deal in common with what you are trying to accomplish: A blank canvas is the starting point for a creative person to visually express his or her ideas.

The parameters that you will use to format your canvas include

- Worksheet cell row height and column width set up specifically for prototyping
- Default font properties: font family, size, style, and colors
- Text alignment properties: horizontal and vertical, orientation, control (such as wrap text)
- Background color or background image
- No visible grid

In this series of exercises you will create an Excel canvas and set the options that make Excel a prototyping tool.

To Prepare a Canvas:

1. Open a new Excel workbook.
2. You only want to make one of the worksheets a canvas, so delete Sheet 2 and Sheet 3 by right-clicking each tab and clicking **Delete** (Figure 3.1, page 40).
3. Right-click the Sheet 1 tab and choose **Rename.** With the name of the tab highlighted, type Canvas.

To convert this sheet to a canvas, you will first hide the grid. The grid will still be there, but the grid lines will be invisible.

Figure 3.1.

Deleting unwanted worksheets.

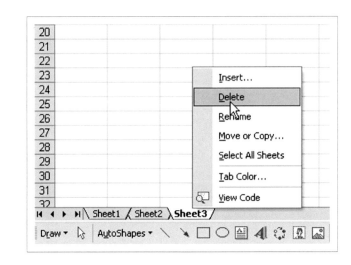

To Hide the Grid:

1. Choose **Tools > Options** from the menu bar (Figure 3.2).
2. In the Options dialog box, select the **View** tab and deselect the **Gridlines** check box (Figure 3.3).
3. Click **OK**.

The gridlines are now invisible.

Figure 3.2.

Choosing the Options function.

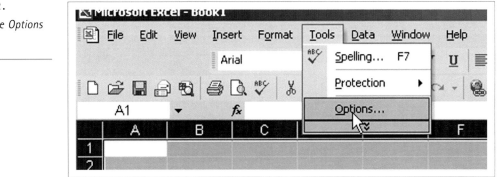

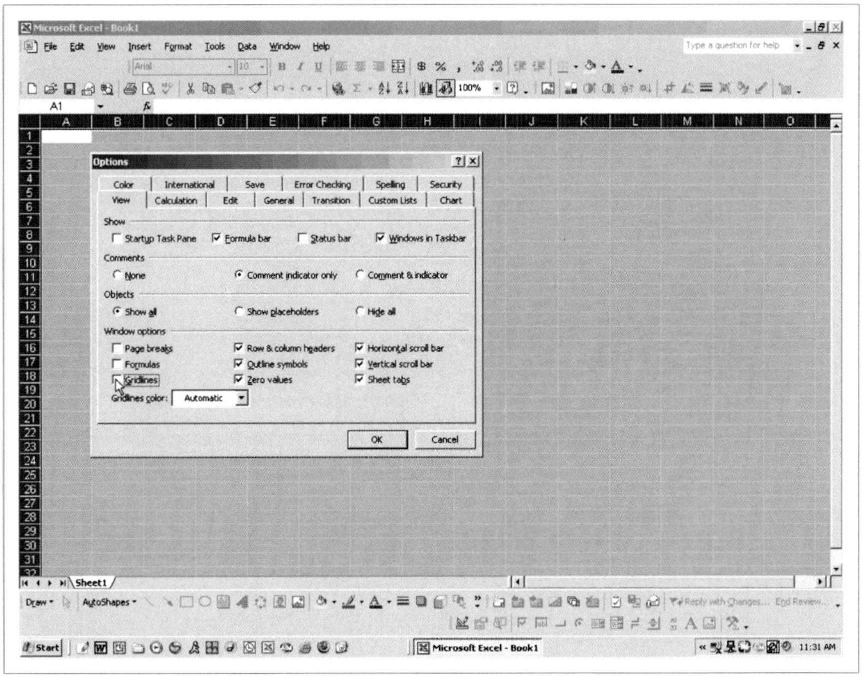

Figure 3.3.
Deselect the Gridlines check box.

Tip

Some prototypers like to switch the grid on and off, using it to help them with alignment; others do not need this visual aid. If you add the Forms toolbar, there is a toggle button to turn the grid off and on.

Now you will change the default Excel row and column dimensions so that they support user interface design and prototyping. Changing the width of the columns creates a much tighter grid, allowing finer control over the layout of text and graphics. A slightly taller row height better accommodates a standard Windows input box or drop-down menu. You will see the value of this change in subsequent chapters. The grid can reflect the flexibility and constraints of either your development environment or your design concept.

Tip

Some experienced Excel prototypers have found it handy when the width of a cell is about the width of a single character of the default font used for their prototype.

To Change the Row and Column Dimensions:

1. Click the rectangle at the upper left of the worksheet, where the column and row headers meet, to highlight the entire worksheet.
2. With the entire worksheet highlighted, choose **Format > Row > Height** (Figure 3.4) and enter 13 for the row height (Figure 3.5).

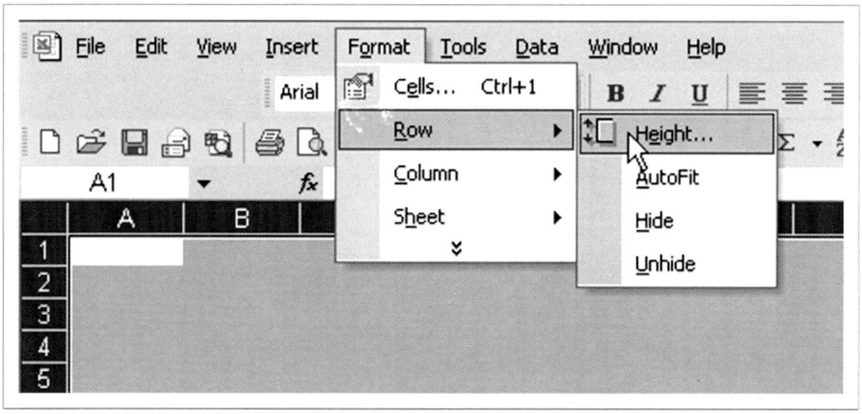

Figure 3.4.

Choose the Height function.

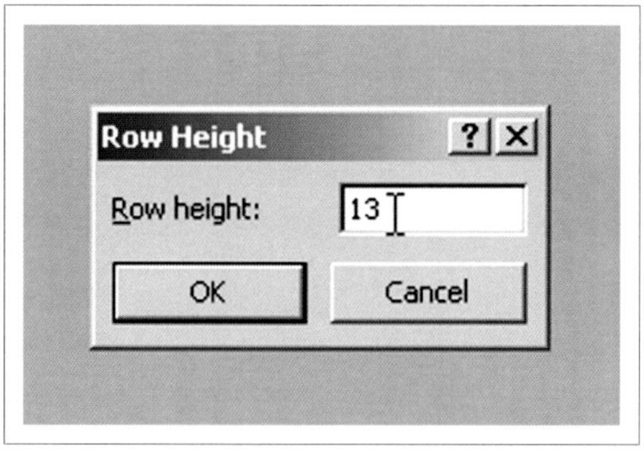

Figure 3.5.

Enter the Row Height value.

3. Choose **Format > Column > Width** (Figure 3.6) and enter 1 for the column width (Figure 3.7).

Tip

- With all the rows and columns selected, you can also click and drag a row or column border to the desired size and it will resize all the rows and columns.

- The Windows shortcut CTRL-1 opens the cell properties sheet and is very useful throughout the entire process of Excel prototyping.

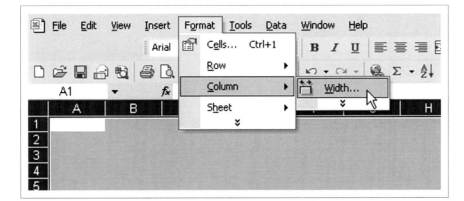

Figure 3.6.
Choose the Width function.

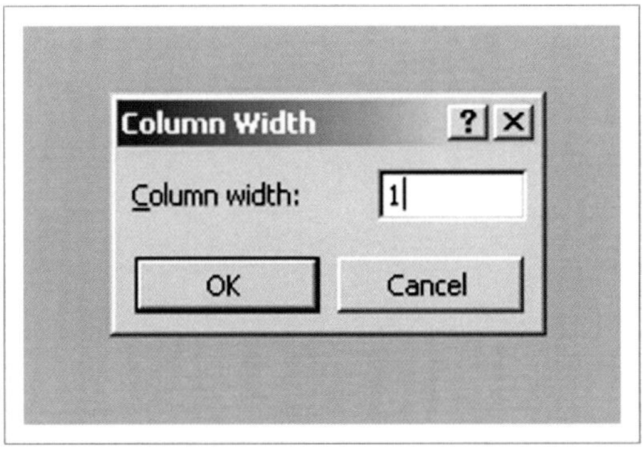

Figure 3.7.
Enter the Column Width value.

The Layers of Excel

A characteristic of Excel is its virtual layers. These layers are laid one over another, which is helpful in designing your prototype. Understanding these layers can help you create different effects in Excel. The layers are

Layer 1: Background image; an imported file can be used as a tiled background.

Layer 2: Cell background color; these colors will cover any part of a background image.

Layer 3: Cell text; the text will appear superimposed on a background image or the background color.

Layer 4: Graphical images, auto shapes, and other drawing elements form the top layers. You can adjust overlap order of graphics within layer 4 by using send-to-front and send-to-back functionality. In practice, avoid using more than three graphical layers.

4. With the entire worksheet still highlighted, right-click any cell and choose **Format Cells** (Figure 3.8).

5. Select **Text** in the Category list (Figure 3.9, page 46).

   Selecting Text from the list stops Excel from autoformatting numbers. Auto-formatting of numbers can result in unintended consequences to the prototype by automatically converting dates, percentages, and other number formats.

6. Click the **Alignment** tab and set the vertical alignment to Top (Figure 3.10, page 47).

   Setting the alignment to top makes text appear at the top of every cell by default. You can set middle or bottom if you prefer. Whatever alignment you choose, it is useful to have as a default across all your prototypes.

7. Click the **Font** tab and set the font to Arial, the font style to Regular, and the size to 10 (Figure 3.11, page 48).

   The font settings become the default whenever you enter text in the canvas worksheet. If you have a style guide for the user interface that you are designing, you can use those font characteristics in your design. Don't worry if you'll need more styles for your design—you can easily override the default setting in individual cells.

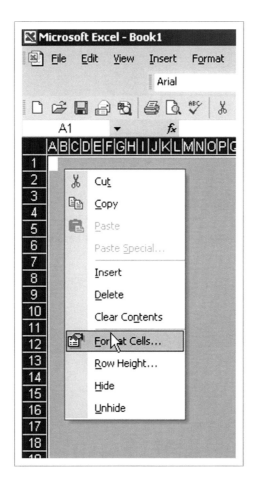

Figure 3.8.
Select the Format Cells function.

Tip

If there are multiple styles that you will use repeatedly throughout your design, make the most common style your default style, as described earlier. You can create a separate worksheet and create these multiple styles in individual cells. You can do this by selecting a cell and then typing in the name of the style.

You can now copy the style and paste into cell(s) in the canvas, and the pasted cells will inherit the styles from the copied cell and override the default styles.

8. Click the **Patterns** tab, where you can choose a color for all the cells if your design calls for a color other than the default white (Figure 3.12, page 49).

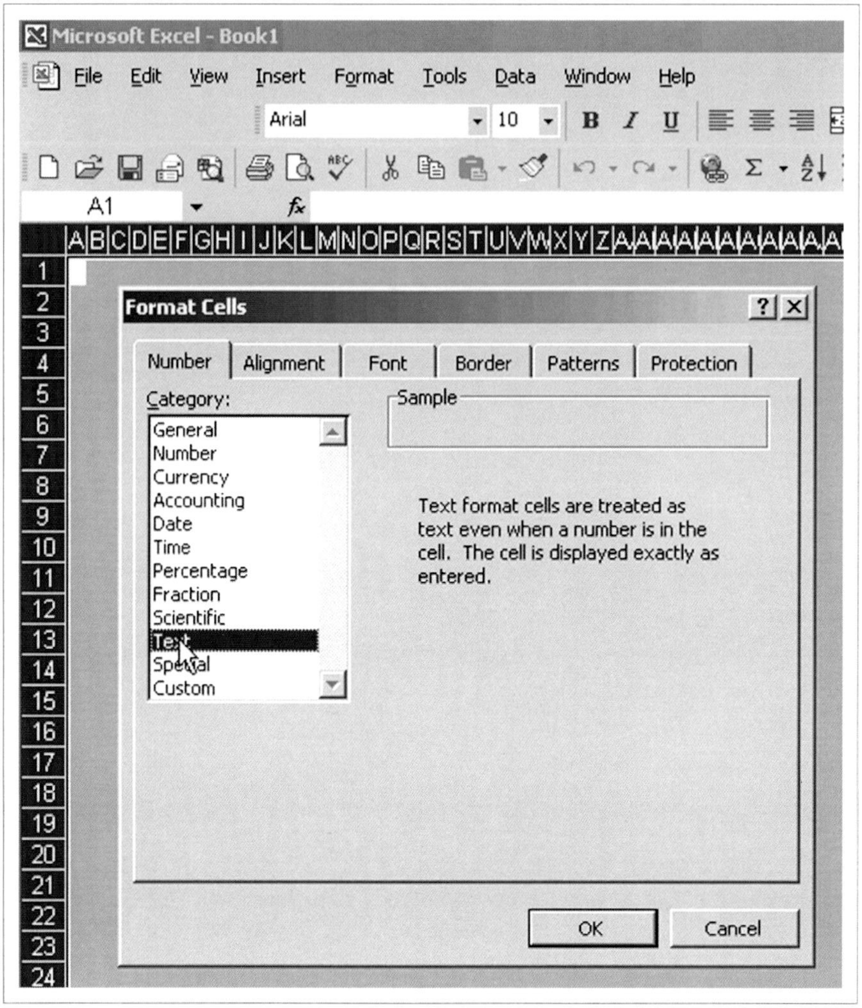

Figure 3.9.

Select Text in the
Number Category.

In the **Patterns** tab you will see the standard Excel palette. Later you will learn how to create your own custom palette for your template so that your designs match your client's or organization's visual branding or house style.

You now have a canvas worksheet. This canvas worksheet has a grid that is optimally formatted for user interface design, font specifications, and background color. Copy all the other worksheets that you create from this worksheet so that they'll have the same specifications built into them. Then any worksheet in your prototype will be interchangeable with any others. If you share your designs with any other users, whether they are across the hall or around the world, this will allow your designs to remain consistent.

9. Now save this file as `Canvas.xls`.

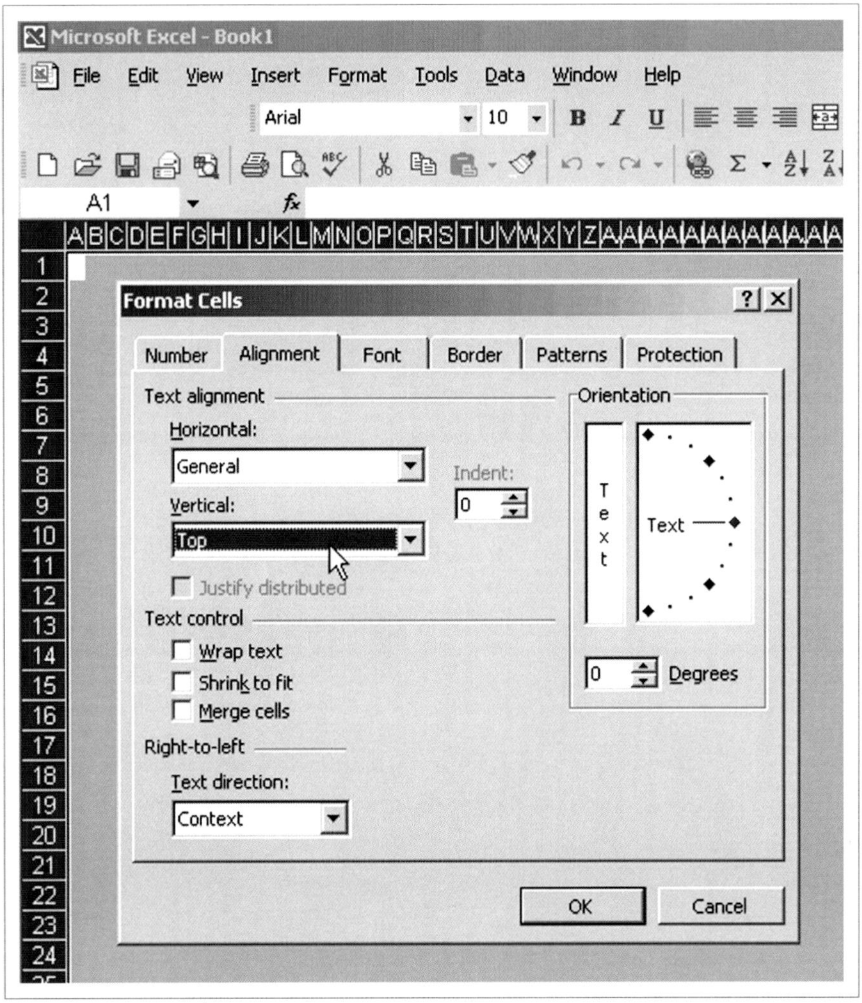

Figure 3.10.
Select Top from Vertical alignment.

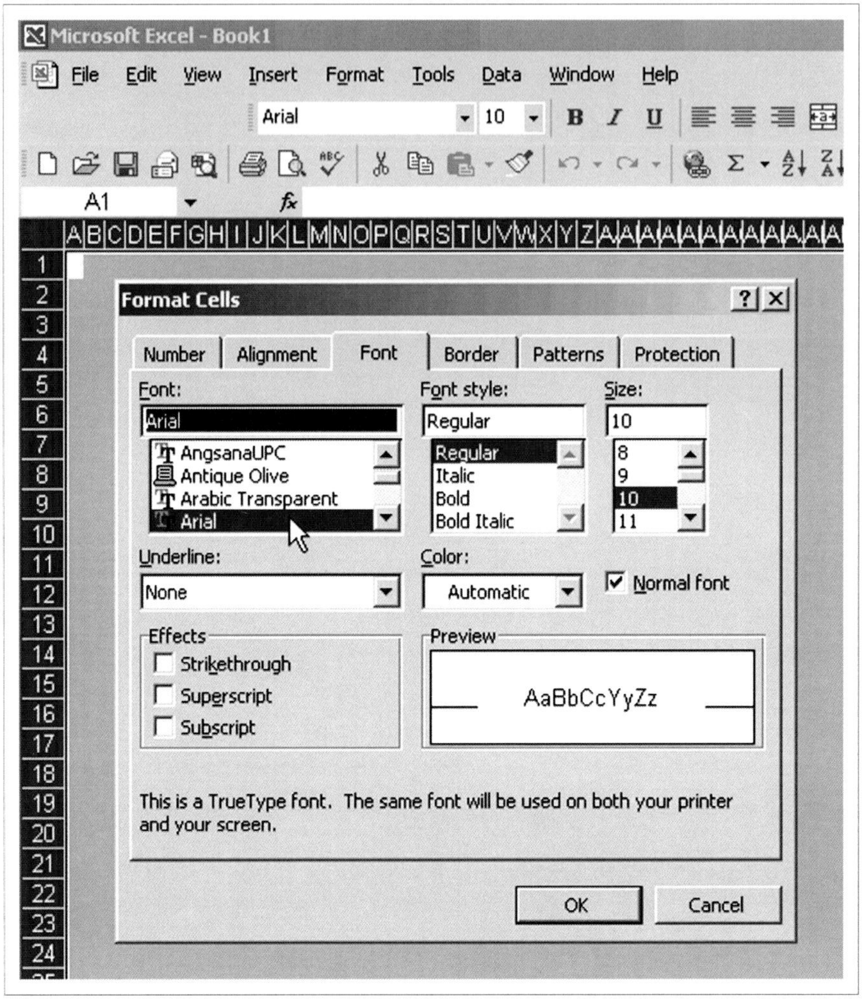

Figure 3.11.

Select Font: Arial.

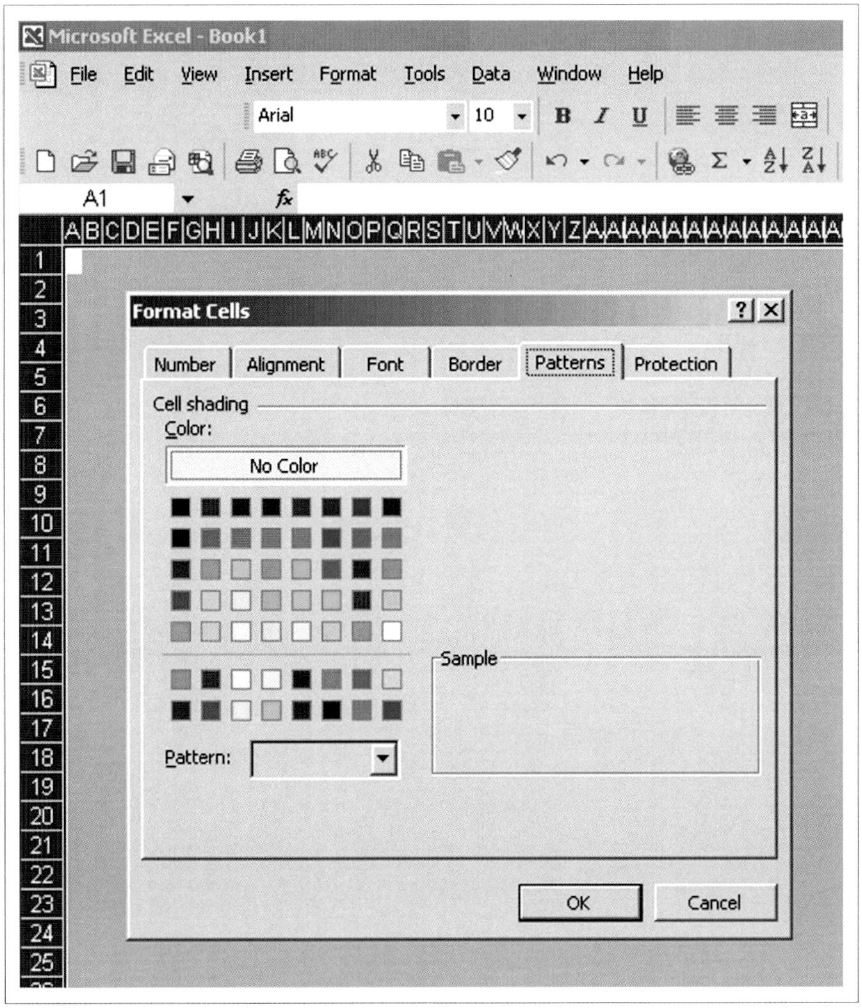

Figure 3.12.

Select a cell color.

Conclusion

You have just completed the most fundamental step in learning to prototype with Excel. You have changed the Excel worksheet from a spreadsheet to a prototyping canvas. Although you could start creating a prototype at this point, with a little more work you can create a prototyping template that makes building prototypes much easier and quicker. In the following chapter you will create a prototyping template.

CHAPTER 4

CREATING AN EXCEL PROTOTYPING TEMPLATE

In this chapter you will learn how to create a prototyping template that includes

- Images and graphics
- Boxes and buttons
- Tab components
- Color key and palette
- Tips and tricks
- Table template
- Prototype starter worksheets

Templates

A *template* comprises worksheets in a special Excel workbook. The template contains user interface elements and useful information that you can use over and over as you build prototypes. By using a template as part of your prototyping practice, you have most of the prototyping building blocks you need available in one document.

The template facilitates collaboration with your team and stakeholders by enabling anyone who has the file to continue with the work that you started. Because the template is built from the canvas worksheet that you already set up, it has default specifications already integrated into the workbook. As you go through the process of building these template worksheets, you will gain a better understanding of how to use Excel for prototyping.

The Image Library

Nearly any prototype that you build will require some graphic elements. For example, you might need

- Logos
- Icons
- Buttons

- Interface widgets
- Illustrations
- Headers or footers

You can store these graphics in an image library worksheet (Figure 4.1) for easy access so you can

- Reserve this worksheet for images that are not created in Excel.
- See the available images together on one worksheet.
- Group them in ways that make sense to you.
- Show them in context with each other; for example, the plus icon goes next to the minus icon.
- Copy many images at a time if needed.

What Graphics Should be Included in Your Image Library Worksheet?

There is no set number of images that you should include in your template. The image library is not intended to contain every graphic that you might ever need,

Figure 4.1.
A worksheet that contains an image library.

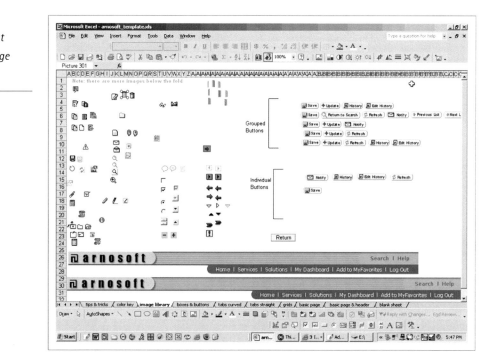

but it is a place to keep the ones you think you will regularly use. In our experience at PeopleSoft and SAP, we found that only a small percentage of all the available graphics was needed to prototype most of the designs. Because the size of your workbook file could become large and cumbersome, take care not to accumulate too many graphics. Too many graphics could slow down your work and make your prototype less readily transportable. As you work on your project and find you need more graphics, you can always add them to the template as you evolve your designs.

Finding the Images You Need

Where can you find the images to put in your template? You have a few alternatives:

- Find appropriate graphics on another Website or application (paying appropriate attention to copyright issues).
- If you are working in a company that has a design or art department, it will often have an image library that you can use.
- Create them yourself.
- For some very simple graphics, Excel and other office applications have clip art that you can use.

When to Use Graphics Instead of Widgets Built in Excel

In subsequent chapters you will learn to build some widgets directly in Excel. How do you decide whether you should make your own each time in Excel or to save a graphic into your image library? Images that are specific to your site, such as logos, icons, or nonstandard buttons, would be good candidates for inclusion in the library. Parts of standard widgets that you will use all the time, such as the down arrow for a pull-down menu, are good to have available, and you can copy those directly from our templates.

Use the right level of fidelity in your prototypes. Not every prototype needs to be pixel-perfect. For example, is it important to have an exact copy of a **Save** button in a wireframe? Or is a generic **Save** button built with table cells in Excel good enough? See "Creating the boxes & buttons worksheet" below. The benefit of table cell buttons built in Excel is that you can change the text in the button at will, whereas you cannot change a static graphic button in Excel.

You will find a file of images on our Website for your use in building an image library: www.effectiveprototyping.com/ep_excel.

Save the file where you can access it easily while using this book.

To Create the Image Library

1. Open the Excel Canvas file that you created and saved earlier.
2. Right-click the **Canvas** worksheet tab and select **Move or Copy** (Figure 4.2).
3. In the **Before sheet** list in the Move or Copy dialog box, select **(move to end)** and select **Create a copy**; then click **OK** (Figure 4.3).
4. With the new tab selected, right-click and choose **Rename**.
5. With the tab text highlighted, type in `Image Library` (Figure 4.4).

Now that you have your Image Library worksheet, we'll show you how to add graphics to it.

To Add Graphics to the Template:

1. From the **Draw** toolbar, click **Insert Picture From File** (Figure 4.5). Alternatively, choose **Insert > Picture** and click **From File**.
2. Browse to where you saved the sample graphics file, exp.xls.
3. Select the graphic called **exp_graphic1.gif**; then click **Insert**. The inserted graphic will appear highlighted on the Image Library worksheet.
4. Do the same for graphics labeled 2–9.

Figure 4.2.

Select function Move or Copy.

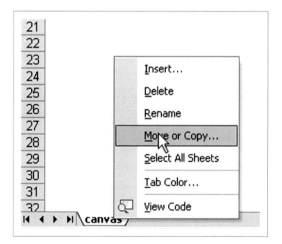

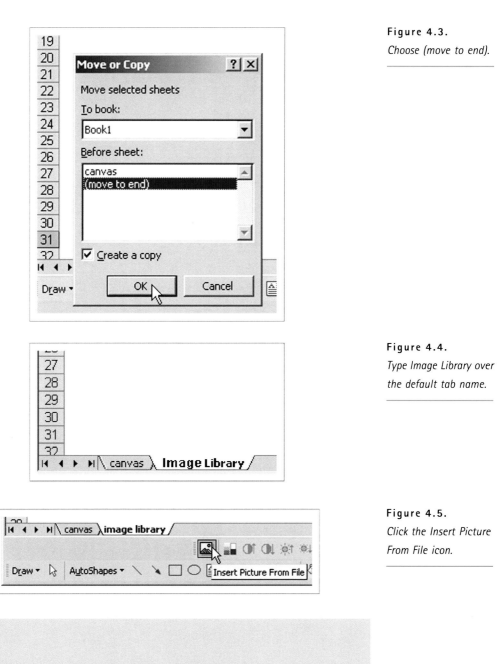

Figure 4.3.
Choose (move to end).

Figure 4.4.
Type Image Library over the default tab name.

Figure 4.5.
Click the Insert Picture From File icon.

Note

If you are copying graphics directly from a Website into Excel, you might inadvertently copy a hyperlink associated with the graphic. To solve this problem, after you have pasted the graphic into your template, right-click the graphic and select **Remove hyperlink**.

To finish your Image Library worksheet, position the graphics in groupings that make sense to you. Keeping your graphics organized will help you to locate exactly what you need. This organization will also help others who use your template to find a specific kind of image.

The Boxes & Buttons Worksheet

This template worksheet includes different types of boxes and buttons that you will need as you design your interface (Figure 4.6). Although you might already have

Figure 4.6.
The boxes & buttons worksheet.

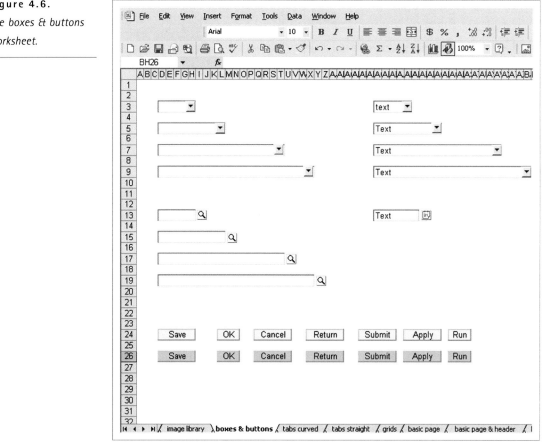

boxes or buttons that you copied on to your image library worksheet, these buttons are made from Excel table cells, borders, and text. You can change their size as well as the text so that they are much more flexible than static graphics.

The boxes (text entry fields, combo boxes, and so on) that are represented in Figure 4.1 were used in a Web application interface. By including this worksheet as part of your template, you will save yourself hours of work in the future.

Creating the Boxes & Buttons Worksheet

Start by opening your Excel template and right-clicking the **Canvas** tab to create a new worksheet the same way you created the Image Library. Name this worksheet boxes and buttons.

Boxes

Your first box is a combo box control that uses bordered table cells and a graphic from the Graphics Library (Figure 4.7, page 58).

To Create the Combo Box:

1. Using your cursor, select a horizontal area of cells.
2. With the cells highlighted, right-click and choose **Format Cells** (Figure 4.8, page 59).
3. Click the **Border tab**.
4. For this exercise you will change the default border color to a dark gray.
5. In the lower-right corner, click the down arrow next to Automatic under **Color**. A color palette will appear.
6. Select the middle gray by clicking it (Figure 4.9, page 60). All the line styles will now be this gray color.
7. Select the two-pixel line (Figure 4.10, page 61). In the center of the dialog box is a white box labeled **Border** with small tick marks. The tick marks represent the table cells that were highlighted on the worksheet.
8. Click in the upper-left part of the box with the arrow (Figure 4.11, page 62).
9. Then click the one-pixel line in the **Style** box.
10. Returning to the **Border** box, click the left and bottom sides of the box (Figure 4.12, page 63).
13. Click **OK**. After you deselect the table cells, you see a box that appears to be recessed, just like a normal input field (Figure 4.13, page 64).

Figure 4.7.

Selecting a canvas area
to place a combo box.

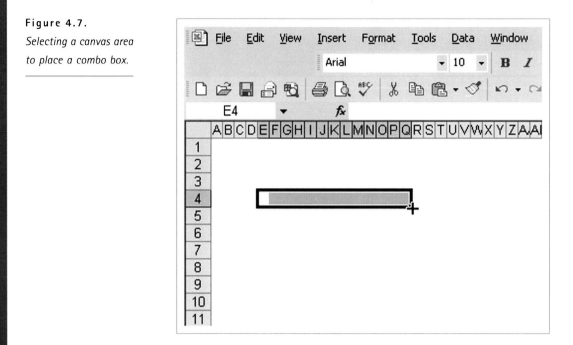

14. Click your **Image Library** tab and find the gray box with the down arrow that you copied into the library previously. Right-click the graphic and choose **Copy** (Figure 4.14, page 64).

15. Return to the **boxes and buttons** worksheet and highlight the cell at the right end of the box that you just created. Paste the down arrow into the table cell (Figure 4.15, page 64).

You just created a combo box control (Figure 4.16, page 65).

To provide a range of boxes, repeat this process with different dimensions to create different variations and kinds of boxes (Figure 4.17, page 65).

Buttons

The buttons you create are also very simple in design. They might not look like the buttons you will end up using on your site, but they will express the idea of a button you'll need for a prototype.

When you built the input boxes, you created a widget that looked like it was inset. To create buttons, you will make a box that looks raised, as though you could click it.

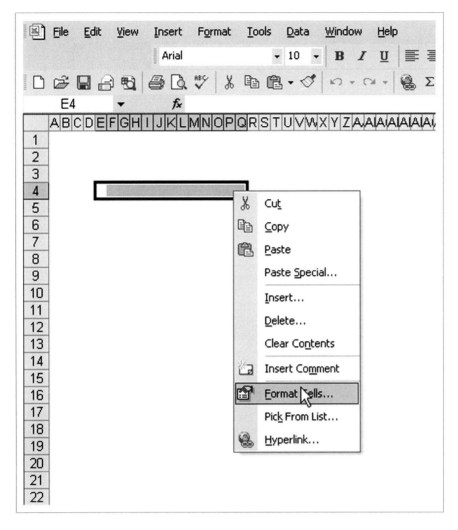

Figure 4.8.

Choosing Format Cells.

To Create a Button:

1. Highlight table cells again, but this time choose only five horizontal cells.

2. Right-click the selected cells and choose **Format Cells**; then choose the dark teal color (Figure 4.18, page 66).

3. Choose the 2-pixel line style and click the bottom and right side of the **Border** box.

4. Return to the **Color** chooser and select a lighter teal color.

5. Still using the 2-pixel line, click the top and left sides of the **Border** box (Figure 4.19, page 67).

Figure 4.9.

Selecting the box fill color.

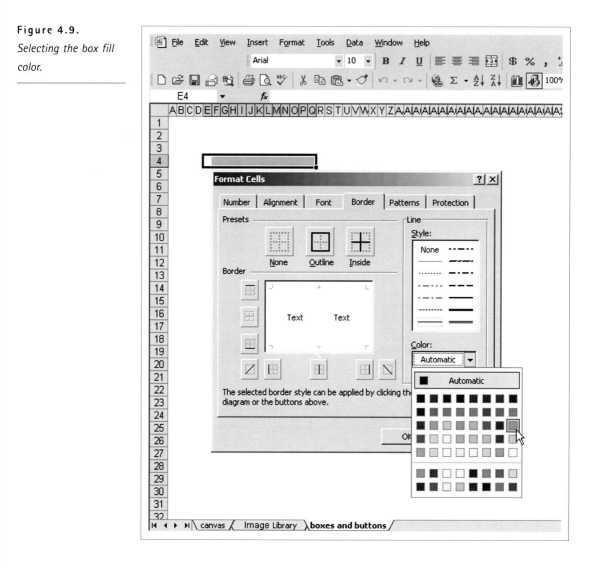

Now you will fill the rest of the button.

6. While still in the **Format Cells** dialog box, click the **Patterns** tab.

7. Select the lightest teal color (Figure 4.20, page 68), and then click **OK**.

8. Deselect the selected table cells and you will see the outcome of the button that you just created (Figure 4.21, page 69).

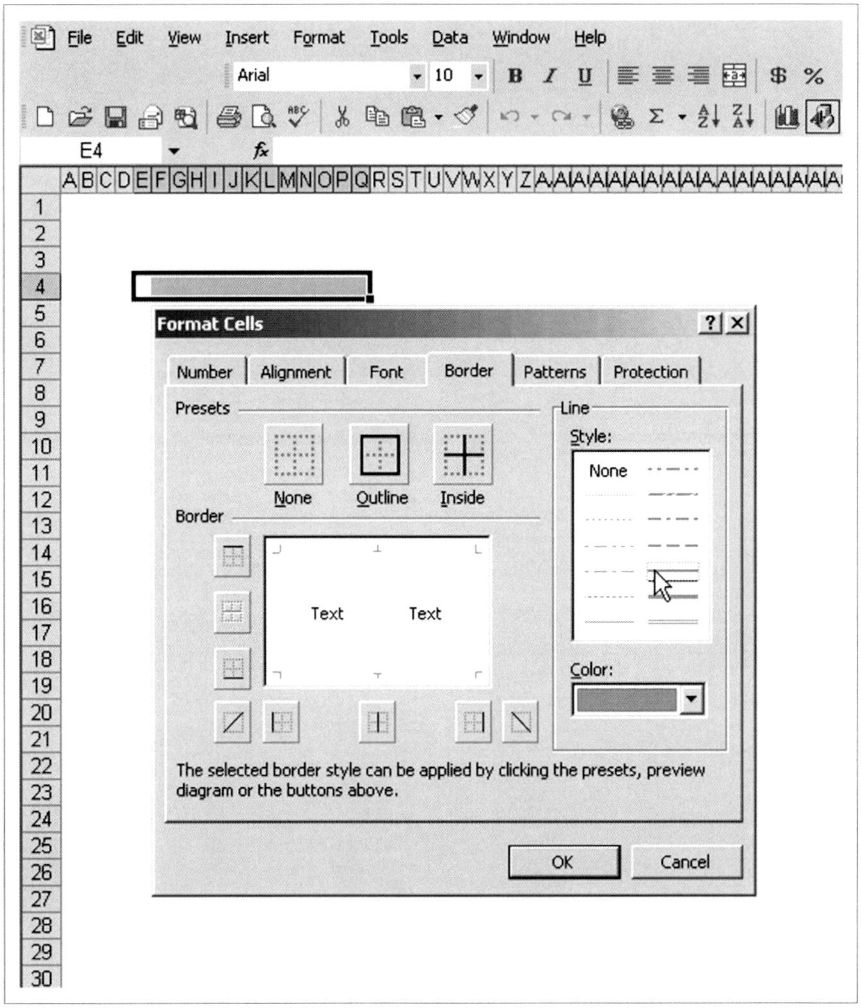

Figure 4.10.

Selecting the line style.

Now add text to the button so that it has some meaning.

9. Highlight the center table cell of the five selected cells (Figure 4.22, page 69) and type in the word Save.

10. Click **Center Text** in the **Formatting** toolbar so that the text you entered is centered (Figure 4.23, page 69).

Figure 4.11.

Applying the border style and color.

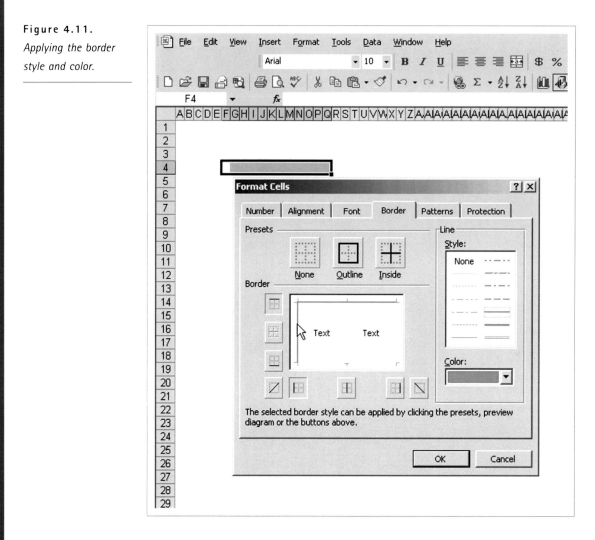

You have created a simple but effective Save button. Using these methods, you can create a wide variety of button styles and types to meet many of your user interface design needs (Figure 4.24, page 69).

Creating a worksheet of boxes and buttons in your template is an easy way to save time and effort when you are on a deadline and need to rapidly finish a prototype design. Remember, you don't have to make every variation of a button you will ever use. Once you are proficient at making these boxes and buttons, it is simply a matter of taking an existing box or button and modifying it to meet your needs.

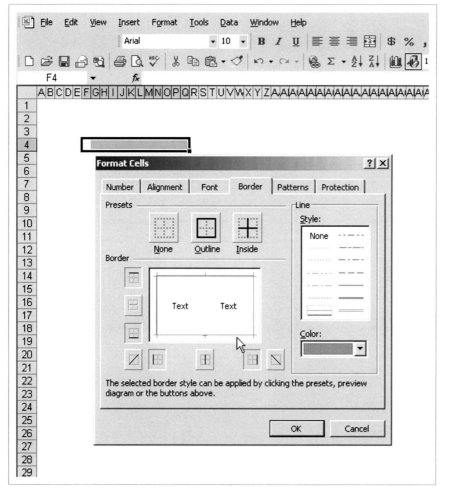

Figure 4.12.

Designating the line border.

The Tabs Worksheet

The tabs worksheet is another template worksheet that, if set up properly, can save you a great deal of prototyping time. As with the boxes & buttons worksheet, you can prebuild these interface features so that when you're in the middle of building a prototype you don't have to stop to figure out how to create tabs; you will already have them ready to use. In this exercise you will create a series of simple tabs, examples of which are shown in Figure 4.25 (page 70).

Follow the same procedure as in the previous sections to create a new worksheet named Tabs Straight.

Figure 4.13.
The finished box.

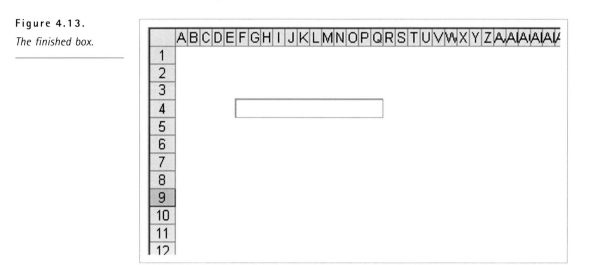

Figure 4.14.
Choosing the Copy function.

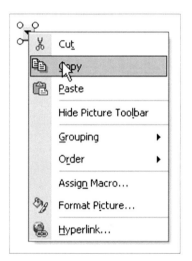

Figure 4.15.
Selecting the cell to insert a combo box control.

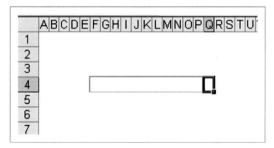

Figure 4.16.
*Example of a combo
box control.*

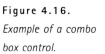

Figure 4.17.
*Examples of various
text boxes and text
box-related controls.*

To Create Straight Tabs:

1. Using your cursor, highlight nine table cells in a single row. This tab will represent the selected tab in the row of tabs you are creating.

2. With the cells still highlighted, right-click and choose **Format Cells**, then choose **Patterns**, select the dark teal color (Figure 4.26, page 71) and click **OK**.

3. In the same way that you inserted text in the button in the previous section, highlight the cell in the center of the tab. Type in `Example Tab` (Figure 4.27, page 71).

4. While you have the text highlighted in the **Format Text** toolbar, choose the **Center Text** icon. Then choose **Bold** and select white for the text color (Figure 4.28, page 72).

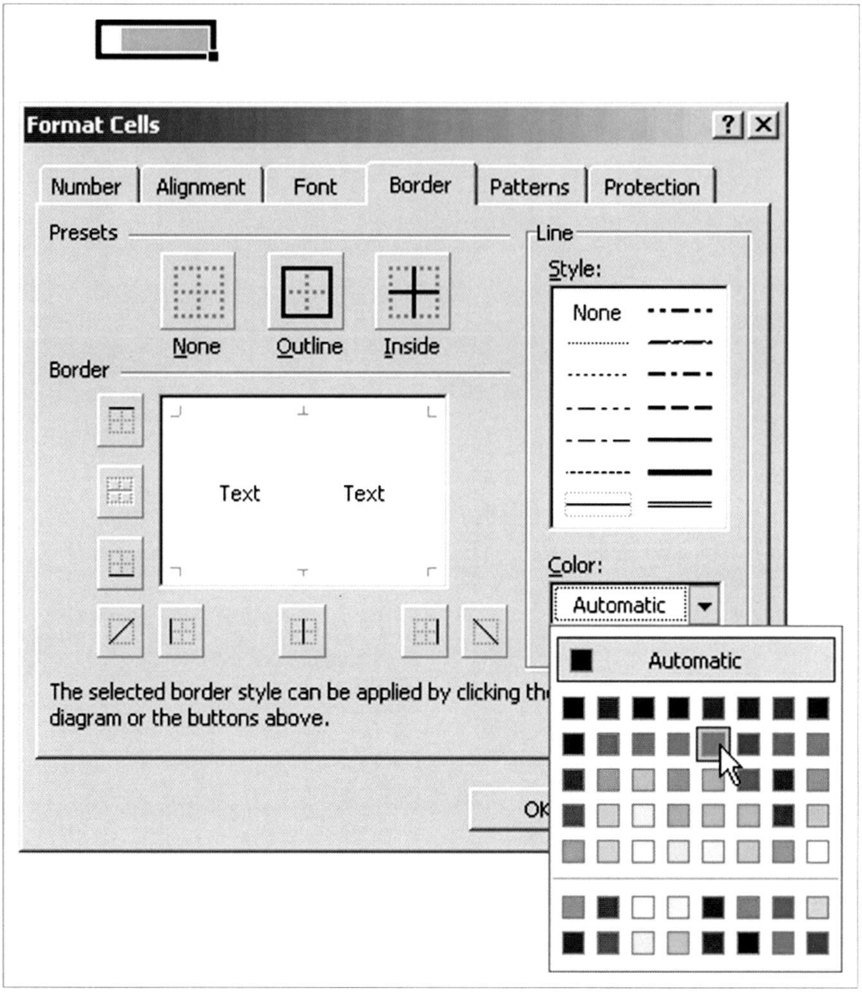

Figure 4.18.

*Selecting the line color
for a button.*

Next you'll create an unselected tab.

5. Skipping one table cell to the right of this tab, select the next nine table cells in the row. Follow the same procedure, except this time select a light gray color (Figure 4.29, page 72). The font style can be the default Arial regular with the default color black.

6. Highlight the light teal tab together with the empty cell to its left and copy these cells (Figure 4.30, page 72).

7. Set the cursor directly to the right of the last gray cell. Using the Paste function (**CTRL-V**), paste in a new light teal tab. Repeat this two more times to finish the row of tabs (Figure 4.31, page 72).

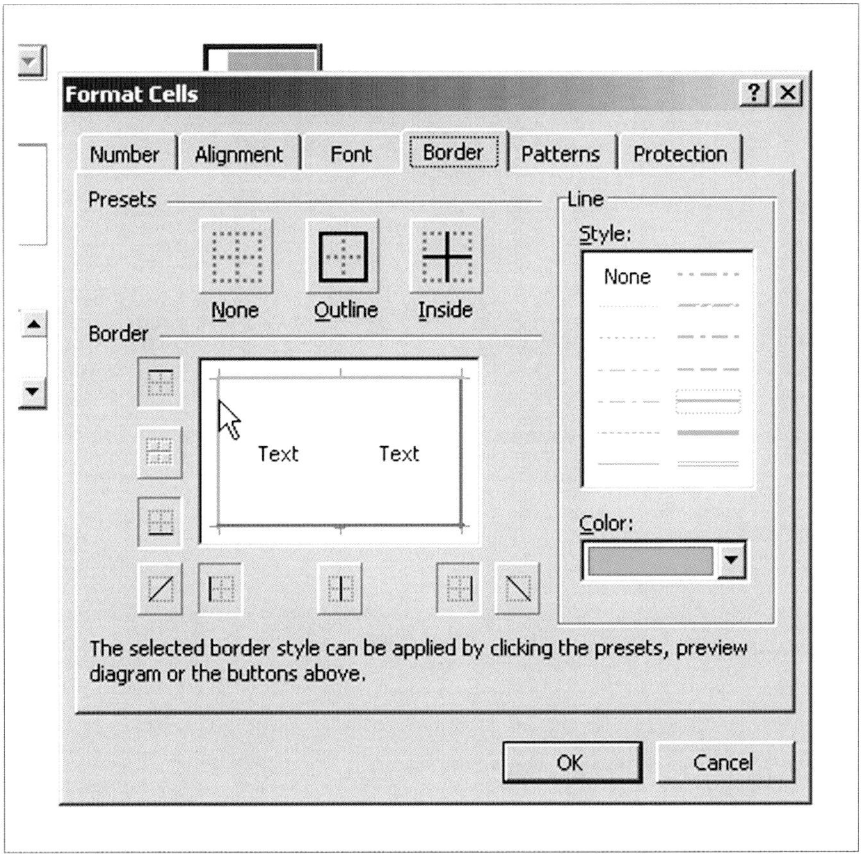

Figure 4.19.

Applying the border style and color for a button.

In this design, you'll include a one-point black line under all the tabs extending across the entire tab area.

8. Select cells on the row of tabs, starting one cell to the left and extending 12 cells to the right of the last tab.

9. While the cells are selected, right-click and choose **Format Cells** and select the **Border** tab. Choose the one-point line style that has the Automatic color choice of black and click the bottom of the **Border** box (Figure 4.32, page 73).

You have created a complete row of tabs, with one of them highlighted (Figure 4.33, page 73).

To finish your tab worksheet, create a series of tab rows with different tabs highlighted. Use copy and paste to quickly create more tab rows.

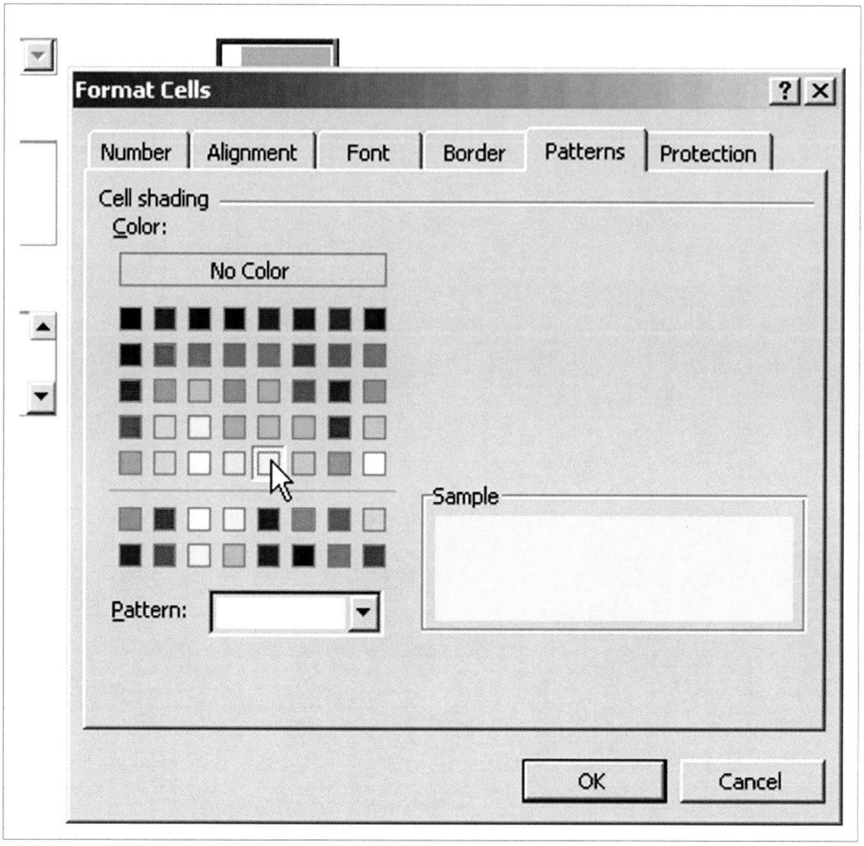

Figure 4.20.

Selecting the fill color for a button.

To Create More Tabs:

1. Highlight the entire row of tabs and copy them.

2. Choose a cell that is two cells below the existing tab row; then paste a new row of tabs (Figure 4.34, page 73).

3. Repeat this three more times until you have created five stacked tab rows.

4. Now copy the highlight tab and paste it in a different sequential position on the remaining tab rows (Figure 4.35, page 73).

5. In each row, replace the extra highlighted tab with a gray tab (Figure 4.36, page 74).

Your tab row worksheet is now complete. You have a simple set of tabs that can easily be copied and pasted into a prototype design (Figure 4.37, page 74).

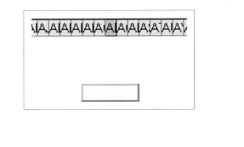

Figure 4.21.
A finished button.

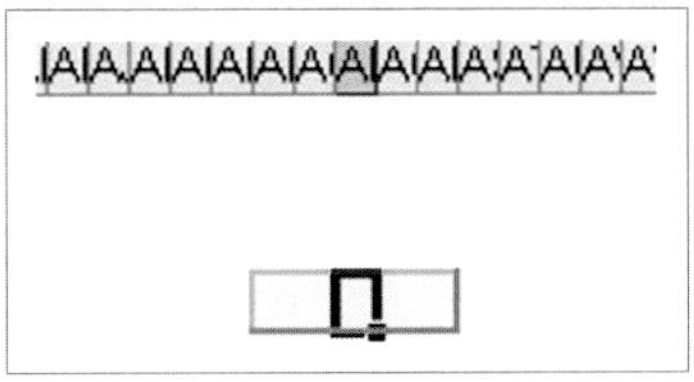

Figure 4.22.
Adding text to the finished button.

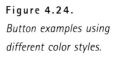

Figure 4.23.
A finished button with centered text.

Figure 4.24.
Button examples using different color styles.

In making your own tabs worksheet, you can change the color or text to match your organization's house style. As you paste the tabs into a design, you can highlight the tab text and replace it with a context-appropriate name. If the tabs are too long or too short, you can add or subtract cells to adjust them.

Figure 4.25.

Examples of finished tabs.

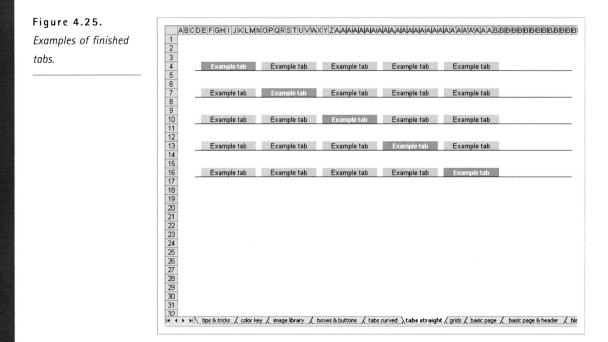

Color Management

The Excel color palette lets you customize a palette for your specific needs and manage these palettes among your various prototypes. The default standard color palette has 50 colors (Figure 4.38, page 74).

You do not have to use only the colors that come with the default palette; you can create your own new custom colors.

To Create a New Color:

1. Click **Tools > Options** to open the Options dialog box.
2. Click the **Color** tab. The default palette opens.
3. Select a color that you want to customize; then click the **Modify** button.

You can choose a new color from a larger color palette or a palette that is made up of white, black, and gray tones. Once you've settled on a new color, you can click **OK** and the new color will replace the color you initially selected (Figure 4.39, page 75).

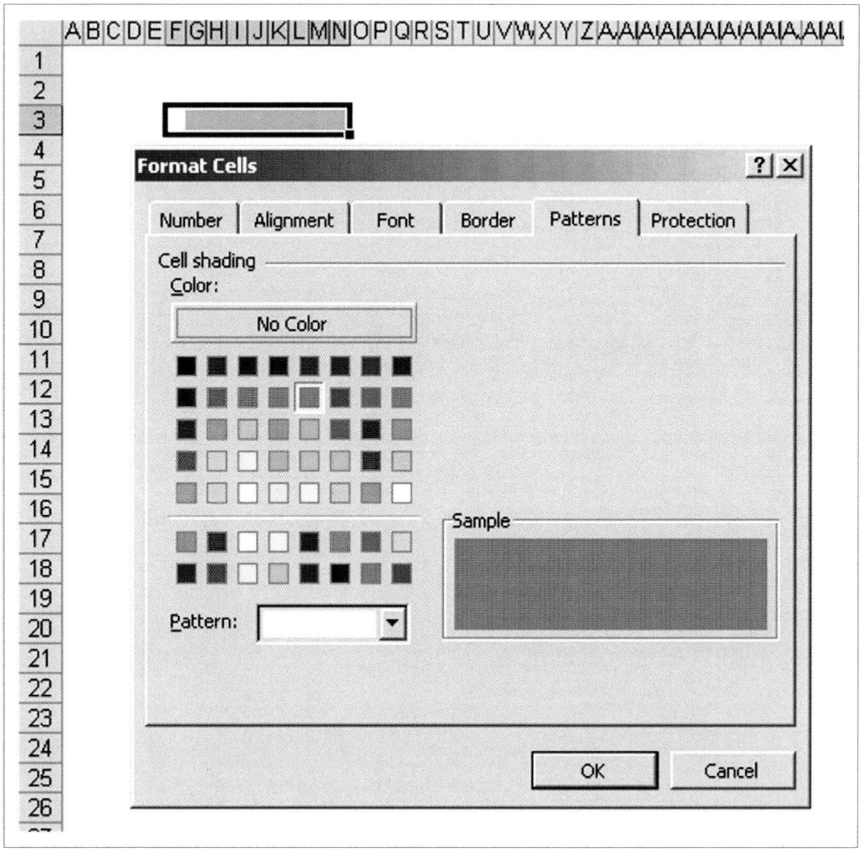

Figure 4.26.
Selecting a tab fill color.

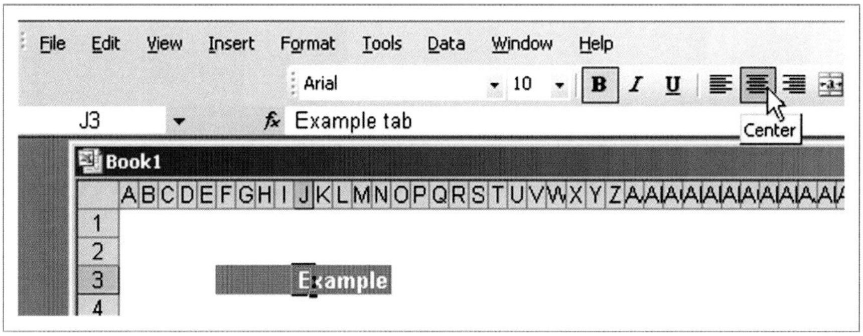

Figure 4.27.
Centering the tab text.

Figure 4.28.
Example of tab centered text.

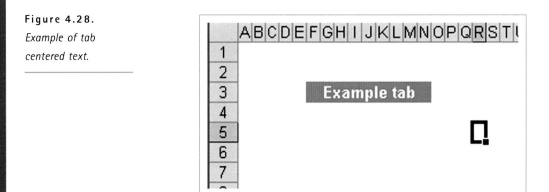

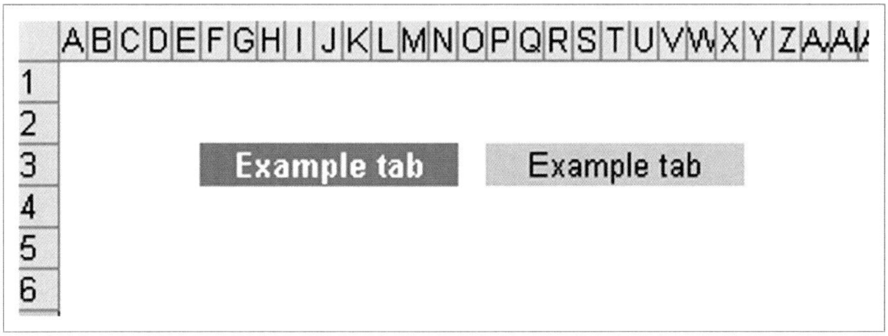

Figure 4.29.
Example of an adjacent gray tab.

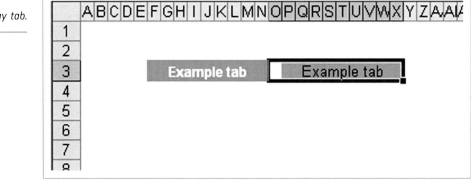

Figure 4.30.
Copy selected gray tab.

Figure 4.31.
Example of a row of tabs.

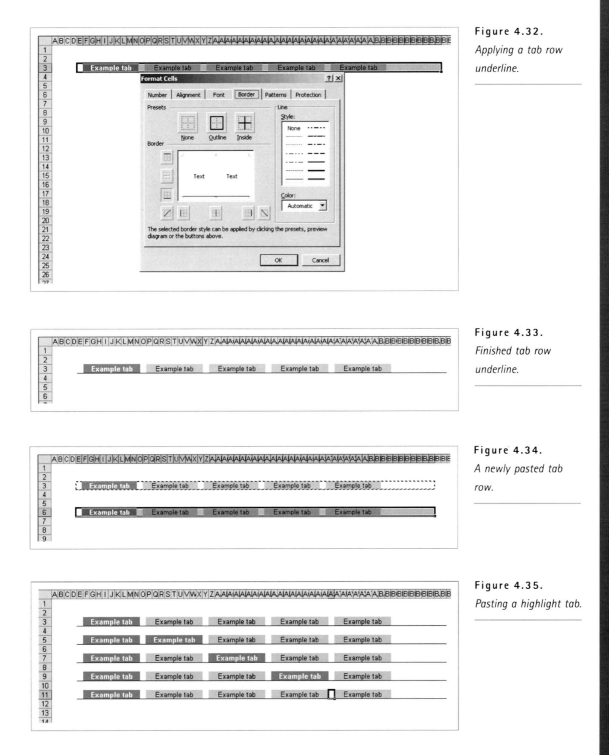

Figure 4.32.

Applying a tab row underline.

Figure 4.33.

Finished tab row underline.

Figure 4.34.

A newly pasted tab row.

Figure 4.35.

Pasting a highlight tab.

Figure 4.36.

Pasting a lowlight tab.

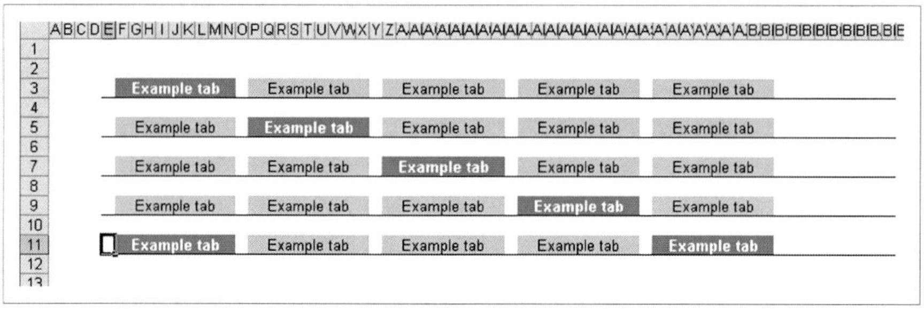

Figure 4.37.

Completed multiple tab rows with different tabs highlighted.

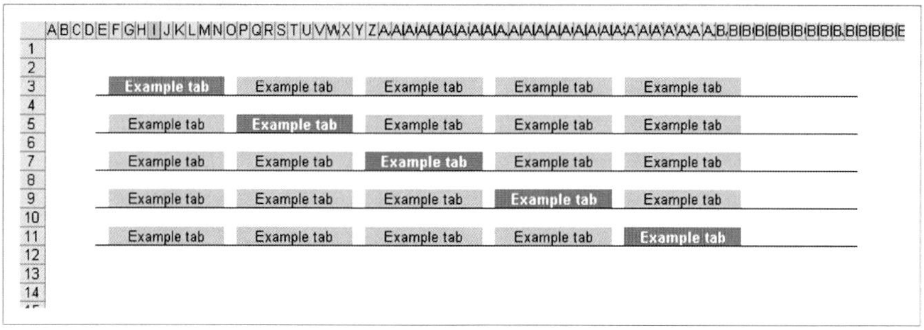

Figure 4.38.

Excel color palette.

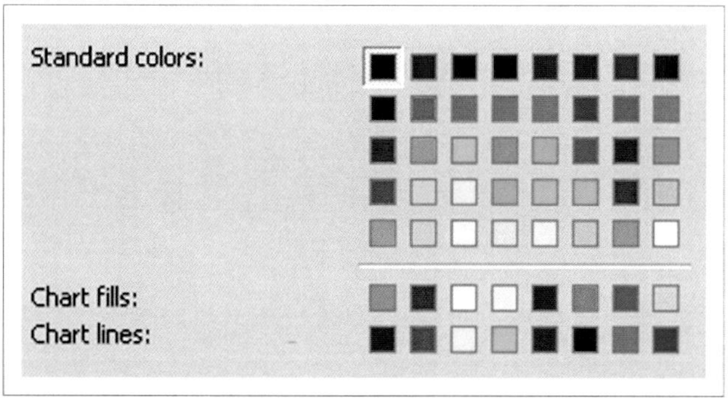

4. To create this new color, click the **Custom** tab (Figure 4.40, page 76).

You see a palette with a much finer range of colors to choose from. The color value scale allows you to take whatever color you choose and move it up or down in the value range, making the color choice darker or lighter. If you want to make color selections that absolutely match specific colors, you can specify their color values in RGB.

5. When you are done creating or modifying colors, click **OK**.

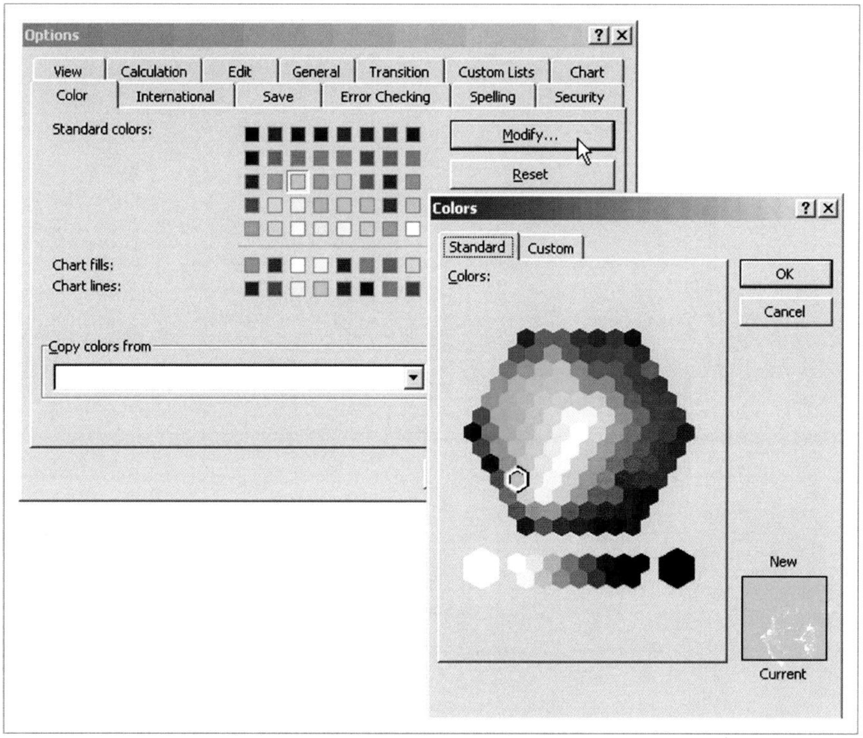

Figure 4.39.
Selecting a new color from the standard Excel color palette.

Tip

Excel uses some default colors that you should not alter. Changing these colors might give you some unexpected results. If you change the blue that is used as the hyperlink color and the maroon (circled in figure) that is used for the visited hyperlink, Excel will use the colors that you changed them to. That might be what you want if the links in your design are not standard and you want them to be a different color by default; otherwise, they could cause unintended color changes (Figure 4.41, page 76).

The custom palette that you create will be saved in the workbook file. If you copy a prototype screen from this file into another workbook that is using the default palette or that uses a different custom palette, the colors in the copied workbook will change to those of the host workbook—which might cause some odd visual results.

Figure 4.40.

Creating a custom color.

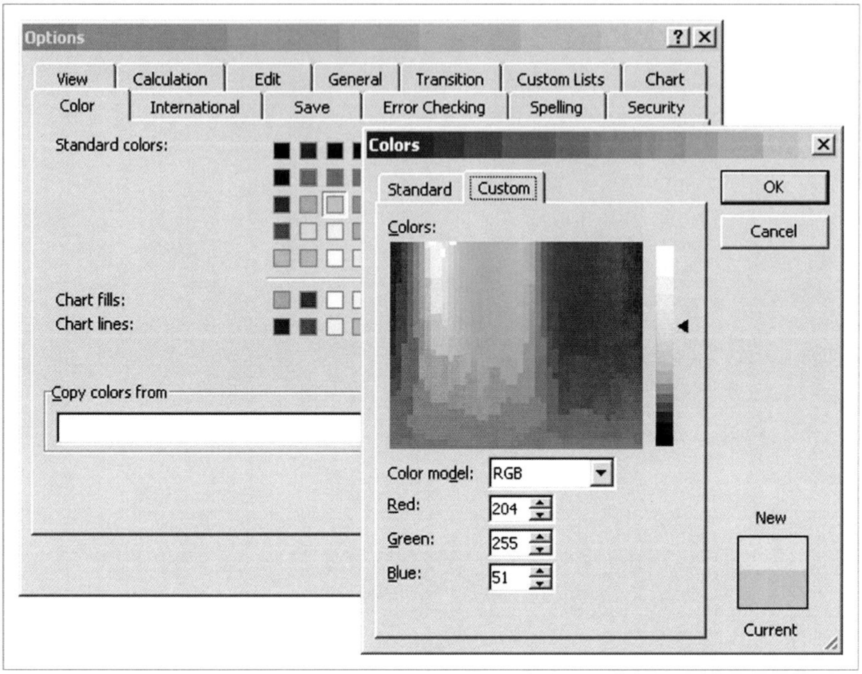

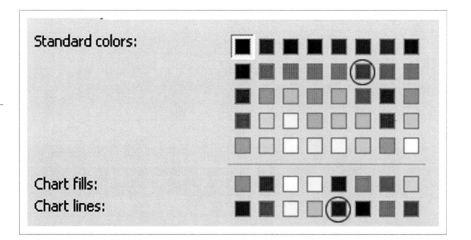

Figure 4.41.

Default colors that Excel uses for hyperlinks and visited link colors.

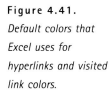

The best solution is that everyone start with the same template. But you can copy and paste a color palette from one workbook to another. Use the **Copy colors from** drop-down list on the **Tools > Options > Color** tab. Select from the workbooks that are currently open, highlight the palette that you want to copy to your current document, and click **OK** (Figure 4.42).

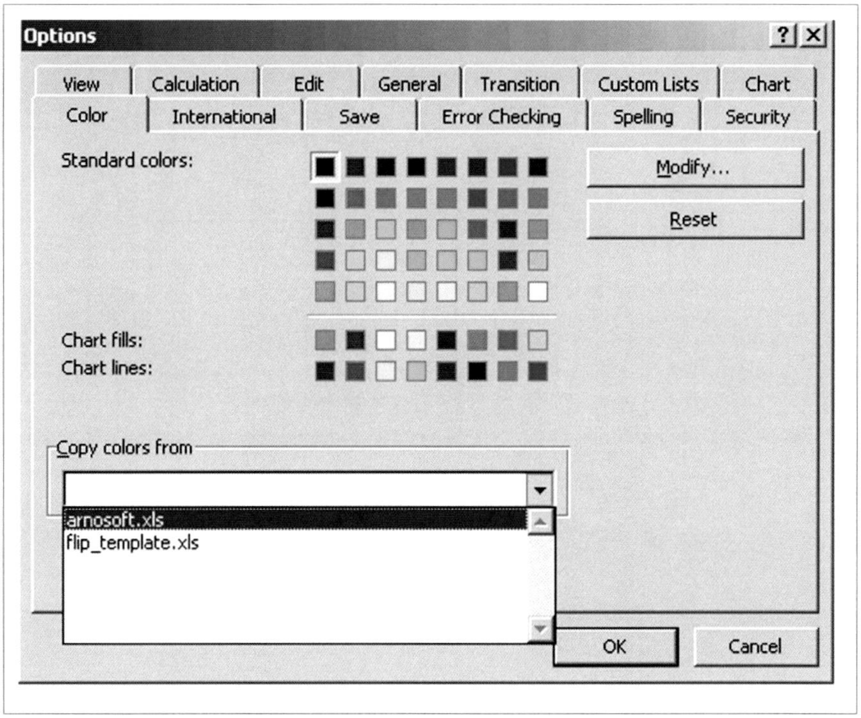

Figure 4.42.
Copying a color palette from one Excel workbook to another.

The Color Key and Palette

The color key worksheet (Figure 4.43, page 78) serves as a color specification guide for anyone who is working on the prototype. You can create a custom palette, and all your collaborators will know exactly what colors should be used for what purpose.

The color key worksheet includes a screen capture of the custom color palette that you created, along with a numbered key that shows each of the different colors in use on a typical prototype screen. You can build this worksheet with any elements that you need to communicate your color palette. A high-fidelity prototype might include a detailed color worksheet, whereas a wireframe prototype that focuses on information architecture and is generally devoid of color might not need a color worksheet at all.

The Tips and Tricks Worksheet

Like the color palette worksheet, a tips and tricks worksheet (Figure 4.44, page 78) for your template will be primarily instructional. Tips and tricks would be a good

Figure 4.43.

Example of a color key worksheet.

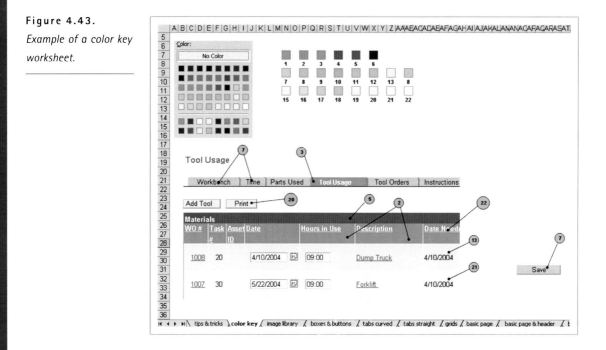

Figure 4.44.

Example of a tips and tricks worksheet.

place to pass on any information that is specific to building a particular design or to include instructions about your process. It's an ideal way to bring your project collaborators up to speed on how to best use this prototyping template.

The Table Template Worksheet

In building prototypes, you might find yourself repeatedly creating tables. The ability to create tables is one of Excel's best features for prototyping. You will be able to describe complex tables, build them very quickly, edit them, and copy and paste them into other worksheets.

You can create a table using patterns, text, and borders. You can

- Paste a table header onto a worksheet
- Change the text
- Paste column dividers
- Add text and widgets into the table
- Configure the spacing between rows

In these examples, the table is made up of a header, a subheader, and table rows. The rows in the table are built using alternating light and dark colors with a one-pixel white line between each row and column. Let's look at how to create the tables shown in Figures 4.45 and 4.46 (page 80).

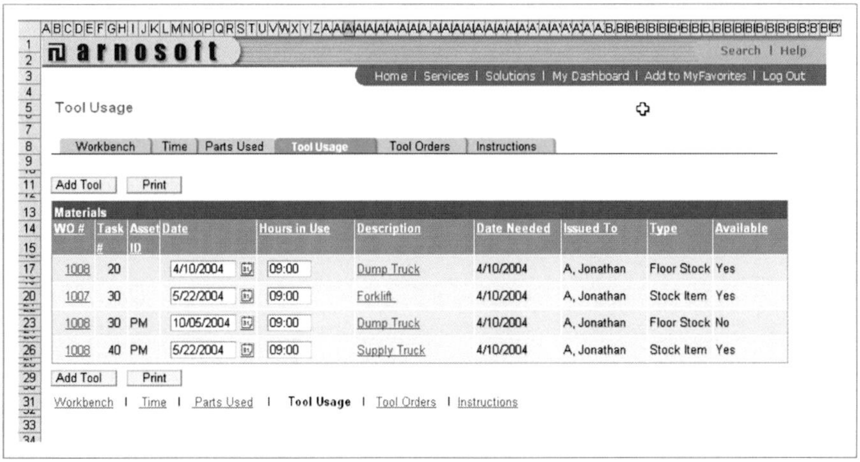

Figure 4.45.

Example of a table built in Excel.

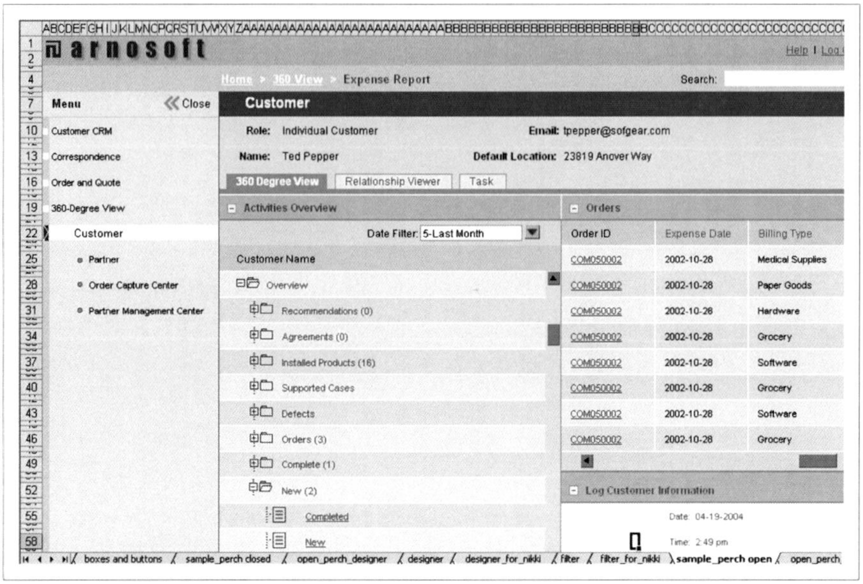

Figure 4.46.

Example of a table built in Excel.

Creating the Table Template

Three rows are dedicated for each table row of one color. Look closely at the examples of the table in Figure 4.47. You will see that each table row is three worksheet rows deep, but two of the three rows are much shorter than the middle row. The middle row is for the content, whether it is text or a widget, such as a combo box. The reason for these added rows is twofold:

- For adequate spacing above and below your text and widgets
- To prevent distortion of your pasted graphics

The next part of the worksheet is made up of the vertical sections of the table. These are built similarly to the rows but have a vertical line and text that will be copied and pasted into the subheader row.

To Build a Table:

1. Create a new prototype screen from a canvas worksheet and call it `Sample Table`.
2. From the Tables worksheet in the provided sample template file, highlight and copy the header into the new worksheet along with all three rows (Figure 4.48).

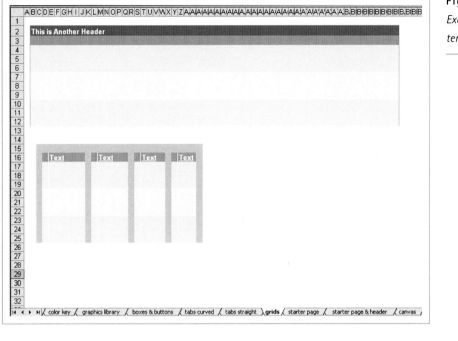

Figure 4.47.

Example of a table template worksheet.

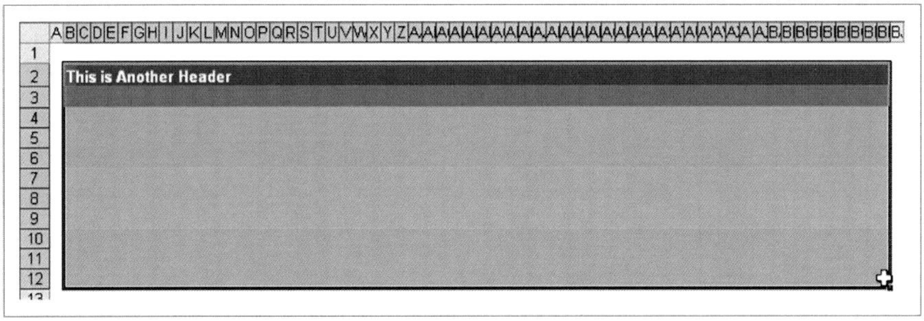

Figure 4.48.

Copying a table component to use on a prototype screen.

3. On the new worksheet, change the header text to `Sample`.

4. In the subheader bar, type in `Text`.

You will notice that the white text style is part of the Table template (Figure 4.49, page 82).

5. Type into your sample table a line of text into each middle row. This will give you an idea of where to place your vertical divider lines (Figure 4.50, page 82).

6. From the **Table Templates** worksheet, highlight and copy a column (Figure 4.51, page 82) and paste it into the new table. Highlight one cell in the subheader to the right of where the text starts (Figure 4.52, page 83).

Figure 4.49.
Table header and subheader text.

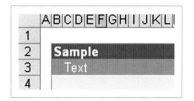

Figure 4.50.
Table row text labels.

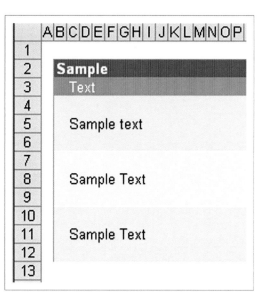

Figure 4.51.
Selecting a column from a table template.

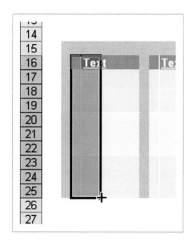

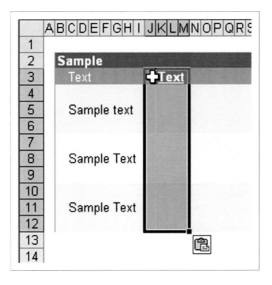

Figure 4.52.
Pasting a column into the Sample table.

Now you can begin to see how the table will grow. You can fill in the rows and then add in new columns as needed. In this case type `Name:` in each row.

7. Next go to the **boxes and buttons** worksheet and copy a combo box. Return to the sample table and paste it next to `Name:`.

You don't have to return to the boxes and buttons worksheet each time. Just paste and reposition and paste again. Change the text in the column header to `Names`. Now you've completed another column (Figure 4.53).

Finish up the table by adding more sample data (Figure 4.54, page 84).

8. To adjust the table row heights, hold down the **Control** key while selecting each row that is above or below a content row, thus highlighting them all (Figure 4.55, page 84).

Figure 4.53.
Two finished table columns.

Figure 4.54.

All table columns finished.

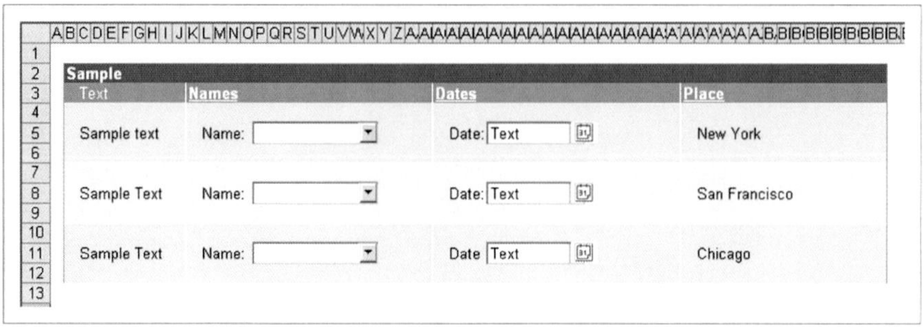

Figure 4.55.

Highlighting table, padding rows for resizing.

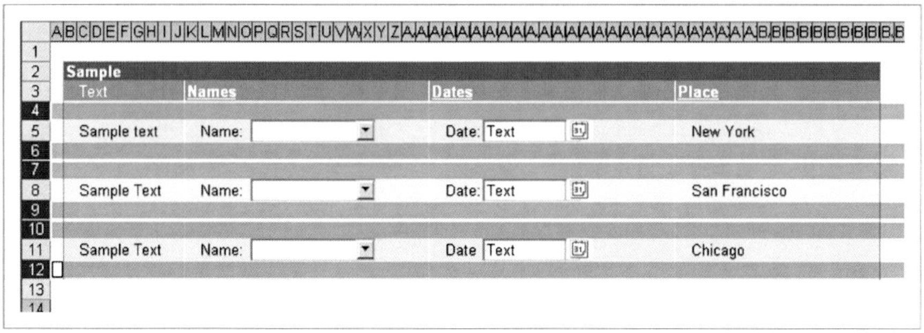

9. Right-click the left column and choose **Row Height** (Figure 4.56); specify **5** and click **OK**.

The results give you a nicely condensed box with spacing around the content.

Finish the table by highlighting the whole table and adding a border by using the Format menu (Figure 4.57).

Modifying the Table

Nothing is ever finished in a prototype. So how will you iterate with tables?

- If you just need to change the content, highlight the text and replace it with new text.
- If the column is too narrow, copy a portion of the column and paste it to the right or left to increase the column width.
- If your changes are complicated, return the table to its original state with three-deep rows per table row. Highlight all the rows from the far left column, choose **Row Height**, and return the rows to the original height of **13** (Figure 4.58, page 86).

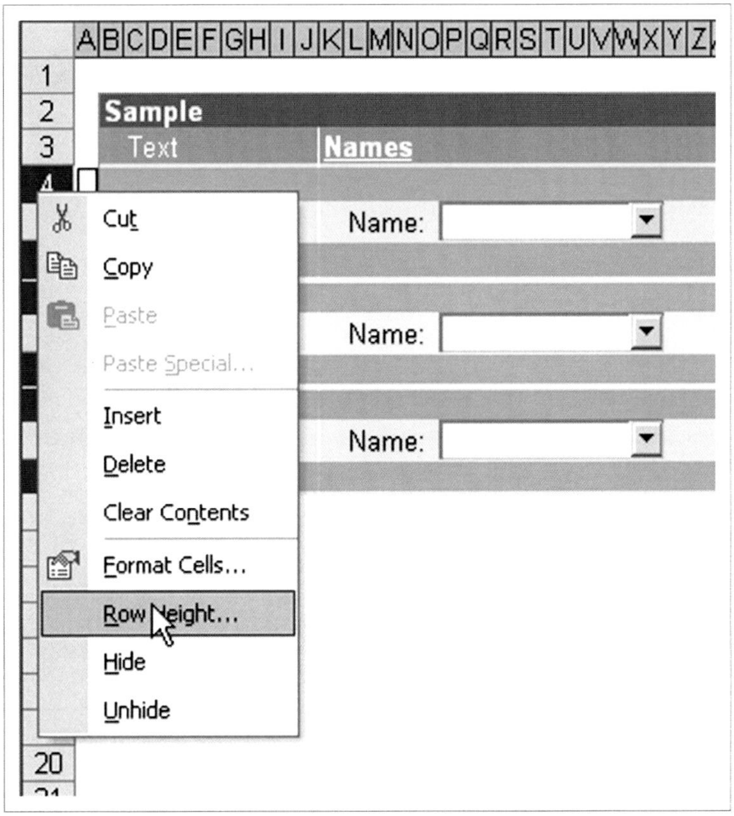

Figure 4.56.
Selecting Row Height to adjust spacing between table rows.

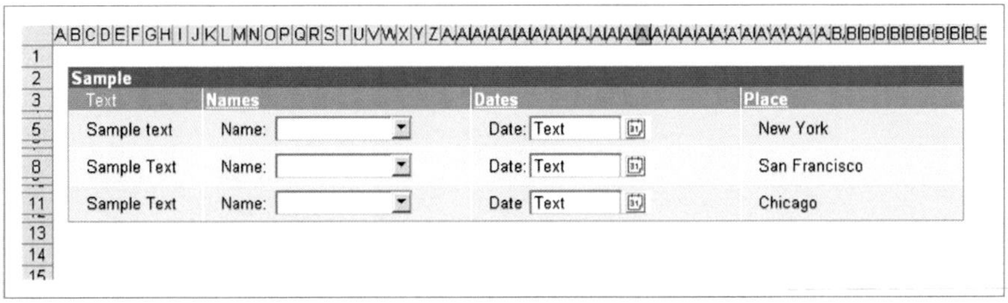

Figure 4.57.
Example of a finished table.

- If you need to add rows, copy two table rows starting with the light row so that you don't change the pattern of light and dark. Then paste the two rows below the bottom darker row.

If you get comfortable with using the Table Template worksheet, you can get the most out of the speed, flexibility, and power of Excel prototyping.

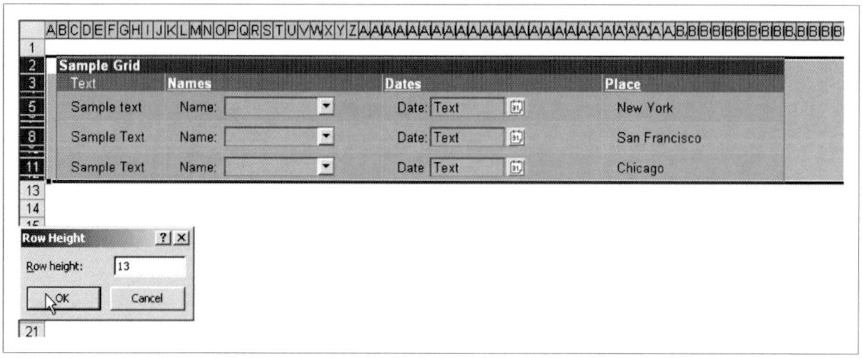

Figure 4.58.

Resetting the row height to make table modifications.

The Starter Worksheet

Another useful template worksheet is a starter worksheet. The example in Figure 4.59 is a starter worksheet from the sample Arnosoft site. Notice the global elements, such as the top navigation bar and logo. The layout of the worksheet follows a design that might be found on many Arnosoft prototype screens. By including a worksheet in your template, which already has many of the global elements, you can use it to start new prototypes without having to start from scratch every time.

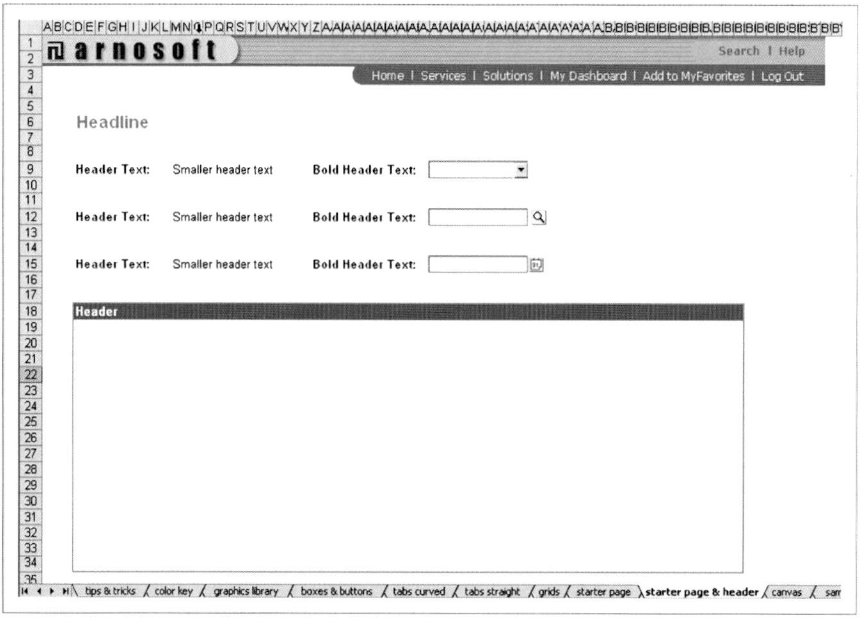

Figure 4.59.

Example of a prototype starter worksheet.

You can save time by having everything placed correctly with many of the widgets you think you'll need.

The contents of a starter worksheet will depend on the design that you are prototyping. You might have more than one starter worksheet, depending on your designs. Don't try to anticipate every starter worksheet that you might need—you don't want to fill up your template with unnecessary worksheets.

You can also backfill as needed. If you start a new design and think that you're going to use that design a lot, copy and save it as a starter worksheet that you can reuse later.

Conclusion

As you worked through the exercises in this chapter, you created your own template. From the canvas, the fundamental starting point for prototyping in Excel, you created the various template worksheets. In the coming chapters we will discuss how you can use this template to create different types of prototypes.

PART 2

PROTOTYPING WITH EXCEL

You have learned the basics of using Excel as a prototyping tool, and you have set up your canvas and template. In Part 2 you will learn how to apply your Excel canvas and template to specific prototyping challenges.

- In Chapter 5 you will use Excel to prototype storyboards.
- In Chapter 6 you will use Excel to prototype wireframes.
- In Chapter 7 you will use Excel for digital interactive prototypes.

CHAPTER 5

EXCEL PROTOTYPING:
STORYBOARDS

In this chapter you will learn how to

- Think about storyboards
- Create a storyboard prototype
- Create a sample storyboard
- Present your storyboard

About Storyboards

The storyboarding process, in the form that we know it today, was first developed for cartoons at the Walt Disney studio during the early 1930s and was subsequently adopted throughout the film industry. Today storyboards are used for planning ad campaigns, commercials, proposals, and other projects intended to convince or compel to action. More recently, the storyboard concept has been adapted to the process of creating software.

Figure 5.1 (page 92) shows a typical entertainment version of the storyboard. Figure 5.2 (page 93) shows a typical software storyboard prototype in a thumbnail format. With the right presentation software, the images can be viewed at a much larger size, in sequence, and with notes, animations, and links to outside files and Websites.

A storyboard prototype for software can be created in different styles. One, which is more like a traditional storyboard, includes a series of sequential illustrated images or sketches based on accompanying narrative text, as shown in Figure 5.2.

This type of storyboard communicates design concepts as a story line or a work-flow. It is generally targeted to internal design team members to align the team's thinking with the goals, behaviors, and conceptual design direction of an idea, product, or service without actually detailing any screen designs. This type of story-board can also be used in focus group studies to validate a concept or workflow with actual users. When representing innovation concepts, storyboards can be tar-geted to both internal and external stakeholders, such as upper management and other strategic influencers inside a company, or to potential investors, members of the media, and other external audiences. This type of storyboard is usually pro-duced using presentation software such as Keynote or PowerPoint.

Figure 5.1.

Traditional storyboard with scanned hand-drawn images used in the making of The Incredibles. Courtesy of Pixar.

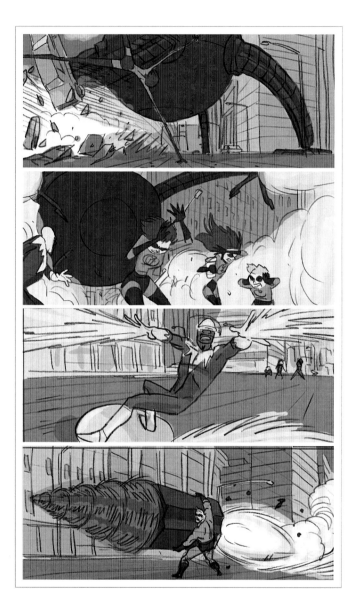

In contrast, what you will learn about here is a second type of storyboard, a storyboard style that mixes text with wireframes, providing a narrative of how a software concept is meant to work without actually implementing any interaction. Instead of a user clicking on the prototype to understand how it works, the audience hears someone describing what the storyboard is meant to represent. The individual

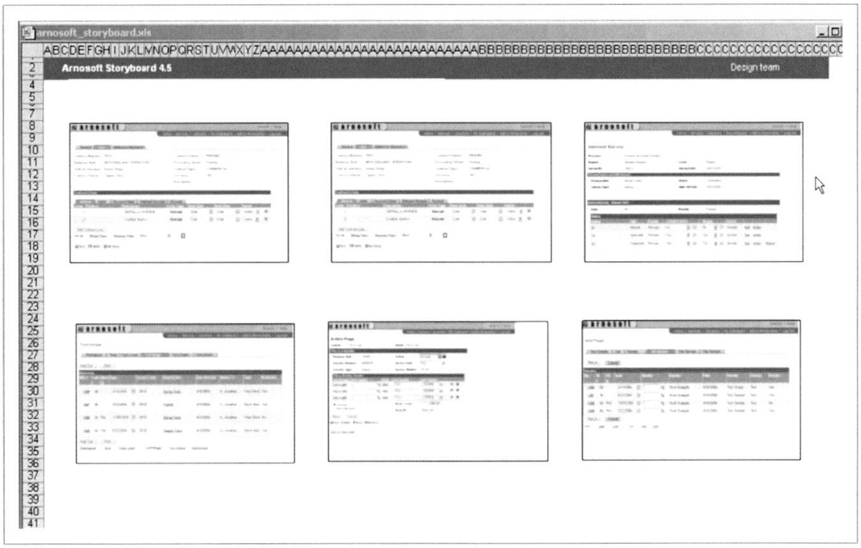

Figure 5.2.
Style 1 software storyboard prototype.

storyboard frames become the talking points, which are held together with a narrative text and supporting graphics (Figure 5.3).

This type of storyboard can act as a checkpoint to keep a software product or innovation team focused on the agreed-to conceptual direction. If, for example, the requirements, scenarios, storyboard frames, and other critical components related to a

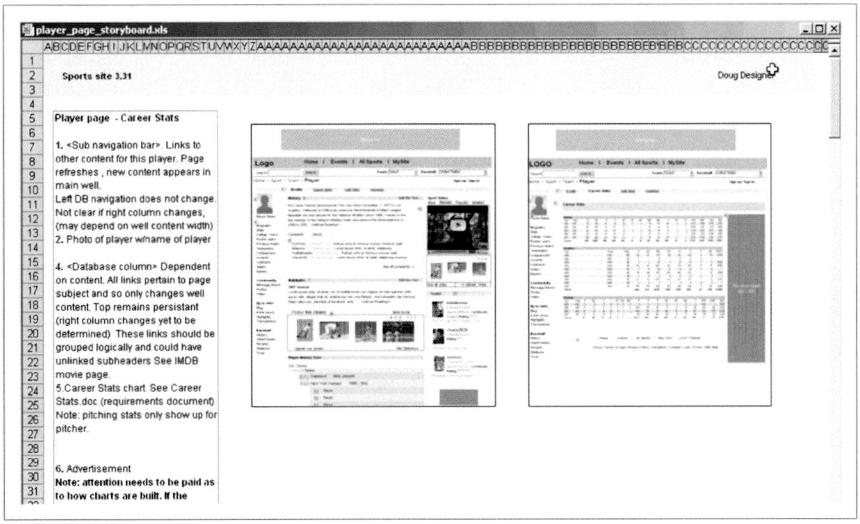

Figure 5.3.
Style 2 software storyboard prototype.

design or innovation scenario are all contained in the worksheets of one Excel prototype file, you can distribute the prototype to targeted audiences for review and feedback and then return later in the design process to review that information. This technique is especially convenient if the team members are geographically disbursed.

Another advantage to having all the pieces of a storyboard project contained in the worksheets of one Excel file is for presentation. You can seamlessly navigate through the various component parts that represent a design or innovation, including the base scenario, storyboard frames, task or process flows, and the like, without having to leave the Excel file that contains the storyboards.

In this chapter you will learn how to make this second kind of prototype using Excel.

Scenario

The scenario that prompts this prototype is based on the initial prototypes needed by a startup online bookseller, Berger Books. Entrepreneur Buzz Berger wants to get seed money for his project from an angel investor. The design team uses wireframes to describe the interface designs, so this storyboard appears early in the software creation process. The storyboard will be used by the team to visualize and understand the functional changes that are being proposed. After they are fully reviewed and iterated, they will be shown to the investor to visualize, in concrete terms, the innovative and competitive ideas on which Berger plans to make a splash in a very competitive marketplace. The team has pitched building the prototype in Microsoft Excel because

- The content inside the worksheets can be scrollable, unlike in PowerPoint, another good storyboarding tool.
- Key ideas and visualizations of the business plan can be included in one or more of the worksheets.
- The story prologue—an overview of the business and transaction concepts—can be contained in its own worksheet.
- The visual storyboard frames can be included in additional worksheets.

How to Create an Excel Storyboard Prototype

A typical storyboard is based on a narrative or story about an engaging topic, innovative concept, or big idea that you want to communicate. The most common storyboard approach begins with writing a story or narrative and then visualizing the key frames of the storyboard with hand-drawn or digital rough sketches.

The narrative can be broken into brief descriptions for each of the key frames. Depending on where you are in the software creation or innovation process, the storyboard drawings can be left rough or can evolve and be enriched with more refined visuals. For example, the drawings can range from simple pictures of users interacting with a system without showing the details of the actual system, or they can be sketch wireframes of the user interface or even screen captures of digital prototypes of the actual interface, as shown in Figure 5.3.

Narrative Writing

We'd like to give you a brief overview of *narrative writing*, the key initial activity for creating storyboards. The goal of narrative writing is to tell the story of an experience, event, or sequence of events while attempting to hold the reader's interest. Narrative writing is usually characterized as

- Written in first or third person
- Including characters, setting, plot
- Perhaps including dialogue
- Organized in chronological sequence (although flashbacks might be used)

The general principles of a narrative include

- *Revealing something of importance.* Narratives make a point that is usually defined in the first sentence but might appear as the last sentence in the first paragraph.
- *Vividly depicting characters and setting.* Bring a story to life by using your senses to depict the events of the story: how does it look, sound, feel, smell, taste? Include the important events that make up the story in enough detail for your audience to understand what happened while avoiding details that do not enhance the main point.
- *Showing, not telling.* Use vivid and precise verbs when describing your events.
- *Presenting events in a clear, chronological order.* Use a logical progression (e.g., beginning/middle/end) with good transitions when moving from point to point.

—Adapted from "Narrative Writing" (TheWritingSite.org) [3]

Storyboards are usually very sketchy (low fidelity) in the beginning and may remain that way, depending on your prototyping objectives. The fidelity of digital storyboards can evolve over time, with screen shots from higher-fidelity interactive prototypes substituted for earlier sketches. One way to determine an appropriate content focus along with the appropriate fidelity is to consult the Storyboard Content and Fidelity Matrix shown in Table 5.1. The content components of a given storyboard can vary in fidelity depending on your objectives for the storyboard, such as portraying rough design and experience concepts on one end of the continuum to presenting innovative concepts in a more refined way to investors at the other end of the continuum. Modulating the content fidelity of a storyboard allows you to place appropriate emphasis on one or more of those aspects.

Table 5.1. Storyboard Content and Fidelity Matrix

Content	Very Low Fidelity	Low Fidelity	Medium Fidelity	High Fidelity	Highest Fidelity
Information design	+	++	++	+	——
Interaction design	——	+	++	−	−
Visual design	++	++	+	+	——
Editorial content	++	+	−	——	——
Branding expression	++	+	+	+	+
System performance	NA	NA	NA	NA	NA

++, Most appropriate;
+, appropriate;
−, not appropriate;
——, completely inappropriate;
NA, not applicable.

You might include this and other helpful decision-making matrices in your Excel template as a worksheet titled Matrices.

Creating the Berger Books Storyboard in Excel

In this exercise you will create a sample storyboard based on the Berger Books presentation.

Start with an outline covering the various worksheets of your storyboard. This will give you an idea of the worksheets you will need. Your storyboards will show wireframes that you have built in an Excel template. To get the assets you need, you will have to go through all the worksheets of your prototype and then capture and save the images to a folder. (For an explanation on how to build a wireframe in Excel, see Chapter 6.) To capture the images, use a screen capture program such as SnagIt or the Macintosh screen capture command, such as APPLE + SHIFT + 4.

To Build a Storyboard:

1. Open the Excel prototyping template that you've already made and save it under a new name.

2. Copy and rename the **canvas** worksheet to `starter page` (Figure 5.4), making this new worksheet the starter page for your storyboard (Figure 5.5).

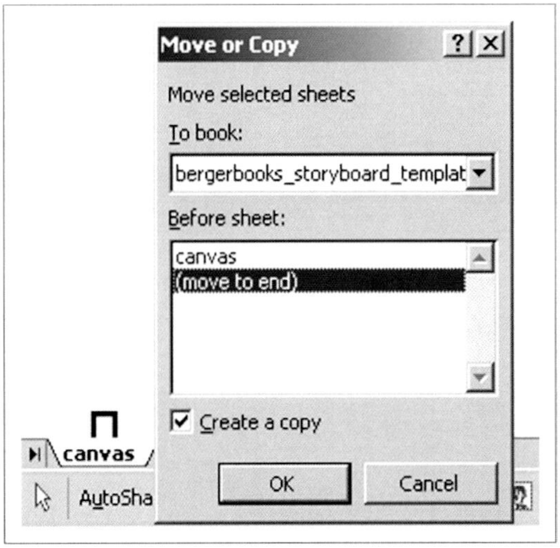

Figure 5.4.
The dialog box for copying the canvas worksheet to move it to the end of the worksheets.

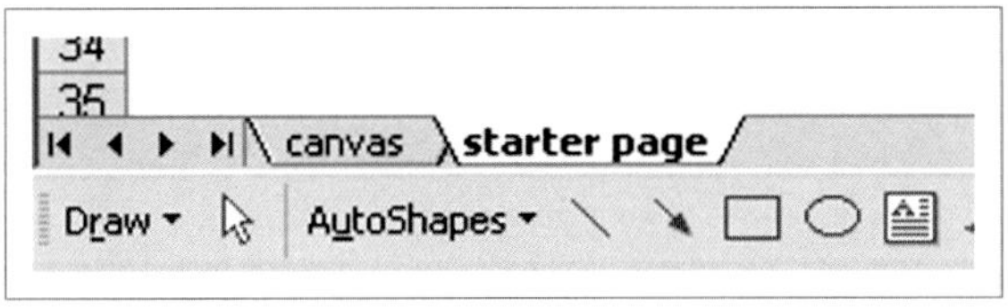

Figure 5.5.
Worksheet renamed to `starter page`.

On this worksheet you will create a header and text box and establish the positioning for the wireframe images. The header will include the name of the company (Berger's Books), the title of the project (Homepage to purchase page), and the author's name. The starter page will then have all the elements built into it that you will need for subsequent worksheets of your storyboard.

To Create the Header:

1. On the starter page, create a header by highlighting the top three rows on the worksheet, then right-clicking the selected rows, and choosing **Format Cells** (Figure 5.6).

Note

You will want to make the header unobtrusive so that it doesn't distract from the overall presentation of your storyboard.

2. In the **Format Cells** dialog box, click the **Patterns** tab, select the lightest gray color, and then click **OK** to confirm the color choice (Figure 5.7).

3. Right-click in table cell B2; then type in the header information (Berger's Books, the title of the project, and the author's name) as a single row with plenty of space between the groups of text (Figure 5.8).

Figure 5.6.
Choosing Format Cells.

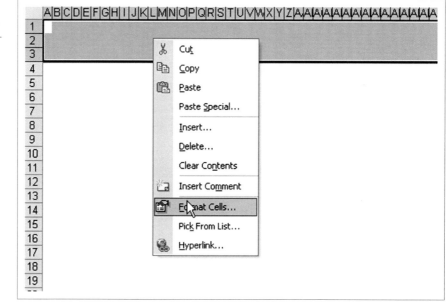

Creating the Berger Books Storyboard in Excel

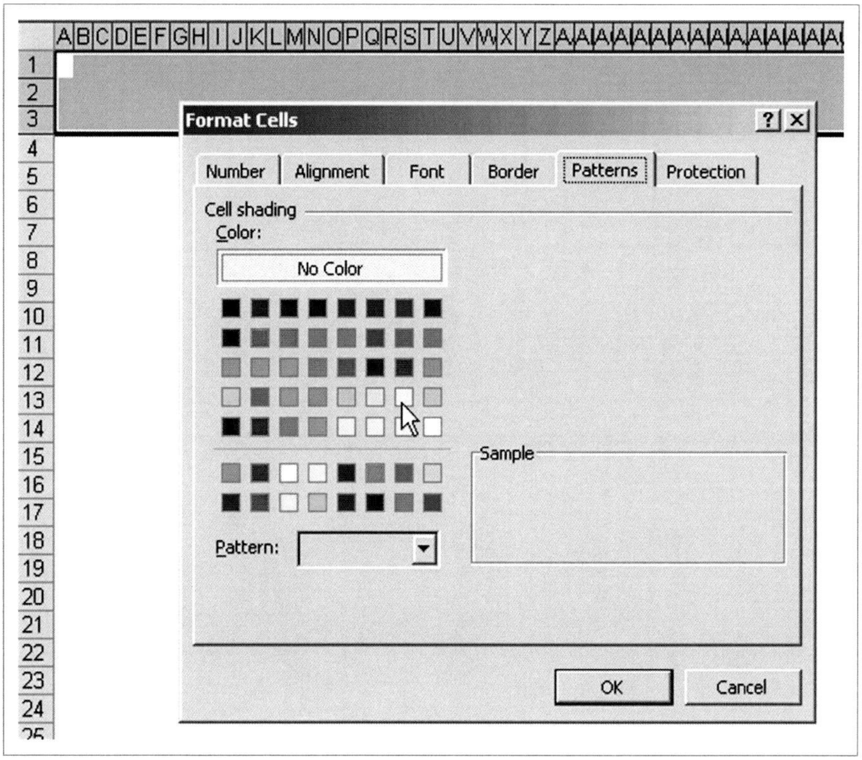

Figure 5.7.

Selecting the lightest gray color for the header area.

Figure 5.8.

Header information, including Berger's Books, project title, and author's name.

Note

You can type each text component into a separate table cell if you want control over precise positioning of each.

4. While the header is still highlighted, select **12 point, Arial bold**, and the color white in the **Format** toolbar.

5. So that the header area has a pleasing height, make the rows above and below the header text smaller by doing the following:

- While pressing the **CONTROL** key, click row 1 and then click row 3.
- Right-click row 3, then choose **Row height**, and then enter 5 in the **Row height** dialog box.
- Click **OK** to complete the header sizing (Figure 5.9).

You have now completed a header for your storyboard. Now you'll place images in your storyboard.

To Place a Wireframe Image on the Worksheet:

1. In the menu bar, click **Insert > Picture > From File** (Figure 5.10).
2. From the folder in your file system that contains all your wireframe images, select the **homepage** wireframe (bb_homepage_wire.gif) as shown in Figure 5.11 and then insert it.

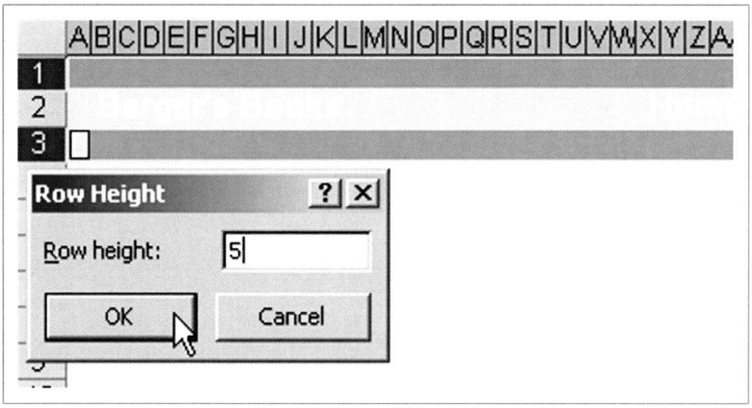

Figure 5.9.

Dialog box for adjusting header row height.

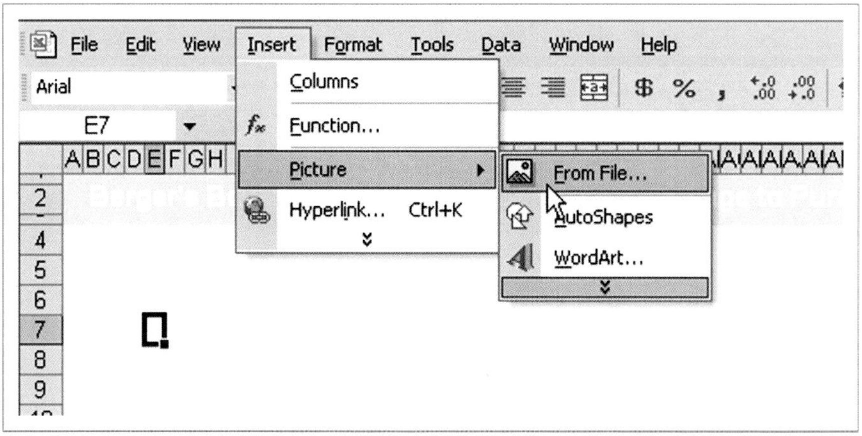

Figure 5.10.

Selecting the commands to place an image from the file system into the starter page worksheet.

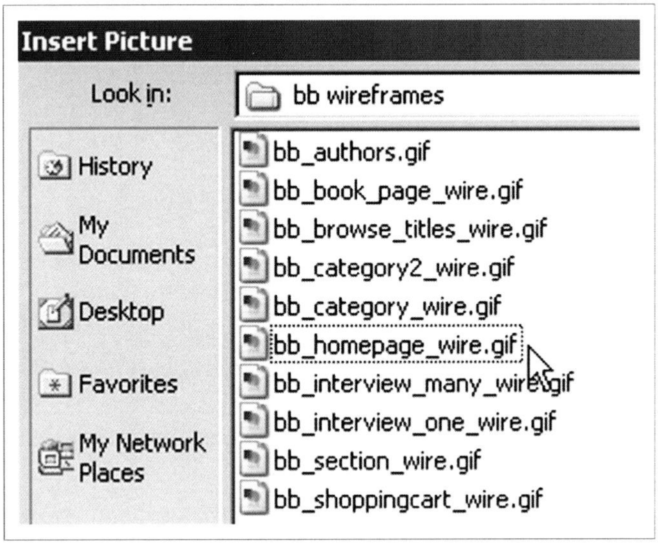

Figure 5.11.
Image of homepage wireframe being browsed in a file list.

This places the wireframe image onto your worksheet. The image is inserted at full size and highlighted (Figure 5.12).

3. Adjust the size of your image by first selecting the lower-right corner of the image. Then, while holding down the **SHIFT** key, drag the corner to proportionally resize the image as desired, leaving enough room to the right of it for some descriptive text.

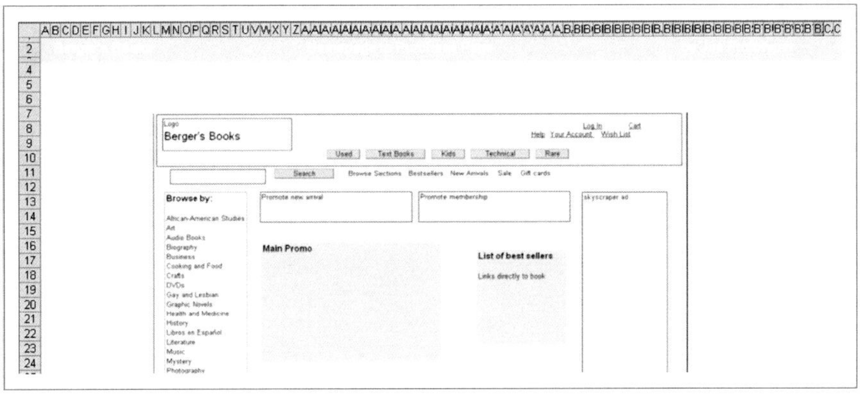

Figure 5.12.
Image of homepage wireframe placed on worksheet.

Tip

To ensure that the rest of your wireframes are positioned and scaled the same way, create some table cell markers as guides (Figure 5.13). To create the markers, highlight a cell just above the upper-left corner of the image; then right-click and choose **Format Cells > Patterns**. Select a light gray to mark the spot. Do the same at the upper-right corner of the image. Now when you insert a wireframe image into a worksheet, you will know that all the wireframes will be aligned and scaled the same.

Now that you have set the position for the wirefame images, you can position the text box for the titles and descriptive text.

To Create a Text Box:

1. From the **Drawing** toolbar, Select the **AutoShape Rectangle** and position it to the right of the wireframe image. Stretch the rectangle down until it seems large enough for the text that you expect to insert (Figure 5.14).

2. Right-click the rectangle and select **Add Text**. Type in some placeholder text for the title and body text. With the headline text highlighted, format it to **Arial bold, 12 point**.

3. Format the box itself by right-clicking the edge of the box and selecting **Format AutoShape**. In the Format AutoShape dialog box, make the outline disappear by setting it to white (Figure 5.15).

This is only one design you might use. By repositioning the elements, you can explore different design variations, as shown in Figures 5.16 and 5.17 (page 104).

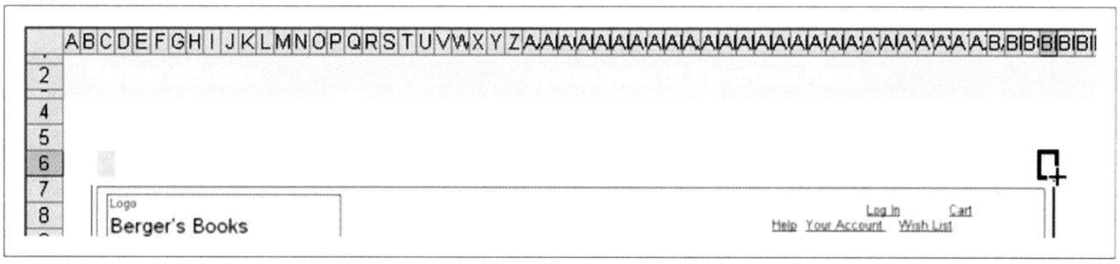

Figure 5.13.
Creating a table cell marker.

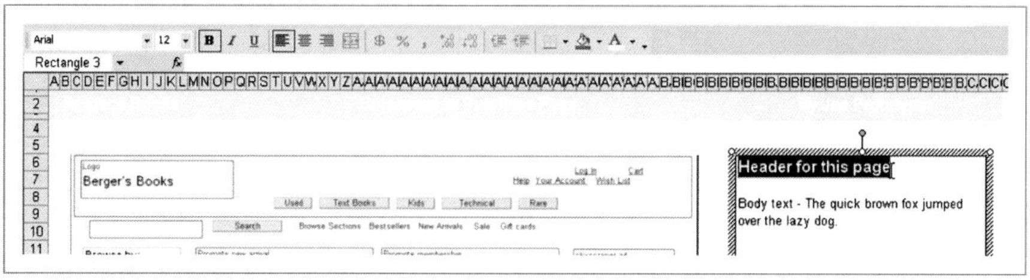

Figure 5.14.
An AutoShape Rectangle used to hold the annotation for a storyboard.

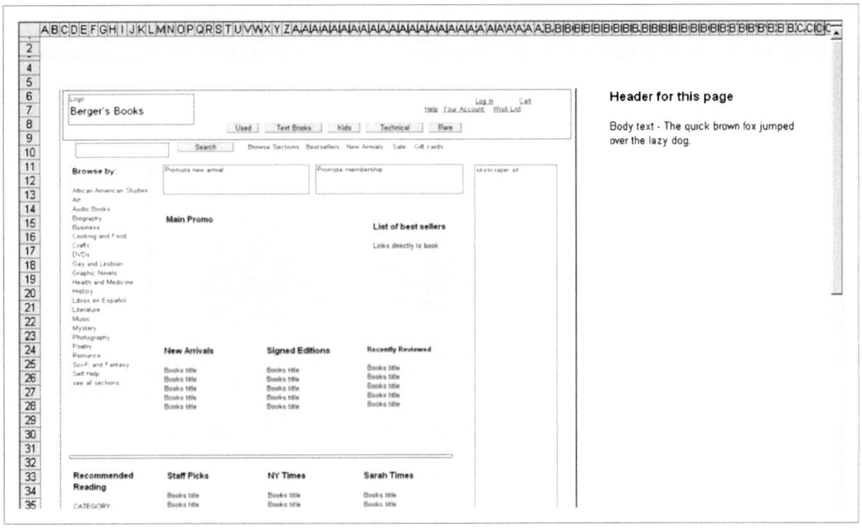

Figure 5.15.
Finished storyboard worksheet with header, placed graphic, and annotation area.

Tip

You know that many further ideas will emerge when you share your storyboard with your design team and project stakeholders. To capture further ideas in your storyboard, you can create a text box below the story text box to serve as a capture space for ideas to act on throughout the design process.

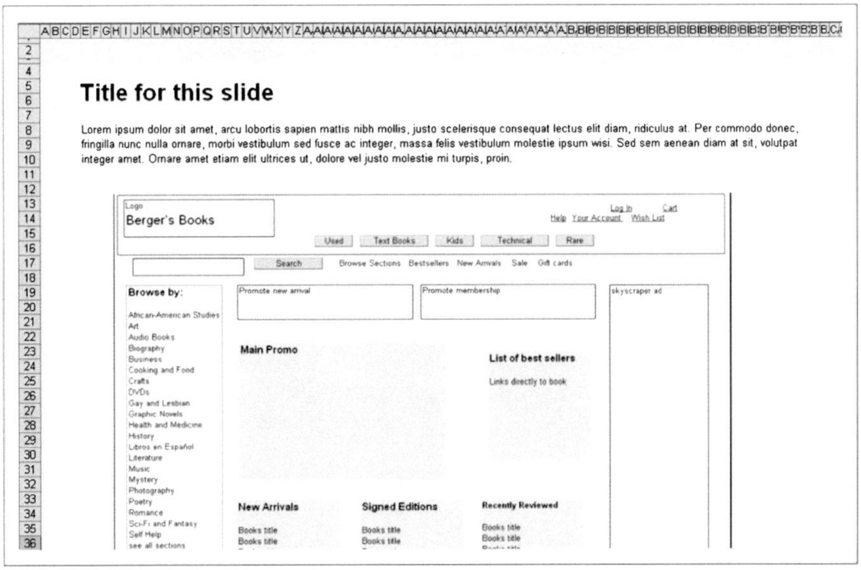

Figure 5.16.
Storyboard worksheet configured with text at the top of the worksheet.

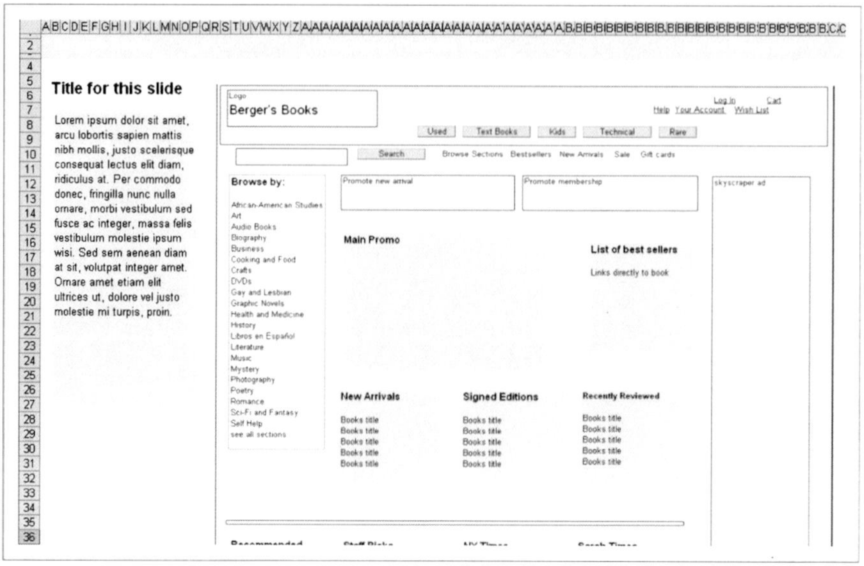

Figure 5.17.

Storyboard worksheet configured with text to the left of the image.

Meanwhile, to finish the worksheet, select and delete the wireframe image that you were using for positioning purposes; then save your storyboard template. Now that this is finished, you can create your storyboard presentation. For each new worksheet that you need, you can copy the starter page and then move the worksheet to the end of the document. Double-click the tab to rename the worksheet. Each worksheet will carry any settings that you have applied into the starter page.

You can add an executive summary, a storyboard outline, or other ancillary information worksheets by modifying a starter page to accommodate those needs.

Options for Presenting Your Storyboard

In the preceding exercise you presented the prototype to your team, so there is little concern that everyone knows it was built in Excel. But if you want a more professional-looking storyboard, you can hide the row and column headers as well as the toolbar(s) on the periphery of your worksheets by navigating the Excel menu to **Tools > Options > View** and then deselecting the row and column headers and Formula bar views. This makes the worksheet appear a little less busy, and as a bonus, no one will be able to guess that your prototype was created in Excel.

Excel is much more versatile than PowerPoint or other similar presentation software applications in that it allows you to present vertically deep worksheets with content below the "fold" via vertical scrolling. Also, Excel allows you to either import wireframes or build your prototype completely in Excel. In the same way you learned how to build a starter page in Chapter 4, you can set up your presentation settings, which can mimic the master page feature found in PowerPoint. In addition, you can use hyperlinks in Excel so that you can link to other worksheets, workbooks, files, or even Websites and pages, thus adding yet another dimension to your storyboard capabilities.

To present your storyboard, the simplest technique is to use the tabs at the bottom of each worksheet. In Chapter 10, "Sharing Your Excel Prototytpe," we cover various ways to color code them and organize them for easier presentation.

Using hyperlinked text within your storyboard is another technique. In this example two text links are positioned at the top of the column used for the annotation area. The standard indicators, Previous and Next, are hyperlinked to either the previous worksheet or the next worksheet in the storyboard.

In this exercise you will learn how to create hyperlinked text to navigate a storyboard.

To Add Navigation Links to a Storyboard:

Follow the steps shown in Figures 5.18 through 5.21 (through page 107).

Figure 5.18.
Indicator <<Previous added above the annotation area.

Figure 5.19.

Highlight all the text in the cell; then right-click and choose Hyperlink.

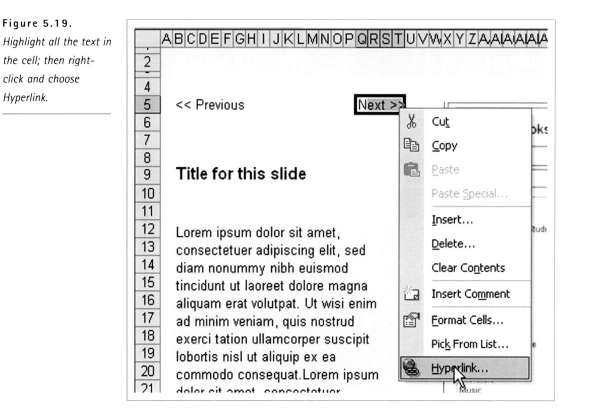

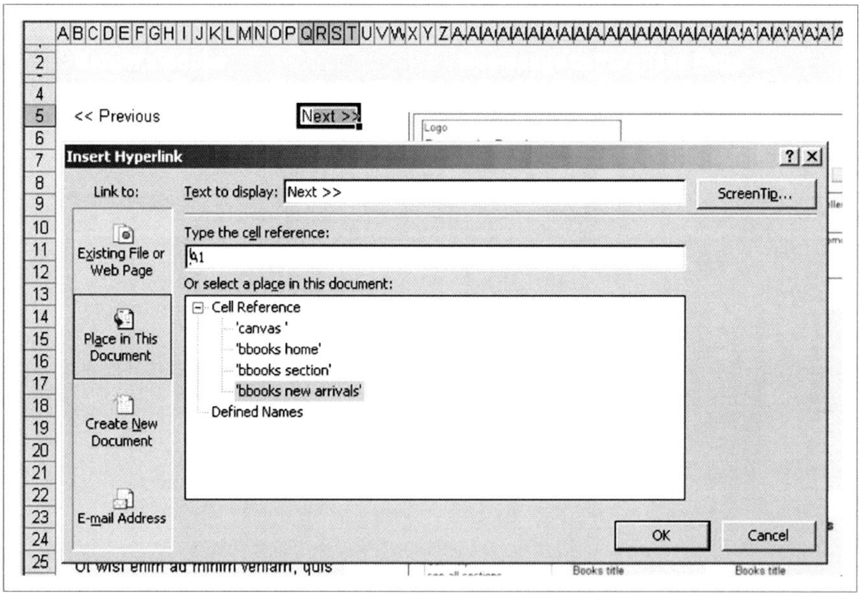

Figure 5.20.

In the Insert Hyperlink dialog box, choose the Place in This Document *button, which will display the other worksheets in the document. Choose the next worksheet in the sequence you want to link to.*

Figure 5.21.
*The indicator, Next >>,
as a hyperlink.*

Conclusion

In this chapter you learned how to use Excel to create storyboard prototypes. The main advantage of a storyboard prototype is its ability to narrate a product's key features without actually implementing designs or interaction in the design. In the next chapter we will discuss how you can use Excel to create your designs in the form of digital wireframes.

References

[1] Storyboard, http://en.wikipedia.org/wiki/Storyboard, August 10, 2007.
[2] Jonathan Arnowitz, Michael Arent, and Nevin Berger, *Effective Prototyping for Software Makers*, San Francisco: Morgan Kaufmann, 2007.
[3] "Narrative Writing" (TheWritingSite.org), 2007.

CHAPTER 6

WIREFRAMES

In this chapter you will learn how to

- Think about wireframes
- Create a task flow or site map wireframe
- Link site map pages to other pages
- Create skeletal and detailed wireframes
- Apply the Excel prototyping methodology to wireframes

Introduction to Wireframes

Wireframes derive their name from the frameworks that sculptors and modelers use to provide the starting shape of three-dimensional work; the artist then "fleshes out" the design with clay or other material, just as you will "flesh out" your design with higher-fidelity content as you progress through the iterative prototyping process. Excel provides the framework for building and refining your wireframes.

You produce wireframes to help explore interactions and flows and to try out different locations for interface elements without spending time and effort on high-fidelity graphics. Your first wireframe might be sketched on a piece of paper or a whiteboard and then further developed in Excel. You can include some simple shading or a few standard colors to liven up the visual aspects, but you don't have to. Your primary audience is your design team and other internal stakeholders. Showing wireframes to customers will often simply confuse them.

When you show these sketch-type wireframes to end users or other external stakeholders, increase the fidelity to the point where they understand what they are looking at, but no higher. These sketch-like wireframes invite end users to comment thoroughly on them. Wireframes that look complete tend to get lighter, less substantial feedback, such as comments on font colors, instead of the more conceptual feedback that the sketch wireframes elicit from users.

Think of your wireframe as a brainstorming tool. Because they are created so quickly, you won't get too attached to your wireframes—you will create and discard many wireframes in the process of designing your site. Wireframes enable people to handle quick design iterations without getting caught up in either the details of high-fidelity graphics or the emotional attachment of having worked on something for a long time. Wireframes are a conceptual tool at the start of the design process, but later on the fidelity can be high enough to be the basis for implementation.

Wireframe fidelity ranges from site maps representing site structure to skeletal user interface (UI) wireframes with placeholders for text and graphics as well as detailed wireframes with actual graphics and text. If you create several wireframes representing related windows in your software, you can link them together to simulate the application flow. Finally, you can include color, high-fidelity graphics, and real text elements that will feed into the high-fidelity prototypes for your software.

Task Flow or Site Map Diagram

A task flow or site map provides a conceptual framework for your software. A task flow provides a diagram of how a user will interact with your software to complete a task. Usually each item in the flow represents a window or the state of a window. Often these task flows help you make key decisions on design and navigation structure before going into detailed design.

A site map, on the other hand, is a visual, hierarchical guide to the organization of a Website. Building a site map helps you determine the relationships and links between various elements and pages of the Website and can facilitate discussion about Website content and task flows. Site maps typically look like corporate organization charts, but be careful that your Website does not simply mirror your company's organization chart. Visitors to your site don't care how your company is organized—they care about locating the information that they came to find and about reaching the goal that brought them to your site, such as buying a book.

In the following procedures we show you how to build these high-level structural wireframes. The techniques are the same for these prototypes, so we provide only an example for a site map. For a task flow you would substitute the task flow diagram for the hierarchical site map.

In this exercise you will build a flowchart using Excel's AutoShapes and Connectors.

To Create Site Map Wireframe Boxes:

1. Begin with a fresh canvas worksheet in a new workbook and rename the worksheet `Site Map`.

2. From the Drawing menu, choose **AutoShapes > Basic Shapes**.

3. Select a simple rectangle (Figure 6.1).

4. Place the cursor near the top of the worksheet; then click and drag to create a rectangle.

5. To label the box, highlight it by right-clicking the border and choose **Add Text** from the menu. Inside the box a line appears, indicating that you can enter text.

6. Enter the text `Homepage`. The default text position will be in the top right. In this example, center the text in the box both vertically and horizontally. Right-click the box and select **Format AutoShape**, select the **Alignment** tab, and choose **Horizontal** Center and **Vertical** Center (Figure 6.2, page 112).

7. Repeat this process, adding three boxes in a line below the Homepage box. Label them `Section 1`, `Section 2`, and `Section 3` (Figure 6.3, page 112).

In a site map you can indicate the relationship between the different boxes that you create. The position of the boxes indicates hierarchy that is usually combined with connector lines. Excel offers automated connector lines as part of the standard AutoShapes menu.

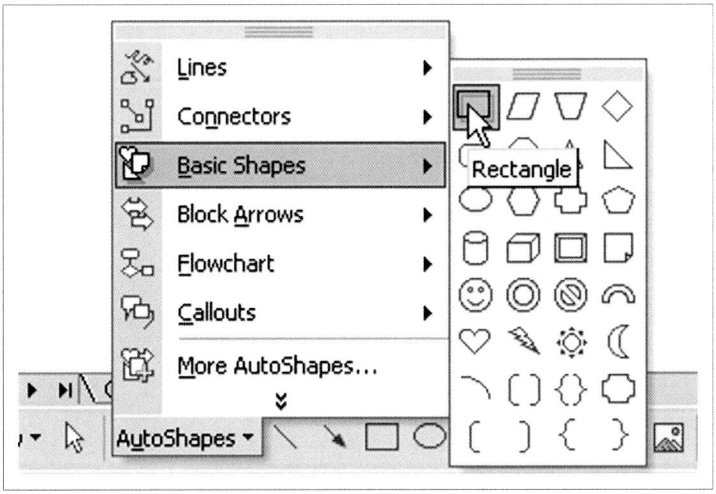

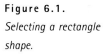

Figure 6.1.
Selecting a rectangle shape.

Figure 6.2.

Selecting the text centering attributes.

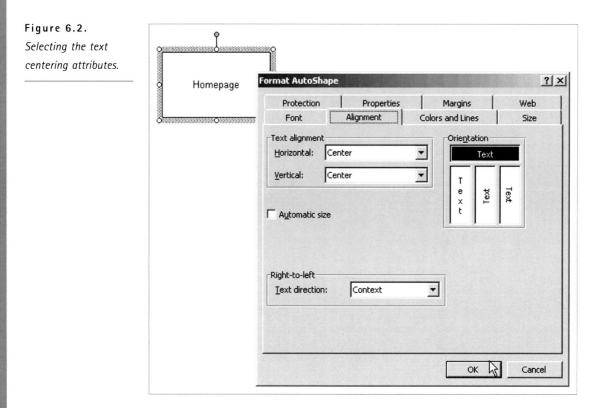

Figure 6.3.

Basic site map boxes.

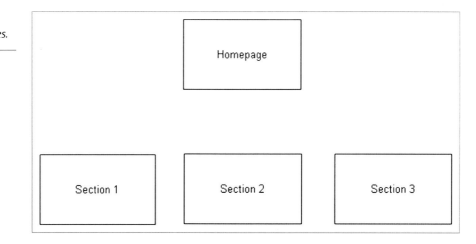

To Add Connectors Between Boxes:

1. Choose **AutoShapes > Connectors > Elbow Arrow Connector** (Figure 6.4).
2. Select the box where you want the connector to begin.

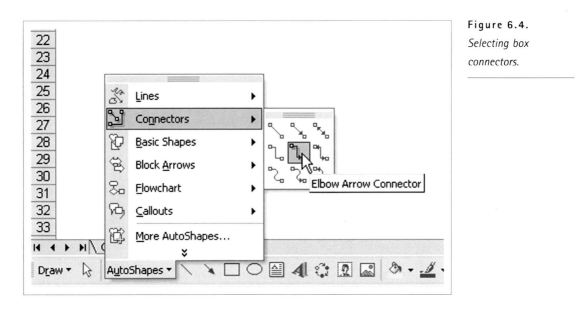

Figure 6.4.
*Selecting box
connectors.*

The active points on the box are indicated by small circles as you position your cursor over them. Click one of the points that indicate position to anchor the connector. Click an anchor point on a different box to position the connector end (Figure 6.5).

Multiple connectors can be attached at a single point to connect one box to several other boxes (Figure 6.6, page 114).

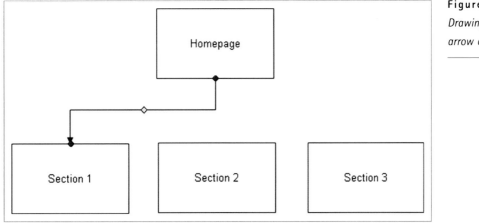

Figure 6.5.
*Drawing an elbow
arrow connector.*

Figure 6.6.

Multiple connectors to a single box.

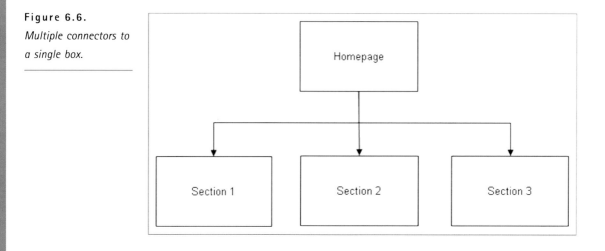

Though there are other ways to create the lines between boxes, the advantage of using the connectors is that they are anchored to the box and will readjust as boxes are repositioned.

The Hyperlinked Site Map

Often a site map is a standalone page among the many pages of documentation. Using Excel, the site map can take on an added dimension or function by using the feature that adds a hyperlink to a shape. Your static boxes can then link to the worksheets that they represent in your designs.

To Create an Interactive Site Map:

1. Create four new worksheets in your site map document, representing the four site map boxes: a homepage and three section pages.
2. Highlight the box labeled **Homepage**, right-click the box, and select **Hyperlink**.
3. In the **Insert Hyperlink** dialog box, select **Place in This Document**, find **Homepage** in the site map (Figure 6.7), and click **OK**.

The Homepage box in the site map is now a hyperlink linked to the wireframe worksheet that it represents. Repeat this procedure for each box. Now your site maps can represent a high-level structure and can also act as an index that links to the page-level wireframes. Use this technique early in the design process as a

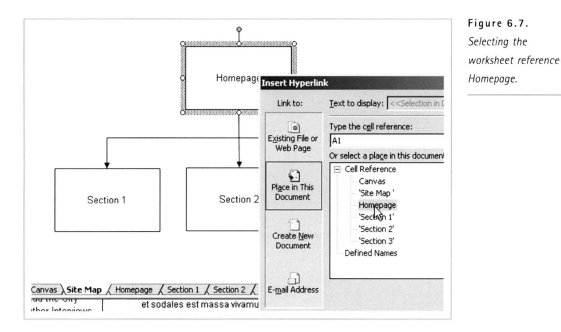

Figure 6.7.
*Selecting the
worksheet reference
Homepage.*

proof of concept for a navigation structure or as a way to navigate across many worksheets in a wireframe, demonstrating the relationship between the different linked worksheets.

Tip

Create a link from each linked worksheet back to the site map worksheet so you don't get lost.

From Skeletal to Detailed Wireframes

Wireframes that describe screen designs can range from the simple to the complex. A good wireframe always remains conceptual and simple in its graphical representation, but it can become more specific in the way it conveys content architecture, structure, requirements, and task flow.

How you approach building a wireframe in Excel depends on the kind of wireframe you need. In this example of a skeletal wireframe, an entire worksheet is built using only cells with borders and colors. Refer to Chapter 4 to see how to format cells.

The minimal descriptive text is written in the cells within the boxes. Working in this manner is quick and easy—a perfect way to describe an interface concept that doesn't need much detail.

Though it is true that this very low-fidelity wireframe (Figure 6.8) could be built in other applications, building it in Excel offers some advantages that other applications do not have. One advantage is keeping all your designs in a single document file, which lets you easily compare different iterations as you try out various ideas. A single file also lets you share all your progress with others on your team. As your ideas begin to take form, you will have them together as tabbed worksheets in your workbook, where they can be rearranged, renamed, and presented as a progression of visual ideas.

To build the more-detailed wireframe in this example, using a combination of table cells and AutoShapes provides greater flexibility and control in what you

Figure 6.8.

Example of a skeletal wireframe.

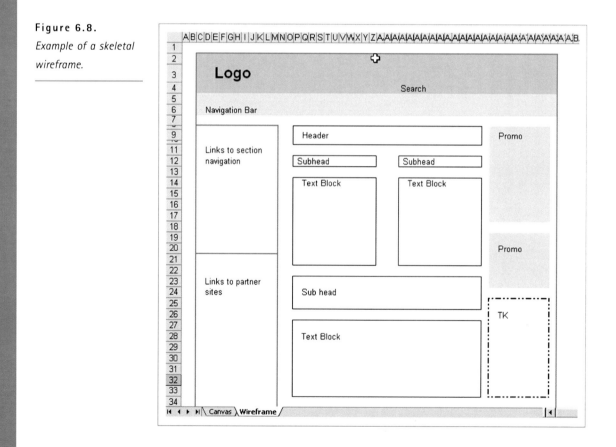

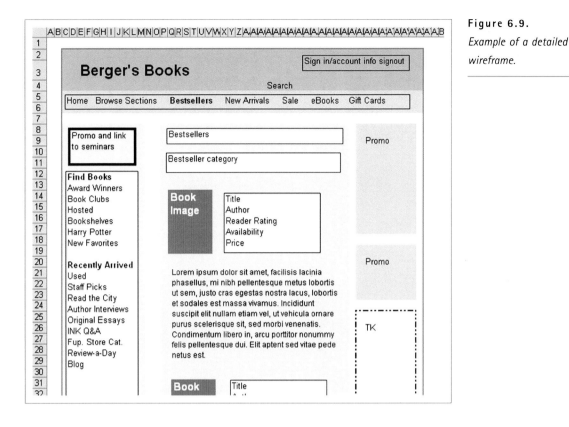

Figure 6.9.

Example of a detailed wireframe.

can describe visually. In the building of this wireframe, the grid structure of the worksheet is built using the previous wireframes' colored and bordered cells. This basic structure remains unaffected by any shape put on top and acts like a background defining the site grid. The content, which is described in greater detail than in the skeletal wireframe, is included in shapes positioned on the worksheet. In some shapes the text shows accurate content, while other shapes are not specific and merely offer greeked text to indicate an undefined content area. Different borders, colors, and border style can emphasize a section of the design or highlight important aspect of the design concept, as shown in Figure 6.9.

The Excel Methodology

Even though wireframes are not detailed, you can still use the same methodology in building wireframes as you would for building more complex design prototypes.

Figure 6.10.

Worksheet with predefined graphics elements.

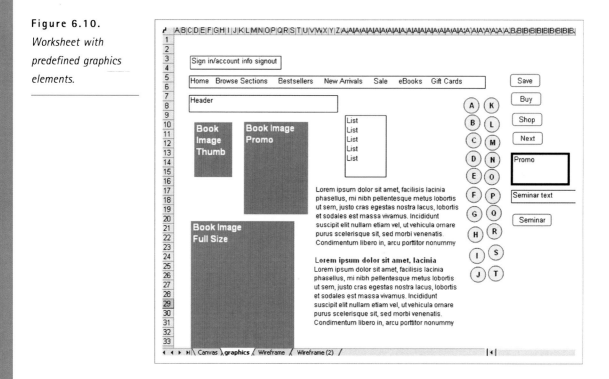

In Chapter 4 you learned how to build template worksheets with a library of widgets and detailed buttons to facilitate reuse in complex worksheets. You can do the same for your wireframe template. The elements that you put in your graphics library might be nothing more than simple boxes or shapes filled with greeked text. You can save time and effort by not having to create new elements; you can copy and paste them from your template worksheets into your wireframes. When you include reusable elements in your wireframe Excel file, other members of your team can work with the same elements that you used, ensuring consistency and a quick turnaround of iterations (Figures 6.10 and 6.11).

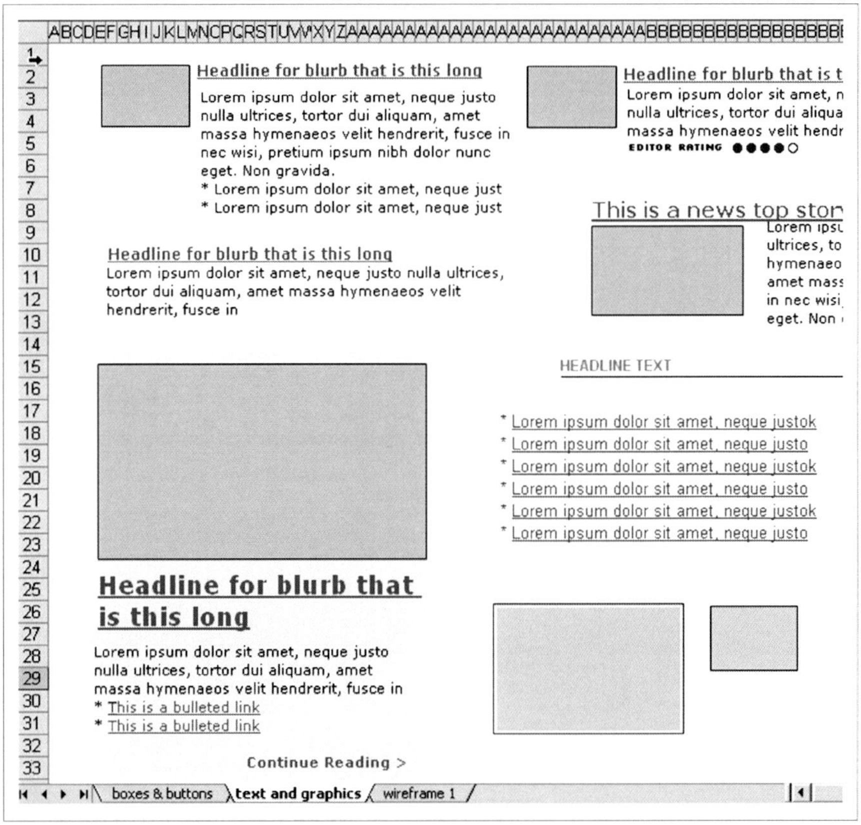

Figure 6.11.

Worksheet with predefined text and graphics arrangements.

Conclusion

In this chapter you have learned about various styles and uses of wireframes and how to create low- and high-fidelity wireframes, including site maps and task flows. In the next chapter you will make the designs interactive.

References

[1] Jonathan Arnowitz, Michael Arent, and Nevin Berger, *Effective Prototyping for Software Makers*, San Francisco: Morgan Kaufmann, 2007.

[2] Carolyn Snider, *Paper Prototyping: The Fast and Easy Way to Design and Refine User Interfaces*, San Francisco: Morgan Kaufmann, 2003.

[3] Jo Ann Hackos et al., *User and Task Analysis for Interface Design*, Hoboken, NJ: Wiley & Sons, 1998.

CHAPTER 7

DIGITAL INTERACTIVE
PROTOTYPES

In this chapter you will learn how to

- Use digital interactive prototypes
- Create a digital interactive prototype with Excel
- Create a digital interactive prototype

About Digital Interactive Prototypes

A digital interactive prototype is an interactive wireframe that is quickly created and iterated using low-tech tools such as Excel, PowerPoint, or Visio. This chapter does not cover the form of digital interactive prototype that is coded or scripted and fully interactive, such as those created in Director, Flash, and so on. Digital interactive prototypes share a good deal in common with paper prototypes in that they can be very rapidly generated, allowing them to be used early in the software creation process. Like paper prototypes, interactive prototypes can be employed for early formative usability testing and stakeholder evaluations. Unlike paper prototypes, these interactive prototypes can range from a series of low-fidelity click-through screens for quick visualization of a design concept to a high-fidelity interactive prototype. Paper prototypes, in contrast, are generally lower fidelity.

An interactive prototype can have the look and feel of the final product. A user can click on a button or menu, and it can appear as though the button or menu is working. The perception of interaction is created by linking to another worksheet in Excel; the change is almost completely transparent to the user. This simulation of interactivity makes interactive prototyping uniquely useful for

- Understanding task flow and context of use by asking a user to directly interact with the prototype as though it were functioning software
- Validating assumptions in scenarios, requirements, and user profiles through its higher interaction fidelity
- Getting more detailed product feedback in usability testing than from paper prototyping, because the prototype has a more natural look and feel
- Getting feedback from remote stakeholders who cannot attend a face-to-face meeting

How Does an Interactive Prototype Work?

An interactive prototype is created from a storyboard scenario, task flow mappings, and a collection of roughed-out window or Web page designs. To simulate navigation and interaction as specified in a scenario and task flow, these designs are linked in sequence with hyperlinks to mimic a working system. In Excel you can apply interaction to text or graphics via hyperlinks and other techniques. You can also simply switch between worksheets using the worksheet tabs.

In Excel, the content of a digital prototype can be easily arranged, rearranged, and modified to allow rapid exploration and validation of design ideas. Because of this flexibility and malleability, interactive prototypes are especially useful during the early to middle stages of design, which are generally more exploratory in nature. Because these prototypes are rendered in interactive format, they are especially helpful for remote usability testing [2] [3], where test moderators and test participants are in separate geographic locations.

Scenario

Welcome to Acme Ceramics, the online retail case study that will help you continue the journey to discovering the value and applicability of effective prototyping. Acme Ceramics is a case study we'll use to guide you through the steps of creating an Excel interactive prototype. Acme Ceramics is a company that's been around for four years. Its core business is selling ceramic dishware products on the Web. The company now wants to expand its market and customer reach by branching out into other household goods. A project team has been put together, including a product manager, a domain specialist, a creative writer, two designers, and three developers. In addition, Acme has external stakeholders in the form of venture capital investors.

Creating Interactive Prototypes with Excel

Excel's strong design layout support and precise grid alignment features make it useful for laying out the screens of an interactive prototype. After you have set up a prototyping template in Excel that meets your needs, you can quickly and easily create interactive prototypes with any mix of fidelities. Why would you choose Excel for interactive prototyping instead of another tool? Let's explore the reasons by using the Acme Ceramics redesign scenario as an example.

As described in the sidebar, the Acme Ceramics business model, branding, and Website are known quantities that need a "facelift and body tucks" to regain some of the customer base lost to competitors. Acme Ceramics has plans to add new products and expand its existing customer base. The team decided to develop digital interactive prototypes in Excel because it offers a complete prototyping environment that already exists and that can be reused and updated.

To begin the prototyping process, the team must update the graphics library with the new look, and introduce new controls and behaviors to the prototyping environment. Because the Excel prototyping environment is reusable, the team does not have to start from scratch.

Gathering and Verifying Requirements for the Prototype

Before starting any design and prototyping activity on the Acme Ceramics Website redesign, the design team must articulate its assumptions about the overall design concept before gathering requirements. The requirements can include business, functional, technical, and user requirements. Not all the requirements can be gathered at the beginning of the redesign project. The design team begins by gathering the ones that are readily available and then continues over time to gather more requirements as they become available and as their design evolves and progresses through iterations.

In the Acme Ceramics redesign, a substantial set of business requirements is available from the product management team in the form of a business requirements document (BRD). The BRD describes in detail these key requirements:

- A new branding scheme, including renaming Acme Ceramics to Arnosoft
- A new overall visual look based on the new branding scheme
- A new look and feel catering to the emerging Gen-X customer base
- A utility to collect marketing data about customers navigating to the site

The product marketing group also provides an updated functional requirements document (FRD) that articulates a new use case that requires the following functions:

- Site hit tracking data aggregation, tabulation (per market segment, geographic location, and navigation origin), and reporting
- Related products configurator

Meanwhile, the Website architecture team provides a technical requirements document (TRD) with the following requirements:

- Technical integration to support a third-party tool for hit tracking
- Business logic that supports the related products configurator

The user requirements are

- The new branding scheme and the new resulting look
- Improvements resulting from recent usability testing
- Other details of the user requirements will be articulated during iterations of design, prototyping, and prototype validation

Creating a Screen Flow Diagram

Before becoming too immersed in screen designs, create a screen flow diagram. The screen flow depicts the flow of tasks required for a user to successfully find and select a desired product or set of products, place them in a virtual shopping cart, and complete the transaction of placing an order (Figure 7.1).

Screen flow diagrams comprise miniature representations of screens, commonly called thumbnails, and interconnecting lines that illustrate the interaction flow paths. A screen flow diagram is useful when you're setting up the interaction and navigation schemes in your prototype. This screen flow will help you decide which parts of navigation and interaction should actually function in your prototype and which can remain static.

Figure 7.1.

Screen flow diagram.

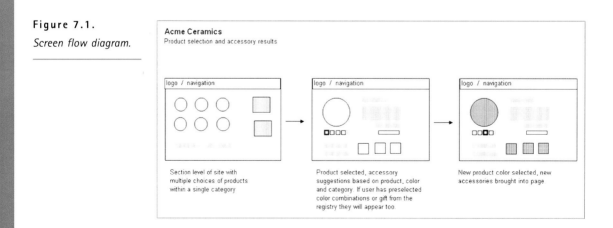

To create a screen flow diagram, begin by creating the thumbnail screen images using one of three methods:

- Hand-draw the screens on paper, scan them, and then reduce them digitally to a desired thumbnail size in a graphics editing tool.
- Create graphic representations of the different screens to a desired fidelity using a graphics editing tool; then reduce them to a thumbnail size.
- Create simple thumbnails in Excel using the drawing and text tools.

To Import Scanned Drawings or Graphics Created in Another Application:

1. From the **Drawing** toolbar, choose **Insert Picture From File**.
2. Browse to the location of the image file.
3. Click **Insert**.

The picture is then inserted into the prototype.

A drawback to using imported images is that you cannot easily modify them after they are imported into Excel. As described in Appendix A, you can scale, crop, and alter the look of imported images. To actually edit the image, you must use a graphics editing tool and then reimport. If you create thumbnail images in Excel, you can change them anytime you need to without having to use another application.

Create a thumbnail of an application window or Web page by adding shapes to a rectangle that represents a page or screen. If you have any pencil sketches or print-outs from other apps, keep them on hand for reference. In this case, refer back to Figure 7.1.

To Create the Thumbnails in Excel:

1. Our first step is to draw the rectangle that will be the basis for the thumbnail. From the **Drawing** toolbar, choose **AutoShapes** > **Basic Shapes**.

From the **Basic Shapes** menu, you can choose from a number of shapes that should cover most of your needs for a simple design. Other menus, such as the **Flowchart** menu or **Stars and Banners**, offer more shapes. Choose **More AutoShapes** for a gallery of clip art images that you can use.

2. Select the Rectangle, as shown in Figure 7.2 (page 126).

Figure 7.2.
Choosing AutoShapes
> Basic Shapes >
Rectangle.

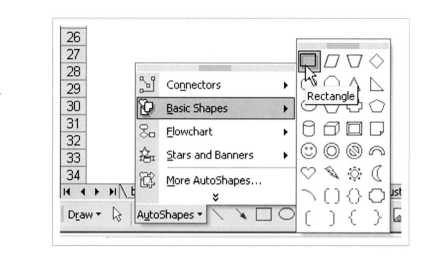

3. Draw a rectangle that is 10 rows tall and about 20 columns wide, as shown in Figure 7.3.

4. To create the header of the thumbnail, choose **AutoShapes** > **Basic Shapes** > **Rectangle** again. Click and drag to draw a small narrow rectangle, as pictured in Figure 7.4.

5. To add text to the header, right-click the header rectangle and choose **Edit Text** (Figure 7.5).

Figure 7.3.
The Basic Shape rectangle.

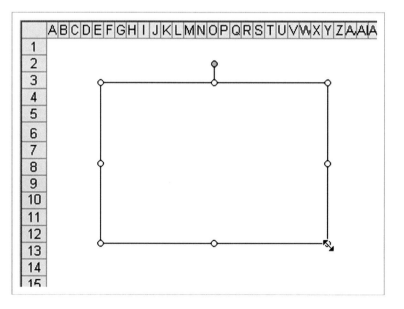

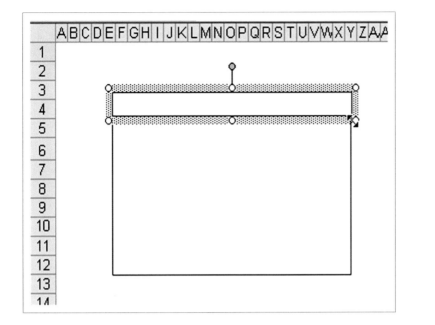

Figure 7.4.
The header rectangle for the thumbnail.

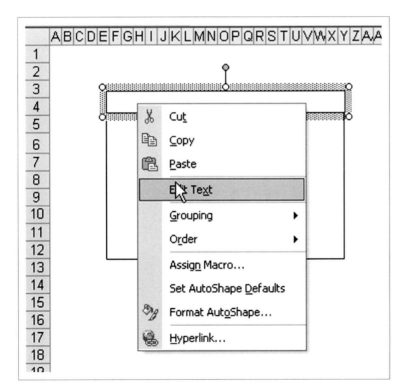

Figure 7.5.
Choosing Edit Text.

Figure 7.6.

Header text is added to the thumbnail.

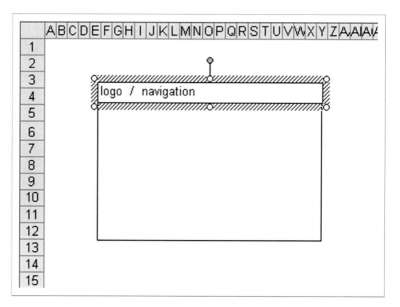

6. Type in the text `logo / navigation` (Figure 7.6).

7. To create the product image placeholders (circles) choose **AutoShapes** > **Basic Shapes** > **Circle**. Holding down the SHIFT key, click and drag a small circle, as shown in Figure 7.7.

8. Repeat step 7 until you have six circles, as shown in Figure 7.8.

Figure 7.7.

The first placeholder graphic circle to represent a product image is added.

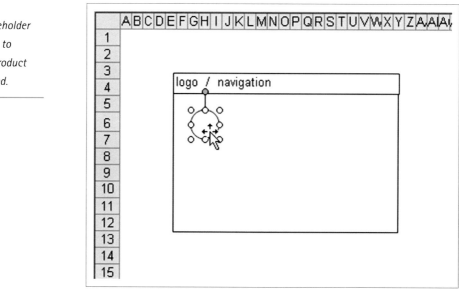

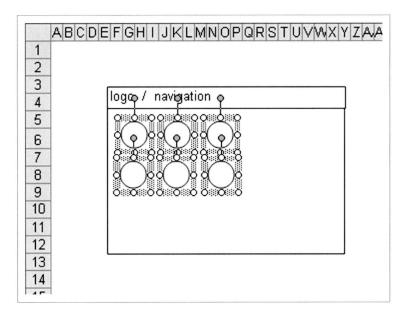

Figure 7.8.

Five more placeholder graphic circles are added to the thumbnail to represent more product images.

Optionally, you can copy and paste the circle, or use the duplicate command, **CTRL-D**.

9. To add the squares that represent an area of descriptive text, choose **AutoShapes** > **Basic Shapes** > **Rectangle**. Holding down the **SHIFT** key, click and drag a small rectangle, as shown in Figure 7.9.

10. To shade the square to suggest that it is filled with text, right-click the box and choose **Format AutoShape** (Figure 7.10, page 130).

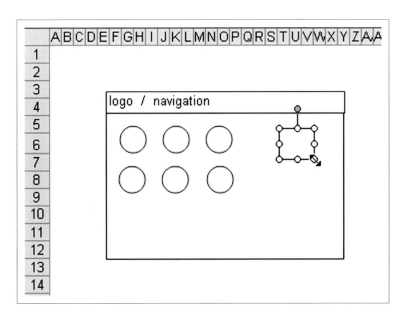

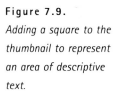

Figure 7.9.

Adding a square to the thumbnail to represent an area of descriptive text.

Figure 7.10.

Choosing Format
AutoShape.

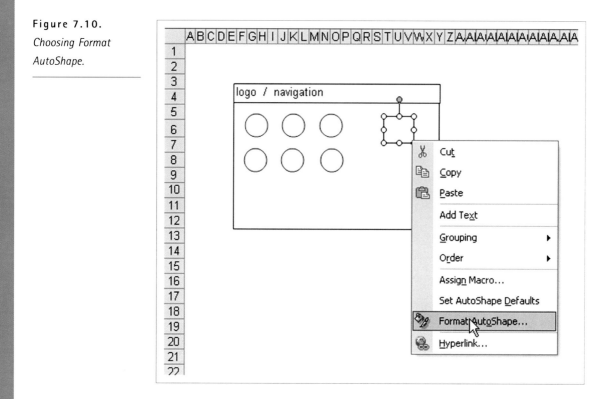

11. In the **Format AutoShape** dialog box, select a gray color for the **Fill Color** (Figure 7.11).

12. Repeat steps 9–11, or copy and paste, or duplicate the square so that two identical squares are added to the thumbnail.

13. To add the lighter text elements at the bottom of the screen, choose **Auto-Shapes > Basic Shapes > Rectangle**. Click and drag a small rectangle, as shown in Figure 7.12 (page 132).

14. To make this rectangle, which is a smaller piece of text, appear less heavy than the other elements, use **Format AutoShapes** to set the gray fill color, as you did in step 11.

15. Remove the line border by selecting **No Line** in the **Line Color** drop-down, as shown in Figure 7.13 (page 132).

16. Copy and paste the small rectangle at the bottom so that the final image is identical to Figure 7.14, (page 133).

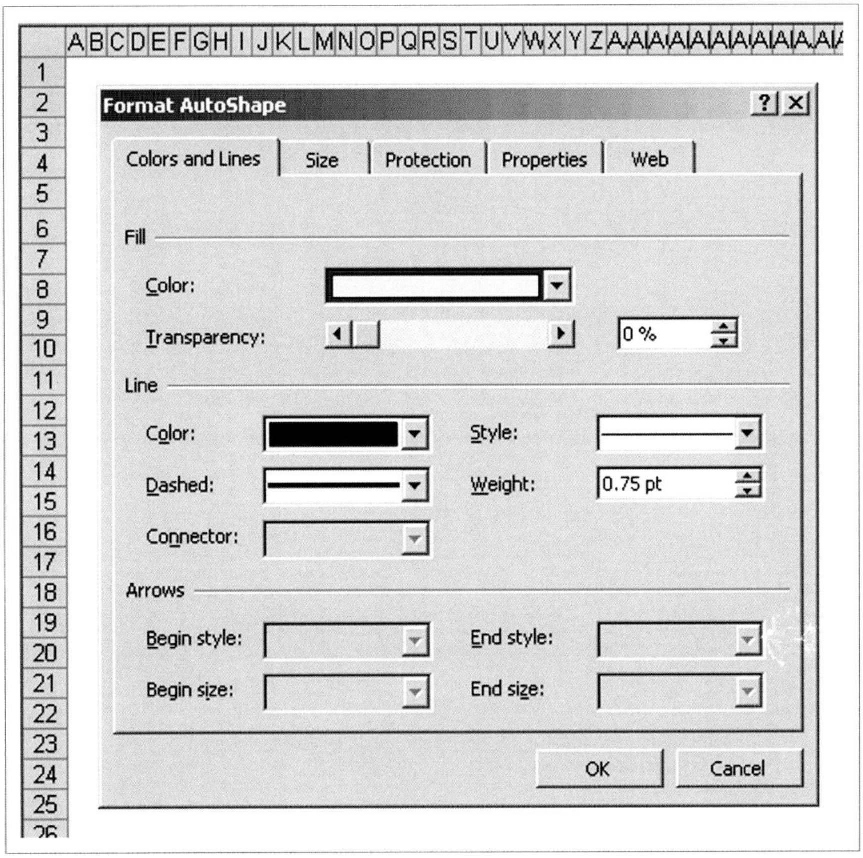

Figure 7.11.

*Selecting a gray color
for the AutoShape
Fill Color.*

In the example shown in Figure 7.1, all the boxes and graphics are AutoShapes that are positioned on the worksheet. The flow lines can be created using the Connectors, as shown in Chapter 6. In this case the lines are made by using the Arrow tool in the Drawing menu.

After you have finished the thumbnail, group together all the different elements within the thumbnail. Excel has a sophisticated grouping feature that makes it easy to work with groups. As you create this scenario, you might find yourself repositioning the thumbnails or copying and pasting them into other worksheets.

In this exercise you will learn how to group, ungroup, and regroup the graphic elements of a thumbnail using AutoShapes.

Figure 7.12.

Thumbnail with the added small rectangle to represent a smaller piece of text.

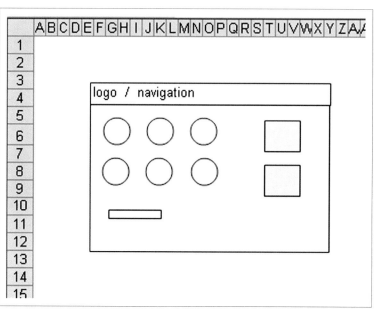

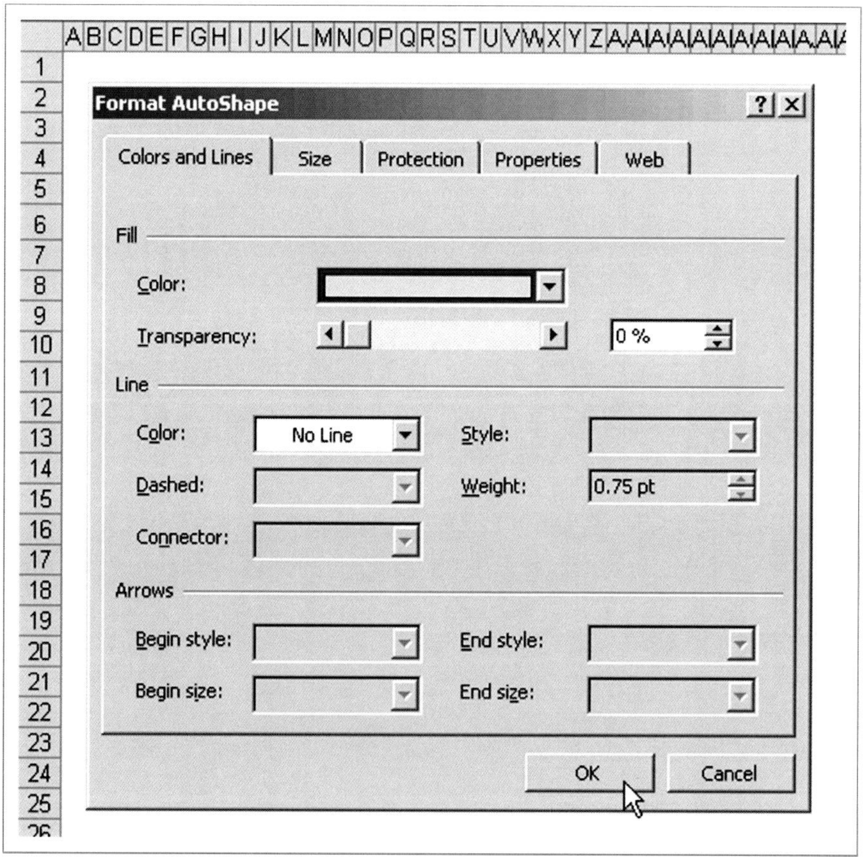

Figure 7.13.

Settings in the Format AutoShape dialog box for the small text area at the bottom of the thumbnail.

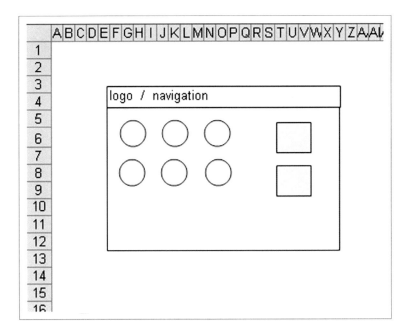

Figure 7.14.
A finished thumbnail for the screen flow diagram.

To Group Shapes:

1. Use the **Select Object** tool in the **Drawing** toolbar to select each individual shape inside the entire thumbnail.

2. With all the shapes highlighted, as shown in Figure 7.15, right-click the selection and choose **Grouping** > **Group**.

All the selected graphics will now act as one graphic.

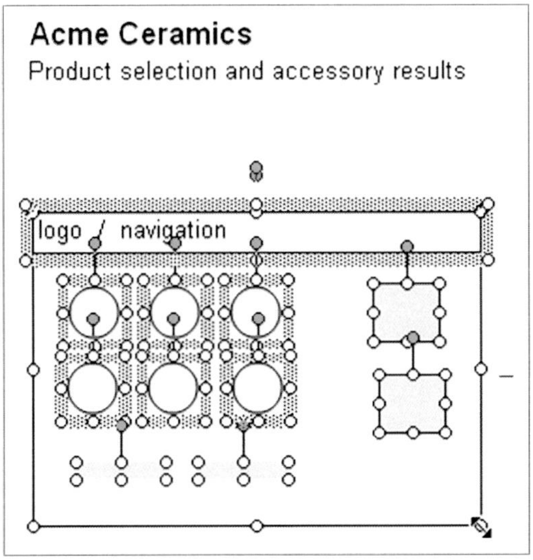

Figure 7.15.
Grouping thumbnail graphic elements.

Use grouping to ensure that all elements are scaled together and that no elements are left behind. You can use the **Ungroup** command to ungroup the graphics; each shape becomes an individual object again. This is particularly helpful when you need to edit an individual item in a group. Then you can use another useful feature, the **Regroup** command, to regroup the individual objects, as shown in Figure 7.16.

If you have ungrouped the graphics, you do not need to select the entire group again to regroup it. You can select one graphic from the original group, right-click it, and select **Regroup**. Excel remembers the prior grouping of graphics and will let you regroup everything again as before. This feature can be very helpful to keep your grouped shapes organized.

As you position the thumbnails for your screen flow, add text descriptions beneath them. How you add text depends on how long the descriptions are:

- If the descriptions are short, type the text into the cells below the thumbnails.
- If you find that you have a substantial amount of text, enter the text into graphics boxes by right-clicking and choosing **Add Text**.

Figure 7.16.

Excel Regroup feature.

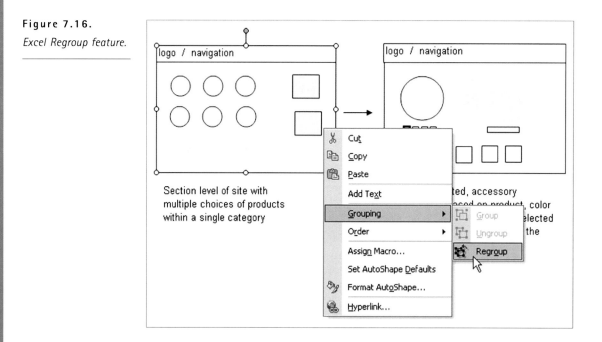

An advantage to using the graphics shapes is that you can group them with the thumbnails, making it easier to keep the thumbnails and their descriptions connected.

Tip

Another way to use grouping is to make groups out of groups. After you have grouped the graphics and while the group is selected, highlight the text box and make a group of both. Now the text is grouped with the graphics and can easily be separated out for editing without having to ungroup the entire graphic.

A screen flow diagram built within an Excel template can be easily shared with others and can be modified or added to by others. The thumbnails can also be ultimately linked to the corresponding full-size screens of the prototype from which it is derived.

Creating an Interactive Prototype

Excel offers a level of interaction that is easy to implement and can be very powerful if used creatively. The two Excel features that enable the interaction are

- Hyperlinking of text and graphics
- Using the workbook tabs

Using these two features together, you can use Excel to mimic a level of interaction that illustrates user interaction from worksheet to worksheet as well as through a complex transaction process. You can show how a button might function or even enable entering text into an input box. You can use Excel to demonstrate interaction functionality to development teams and to test interactive features with users.

In the scenario for this chapter, the designer who is building the interface for Acme Ceramics wants to portray how a feature in the flow of Web pages will work. The feature, which appeals to Gen-X users, allows the user to view a product in different colors. The designer wants to demonstrate the use of the interactive color palette in the interface. The designer has mapped out the process in a screen flow diagram, but to really demonstrate to the team how this will look and feel, the designer will create a simple interaction in Excel. This requires only two worksheets in Excel.

A user requirement carried over from the existing Website is for the system to automatically present different accessories depending on the color and style of a product chosen by a user.

The two worksheets illustrated in Figures 7.17 and 7.18 are identical in size and layout of the content, except

- The products are displayed in a different color.
- The color highlighted in the color selector palette is different.
- The accessories for each are different.

The designer can use graphics from the existing Website, but the designer could just as easily have used simple graphics created in Excel or found graphics from the Web to use for demonstration purposes. The two Web pages are in different worksheets in the same Excel workbook.

In this exercise you will create an interactive digital prototype using graphics and hyperlinked images.

Figure 7.17.
Worksheet displaying maroon dishware products.

Figure 7.18.
Worksheet displaying mustard dishware products.

To Create the Interactive Digital Prototype:

1. Open the workbook **EXP_CH7.xls**.

2. Select the Worksheet tab **maroon plate**.

3. Select the color selector graphic, which has the maroon color highlighted.

4. Right-click the color selector graphic and choose **Hyperlink** (Figure 7.19, page 138).

5. Click **Place in This Document;** then select **'mustard plate.'**

6. Click **OK** to create the link.

The mustard color on the color selector graphic of the maroon dishware worksheet is now a hyperlink to the mustard dishware worksheet. When hovering over the graphic, the cursor becomes a hand to indicate it is an active hyperlink. Clicking it instantly navigates the user to the mustard dishware worksheet from the maroon dishware worksheet. By adding a link on the mustard dishware worksheet that links the color selector graphic back to the maroon worksheet, you create an interaction that vividly demonstrates the functionality to the audience (Figure 7.20, page 138).

Figure 7.19.

Choosing Hyperlink.

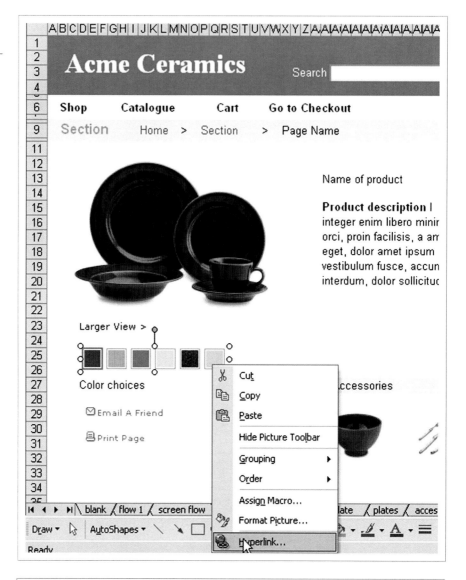

Figure 7.20.

Selecting the hyperlink cell reference 'mustard plate.'

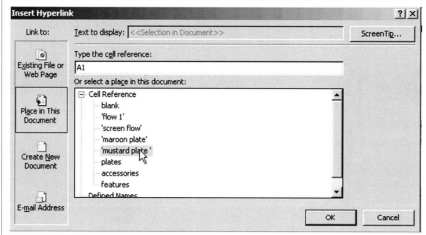

Note

The Insert Hyperlink dialog box gives you a number of choices that highlight some more important features in Excel. For example, you can link to a different file if you want to link to a different Excel document or to any document that could be part of the design, such as a requirements document.

Linking to a Web page offers many opportunities. If your design is part of an existing site, being able to link to that site can show how the prototype might interact with existing Web pages. You can also make links to Web pages that contain support material or examples of similar functionality that you want to show to help bolster your ideas.

Creating a Drop-Down Menu in Excel

In this exercise you will mimic interface widget interaction and functionality by using hyperlinks together with graphic shapes.

The product manager feels that although it is nice to show two or three accessories, there are whole categories of accessories that need to be displayed in the finished coded site. In your next iteration you can try another approach to introducing the accessories by building a drop-down menu.

To implement a drop-down menu, you will create a series of interactive worksheets. The first worksheet will include the hyperlinked widget, which links to the second worksheet. The second worksheet will be a duplicate of the first, except with the drop-down menu added. Clicking the drop-down list on the first worksheet moves to the second worksheet, appearing to the user as though the menu opened when in reality the user simply moved from one worksheet to another. The third worksheet is a destination for one of the links in the drop-down menu, which is the Mustard Accessory worksheet mentioned at the beginning of the chapter. This interactive relationship among the worksheets will determine the way the links in the drop-down list should be created.

To Create a Drop-Down Menu:

1. Starting with the **mustard dishware** worksheet, copy it to create a duplicate worksheet and name it `mustard dropdown1`.
2. Copy the three accessories and their header, Accessories, to a new position to the right of the descriptive text and change the header font to bold.

3. To the right of the Accessories header, add new text, `See All Accessories`.

4. Copy a down-arrow graphic from your image library worksheet and paste it into the header on the far right of See All Accessories, to serve as the widget that will reveal the drop-down menu when it's clicked (Figure 7.21).

5. Copy the worksheet **mustard dropdown1** to create another mustard drop-down worksheet, which you will name `mustard dropdown2` (Figure 7.22).

6. On this newly created worksheet, create a drop-down menu that will display the accessory list.

All the elements of this new worksheet, mustard dropdown2, must exactly align with all the elements of the worksheet mustard dropdown1 so that the added drop-down menu will be the only thing that will appear differently between the two. It is this single difference that makes it seem as though an actual coded drop-down menu has opened.

7. On the **mustard dropdown2** worksheet, choose a rectangle **AutoShape**; then draw a rectangle that extends from the drop-down widget to the width of the header to look like the rectangle shown in Figure 7.22.

8. Right-click the newly created rectangle, choose **Format AutoShape** from the pop-up menu, and then select the desired line color, style, and weight to give the box a gray 1.75 point border.

9. Right-click the rectangle and add text, as shown in Figure 7.23 (page 142).

Figure 7.21.
Down-arrow graphic pasted into position.

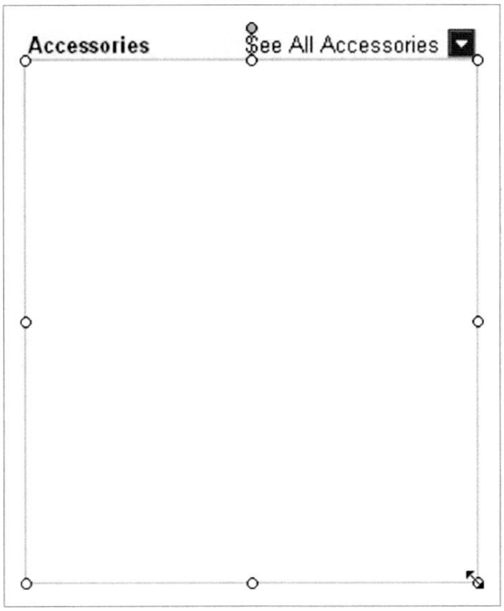

Figure 7.22.
Accessories drop-down menu outline border rectangle.
Excel worksheet Move or Copy dialog box to copy mustard dropdown1.

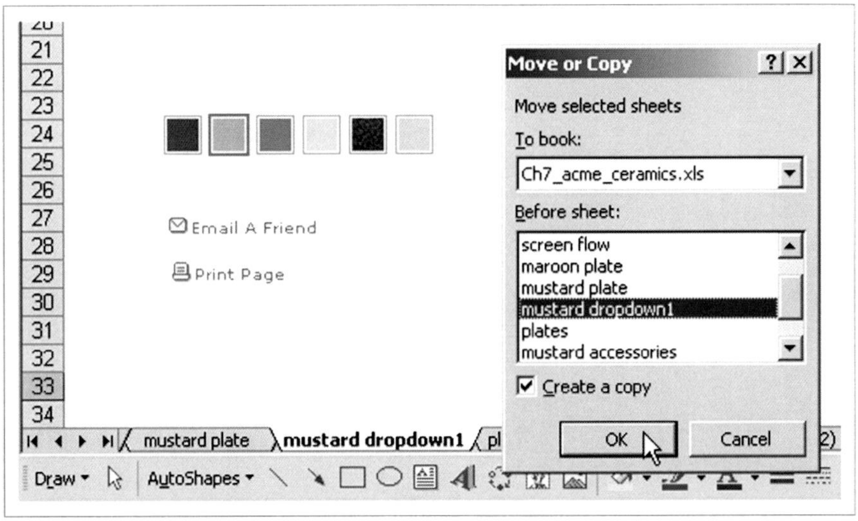

While typing in the product list items, you might notice that the box you created appears too wide and too deep for the list.

10. Reduce the size of the menu border rectangle by clicking it and then resizing it to the size of the drop-down menu, as shown in Figure 7.24 (page 142).

Because the menu box no longer covers the accessories, it makes sense to add a drop shadow to offset it from the surface of the worksheet.

Figure 7.23.

Menu border rectangle
ready for resizing.

Figure 7.24.

Menu border rectangle
resized to the size of a
drop-down menu.

11. To create a drop shadow, draw another rectangle over the box, but offset it by a few pixels equally to the right and down (Figure 7.25).

12. Right-click the drop-shadow rectangle that you just created and choose **Format AutoShape** from the pop-up menu. From the **Format AutoShape** dialog box, remove the rectangle's outline; then give the box a light gray fill tone (Figure 7.26).

13. With the drop-shadow rectangle still highlighted, right-click it again and choose **Order** > **Send Backward** (Figure 7.27, page 144).

Figure 7.25.
Creating a drop-shadow rectangle.

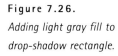

Figure 7.26.
Adding light gray fill to drop-shadow rectangle.

This will place the drop-shadow rectangle behind the menu box rectangle. Do not use **Send to Back**, because the drop-shadow rectangle would be positioned too far behind other elements on the worksheet.

14. To ensure that the menu and drop-shadow rectangles stay together, select both boxes, right-click them, and select **Group** (Figure 7.28, page 144).

Now you can create the hyperlinks that will bring the interaction to life.

15. Right-click the down-arrow graphic in the worksheet **mustard dropdown1** and choose **Hyperlink**. In the **Insert Hyperlink** dialog box, click **Place in This Document**; then select the **Cell Reference 'mustard dropdown2'.** See Figure 7.29 (page 145).

Figure 7.27.
Send Backward selected from the Order submenu.

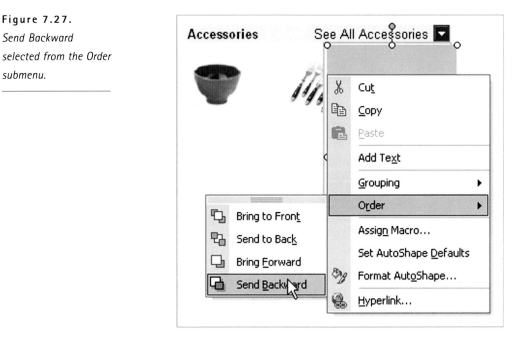

Figure 7.28.
Group > Grouping commands selected.

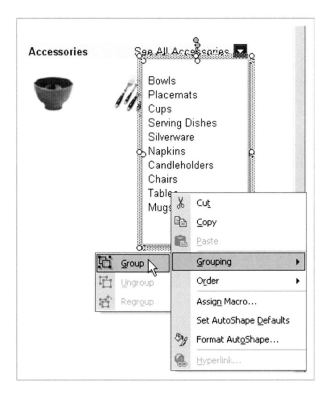

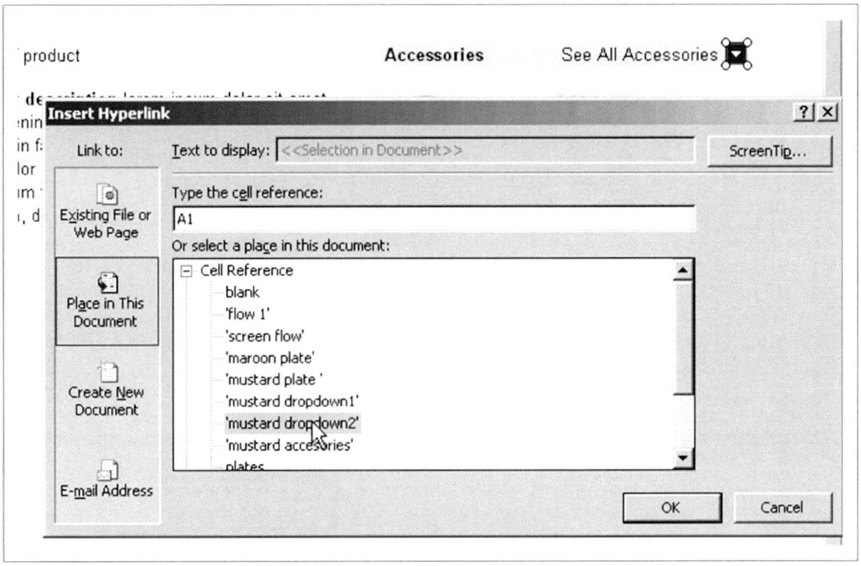

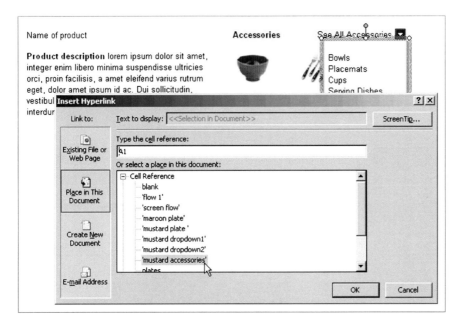

Figure 7.29.

Selecting the hyperlink cell reference 'mustard dropdown2.'

16. On the **mustard dropdown2** worksheet, highlight the drop-down box rectangle. Right-click, select **Hyperlink**, and click **Place in This Document**, but this time select the **Cell Reference 'mustard accessories,'** which is the destination. See Figure 7.30.

With these worksheets you created not only a sequential visualization of actions but an interactive experience that simulates the interaction behaviors that would occur if these worksheets were actually coded (Figure 7.31, page 146).

Figure 7.30.

Selecting the hyperlink cell reference 'mustard accessories.'

Figure 7.31.

The three Web pages that portray the key dishware products interaction sequence.

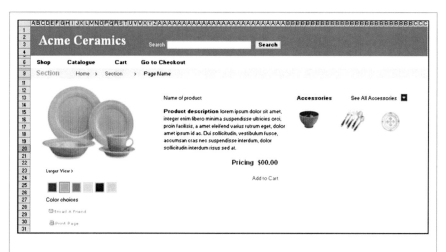

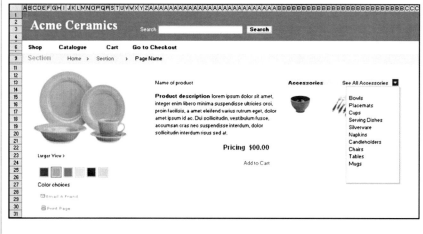

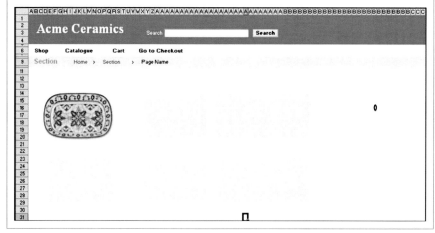

Conclusion

We cannot demonstrate in the static paper pages of this book the power of interaction, navigation, and their accompanying behaviors. When an audience first observes hyperlinking and the resulting interaction behavior in an Excel-based interactive prototype, they experience an epiphanical "Aha!" moment. We've observed them suddenly sitting up attentively in their seats. You can have your own "Aha!" moment by downloading this sample prototype from our complementary Website: http://www.effectiveprototyping.com/excel/interaction. On this Website you can also find other examples of interactive prototypes that demonstrate such interactions as

- Navigation menus opening and closing
- Interactive drop-down menus
- Interactive submenus
- Alphanumeric text entry boxes in a form
- Interactive graphical buttons

References

[1] Jonathan Arnowitz, Michael Arent, and Nevin Berger, *Effective Prototyping for Software Makers*, San Francisco: Morgan Kaufmann, 2007.

[2] Dabney Gough and Holly Phillips, "Remote Online Usability Testing: Why, How, and When to Use It," www.boxesandarrows.com/view/ remote_online_usability_testing_why_how_and_when_to_use_it#comments, accessed April 26, 2008.

[3] Nate Bolt, "Guide to Remote Usability Testing," www.ok-cancel.com/archives/article/ 2006/07/guide-to-remote-usability-testing.html, accessed April 26, 2008.

PART 3

PUTTING YOUR EXCEL
PROTOTYPE TO WORK

You have learned to apply your Excel canvas and template to specific prototyping challenges. In Part 3, you will learn how to develop a design through iterations with your team and how to put your prototype to work within your team and with stakeholders.

- In Chapter 8 you will learn how to develop your prototypes through iterations.
- In Chapter 9 you will learn how to communicate your design to others.
- In Chapter 10 you will learn how to share your prototype with shakeholders.

CHAPTER 8

ITERATING PROTOTYPES WITH EXCEL

In creative design the role of context and the designer's perception of it play an increasingly important part. Since design is being viewed as a process here it could be argued that all new variables are already implicit in the processes to be used. In order to counter such arguments, it is suggested that designers work, of necessity, within a well-defined context of their choosing. The context is defined by the available design prototypes. However, there comes a time during the design process when the designer decides that he or she wishes to move outside the available design prototypes in order to find new variables. This can be seen as the designer changing the context in which he or she is working.

—John S. Gero, "Design Prototypes:
A Knowledge Representation Schema for Design" [2]

In this chapter you will learn how to

- Prepare for design iterations
- Create iterations of your Excel prototype

Preparing for a Design Iteration

The exercises that you've completed in the previous chapters converge as key activities of an iterative design process that helps you achieve your design goals. You have learned about gathering and defining requirements as well as creating task and screen flows in Excel, and you've started your first prototype of a design in Excel. In this chapter you will identify a high-priority screen—a contact information screen—and refine the design through iteration. But first you want to identify the kind of iteration you will be doing. Though there are many perspectives on the types of iterations you can perform, for our purposes we will focus on two:

- Will this iteration be a more detailed version of a more conceptual predecessor?
- Will this iteration be an improvement or change of a prior version based on stakeholder feedback or new and ostensibly improved ideas?

After establishing this kind of an iteration, on that basis you will want to define your requirements, your design criteria, the content, and audience. Some examples of design criteria include

- Evaluate and verify the target audience (for example, better understand the Gen-X market and its potential for sales)

- Reevaluate users' needs (for example, what attracts both current and new users to your site to find something they want? Who exactly are the users you want to attract to your site?)

- Make your design look uncluttered, and improve the information architecture and interaction flow (for example, how can complex information presentations and the related interaction experiences appear simple and easy?)

- Improve grouping of content (for example, how can related and unrelated screen elements be presented logically to users?)

- Apply a more balanced color scheme that reflects your new branding scheme and strategic objectives (for example, how can the new branding, reflecting company values, be reinforced throughout the Website experience?)

Creating Iterations of Your Excel Prototype

... designers may, in an iterative manner, explore the consequences of various design decisions.

—Thomas Erickson, "Notes on Design Practice:
Stories and Prototypes as Catalysts for Communication" [3]

Evolving the Arnosoft Design

The following steps for designing and building a prototype help you evolve the Arnosoft design concept and rationale, develop design patterns and guidelines through iterations, and then converge on a design solution and a set of design specifications:

- Determine the highest-priority screen.
- Block out the most important regions of your screen.
- Lay out the highest priority screen with the required elements.
- Lay out remaining high-priority screens.
- Specify each screen, overall interaction flow, and the various screen elements with a design rationale.

In previous chapters you have learned how Excel can help you quickly build designs to visualize your ideas. But an iterative design process requires that there be a number of trial design attempts and divergent changes that will ultimately converge on a design solution. New requirements and content are added, features are changed or deleted, and then design elements are arranged and rearranged. Just seeing the layout of a page triggers changes as each team member evolves his or her own ideas on what the design should look like. The following four progressive iterations of the new Arnosoft redesign result in a final design:

1. Simple wireframe
2. Wireframe with some details
3. Wireframe updated with design team feedback
4. Final wireframe

The template methodology that you learned in Chapters 3 and 4 makes the iterative process quick and easy in Excel prototyping. If you spent the time to build a template before beginning your design, the template environment will include everything that you'll need to iteratively build the worksheets for your wireframe designs. The template worksheets include the specifications for your site built into them. The grid matches the site size specifications, and the color palette uses the specified colors. There are also premade boxes and buttons and a library of images and widgets at your disposal. By copying and pasting, you can use the different template worksheets to construct your designs out of the predefined component parts and design patterns.

Iteration 1: Simple Wireframe

To begin your design journey for the Contact page, first build a simple wireframe that includes all the initial requirements as defined in your design kickoff meeting. Because it will undergo changes as the design process unfolds, you'll want to use the simplest of methods for this initial wireframe (Figure 8.1, page 154).

In this first iteration, build the boxes using borders from the Format Cells menu. You can add tones using the Patterns menu found in Format Cells. Add text to your design by typing into the cells without formatting the text or worrying about exact positioning. Your goal with this first iteration is simply getting the worksheet done quickly so that you can see how the various user interface elements work in the layout.

Rather than run through this basic process, you can refer to Chapters 3 and 4 and Appendix A for techniques to build this design.

Figure 8.1.

Simple wireframe.

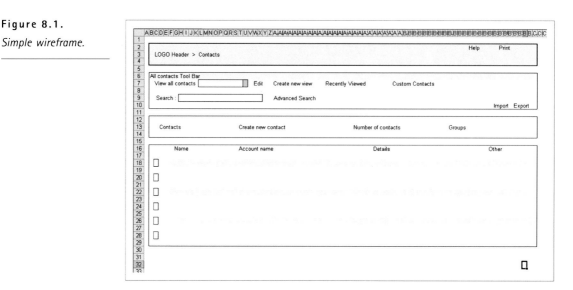

Iteration 2: Wireframe with Some Details

Your first wireframe could be shown to the team as-is, but you might realize that it is not articulated enough and could lead to many questions. You might decide to improve the affordances [4] of the design. Of the various elements on your worksheet, you might want to depict which elements are links or give a little more clarity to some of the widgets.

In this exercise you will create a wireframe with some details by using your template to create a fresh canvas, wireframe2. You will use the image shown in Figure 8.2 as your guide for building the new wireframe.

Figure 8.2.

Wireframe with some details.

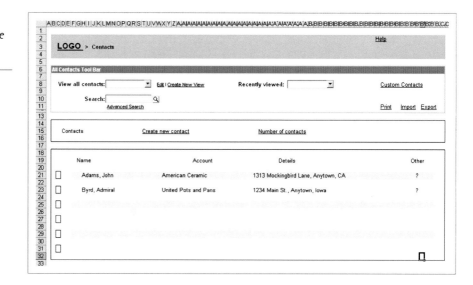

1. In Iteration 2, create the logo area at the very top of the worksheet and apply the site color to distinguish it from the rest of the worksheet (Figure 8.3).

2. For the text that reads **LOGO,** choose a large font and select the word **LOGO.** Choose **Underline** in the Type menu to indicate that this will be a link. Since the client for your wireframe is internal, don't use a graphic logo from your image library—everyone knows already what the logo looks like.

3. If the text is too tall for the row height, increase the row height (Figure 8.4).

4. To create the next box, go to the **basic page** worksheet tab in your template and copy the header bar; then paste it into position in the wireframe (Figure 8.5, page 156).

5. The header bar isn't the correct width. You can add to the width by copying the right end of the header bar and then pasting it to the right of the existing bar. Copy and paste an additional chunk of the header to fill in any gaps. Now you can type in the header text, which uses the correct type specification for a header in a box because it comes from your template (Figure 8.6, page 156).

6. From the **boxes and buttons** worksheet, select and copy the required widgets; then paste them into your design to match the reference worksheet in Figure 8.2 (Figure 8.7, page 156).

7. Copy the table from the first iteration wireframe and paste it into this new worksheet, as shown in Figure 8.8 (page 157).

8. To finish this design iteration, add some placeholder content text to the table, as shown in Figure 8.2. At this point your wireframe has enough information to share with the team and get some feedback.

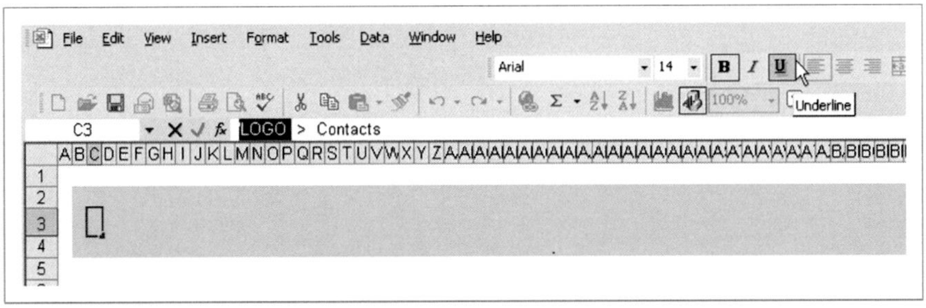

Figure 8.3.
Indicating where to add the logo text.

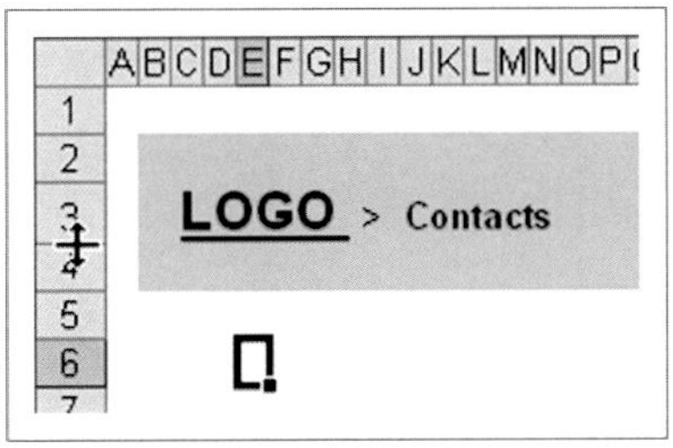

Figure 8.4.
Adjusting the row height to accommodate text.

Figure 8.5.

A header bar copied from the basic page worksheet.

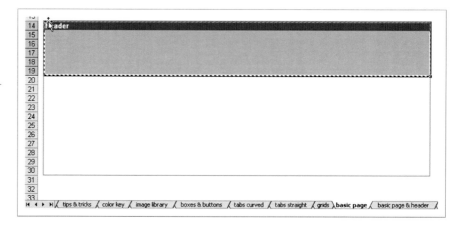

Figure 8.6.

Pasted piece of the header bar to increase its width.

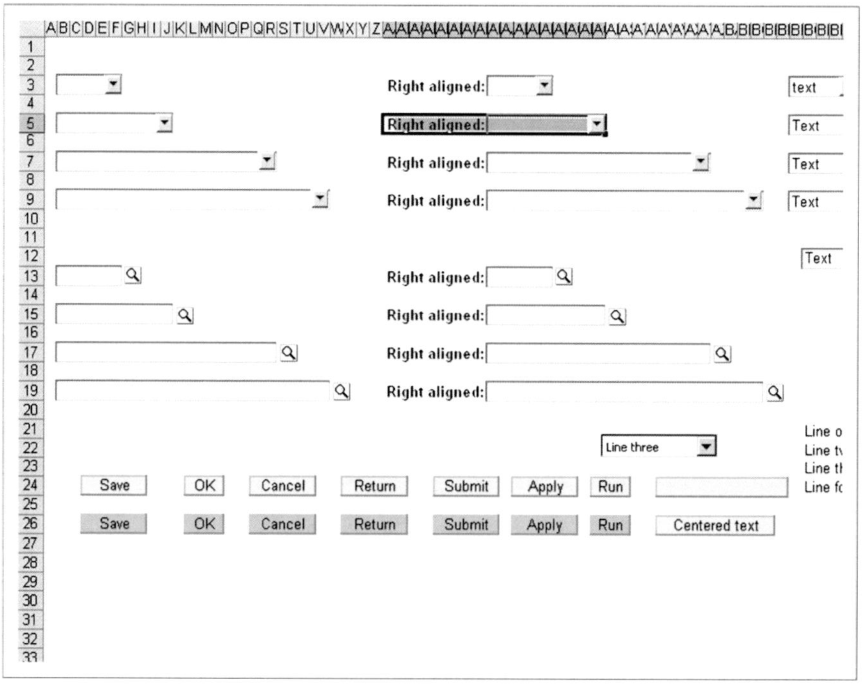

Figure 8.7.

The boxes and buttons worksheet.

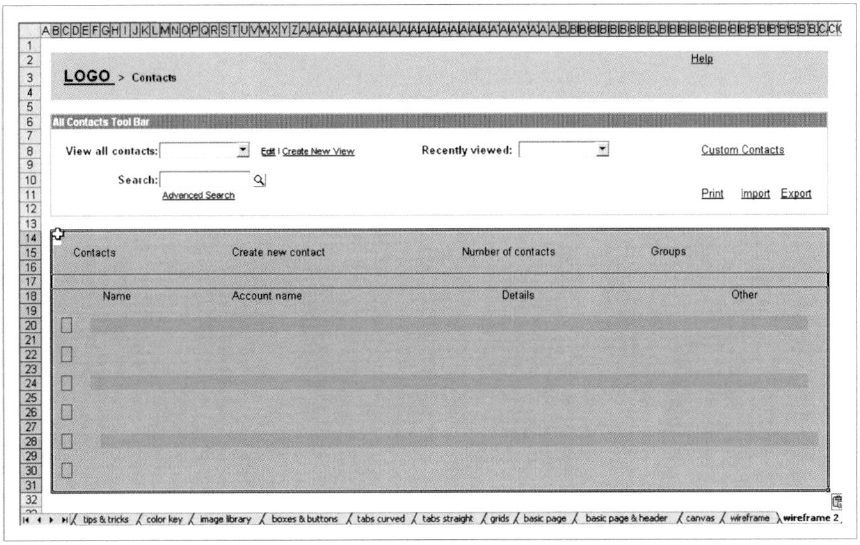

Figure 8.8.

Table design copied from first iteration wireframe and then pasted into position.

Iteration 3: Wireframe Updated with Design Team Feedback

In the meantime, you received feedback from the team that the worksheet should be reconfigured because the All Contacts toolbar at the top of the worksheet has so many boxes that it's hard to understand. The sales team has asked that the Contact Groups feature be more prominent, and they want a quick list of recent groups to be exposed somewhere on the worksheet.

In this exercise you iterate the design again by repositioning, editing, and adding whole sections to the design. You now create a left-hand column for the search features that will also provide a place for the group features (Figure 8.9, page 158).

1. To clear room for the new column, highlight the entire worksheet below the main header; then cut the selected area and paste it in position at cell M6.

2. You haven't left enough room for the new content. Undo the paste action; then repaste at cell S6. If you are satisfied with this spacing, move on.

3. Now you can reposition the search widget by cutting it from its current position (Figure 8.10, page 158) and then pasting it into its new position, as shown in Figure 8.11 (page 158).

Figure 8.9.

Copy and paste All Contacts Toolbar area into its new position.

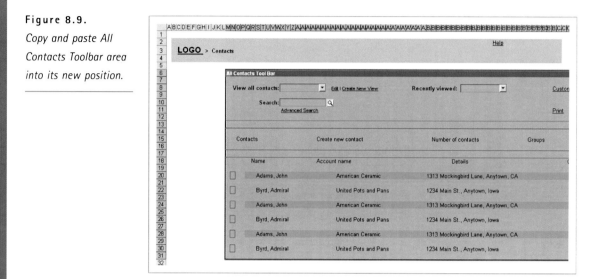

Figure 8.10.

Copy the search widget.

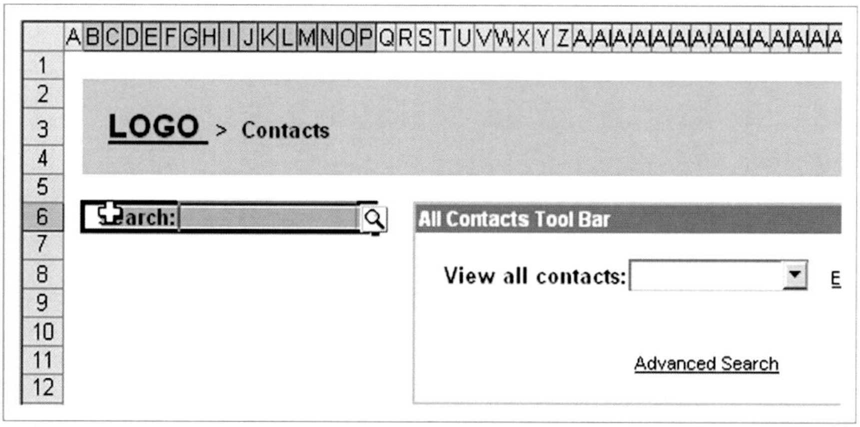

Figure 8.11.

Paste the search widget into new position.

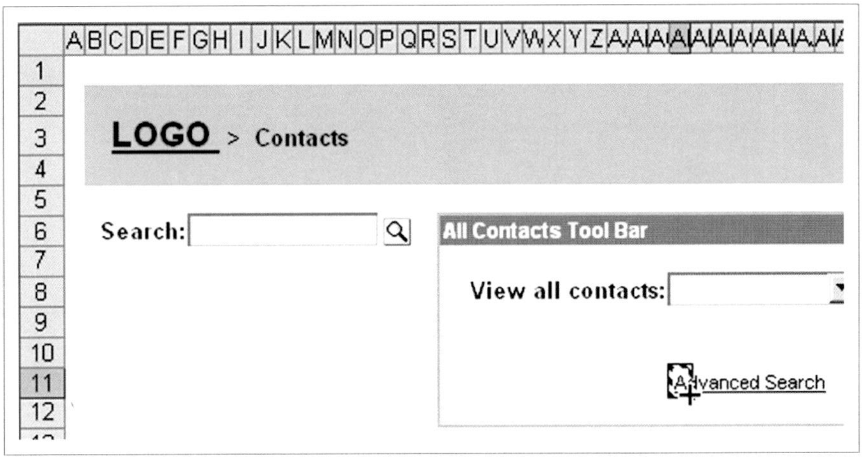

Figure 8.12.

Copy text, Advanced Search.

4. You can also reposition the Advanced Search hyperlink by cutting it from its current position (Figure 8.12) and then pasting it into its new position below the search widget, as shown in Figure 8.13.

5. Make the features Custom Contacts and New Contacts into buttons rather than links. From the **buttons and boxes** worksheet tab, select a premade button that already has centered text. Copy the button from the template worksheet; then on the prototype worksheet, paste two buttons into the new column, as shown in Figure 8.14 (page 160).

6. Select the text and type in the button names Custom Contacts and New Contact; then delete the original text on the right side (Figure 8.15, page 160).

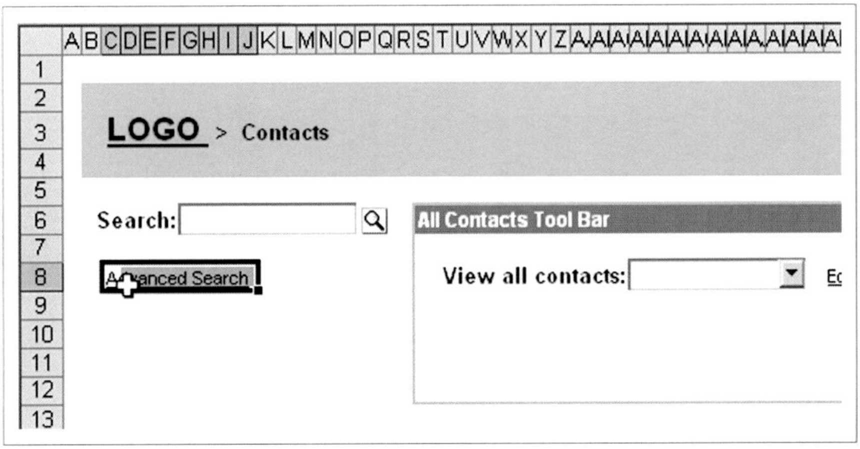

Figure 8.13.

Paste text, Advanced Search.

Figure 8.14.

Button selected on boxes and buttons worksheet.

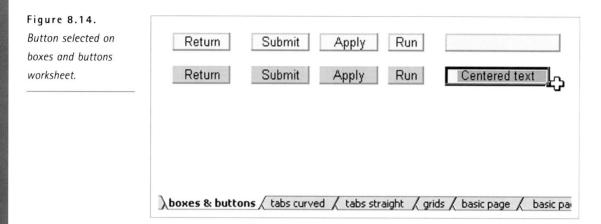

Figure 8.15.

Type correct text into the generic button.

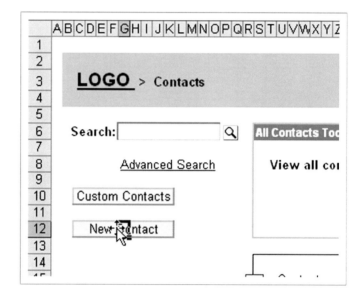

7. To create the Contact Groups box, highlight an appropriate area in the new column under the **Custom Contacts** and **New Contacts** buttons. To save time, go to the **Formatting** toolbar and select **Borders**. Using the pull-down menu, highlight the icon that places a one-point black outline border around the selected area and click (Figure 8.16).

8. Now that you have created the new left column, narrow the rest of the layout so that it fits within the worksheet grid. Scroll to the right to see what is beyond the window area; then cut any elements that lie outside the window area and paste them into a position within the boundaries of your design.

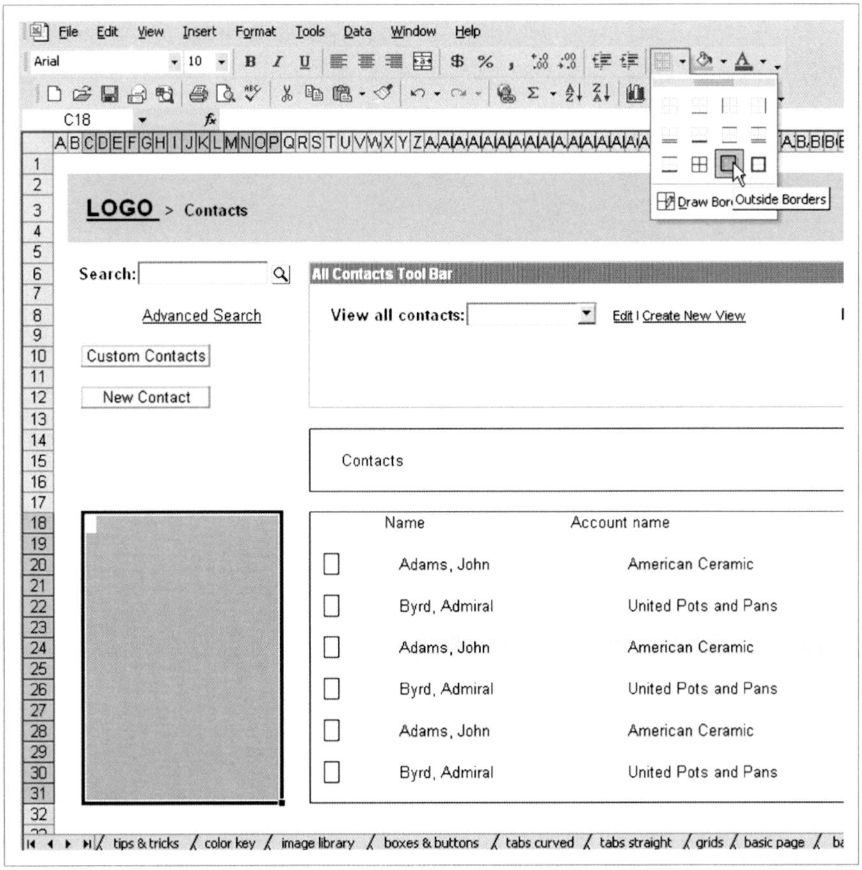

Figure 8.16.

Select cells for Contacts Groups box.

9. Now highlight the right edge of the table (Figure 8.17, page 162); then cut the left edge of the table and paste it into the correct position (Figure 8.18, page 162).

10. An easy way to delete the remaining unwanted table elements is to highlight the area that you want to clear (Figure 8.18), including one row of empty cells above the table and data entry area, then press **CTRL-D** (duplicate). The top row of cells is duplicated within the highlighted area, clearing all the cell attributes (Figure 8.19, page 163).

11. Finish this design iteration by cutting, pasting, and entering text to match the design shown in Figure 8.20 (page 163).

All these changes might take less than an hour. You are ready for a second review after iterating some of your other designs.

Figure 8.17.

Right edge of the table selected.

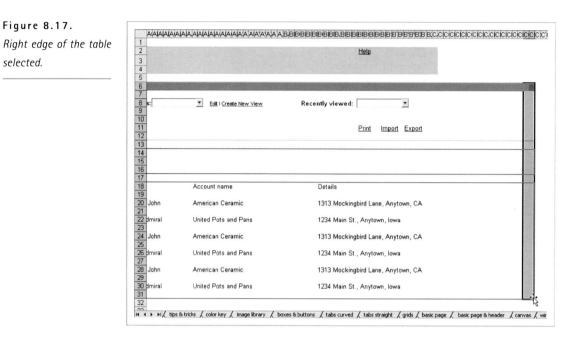

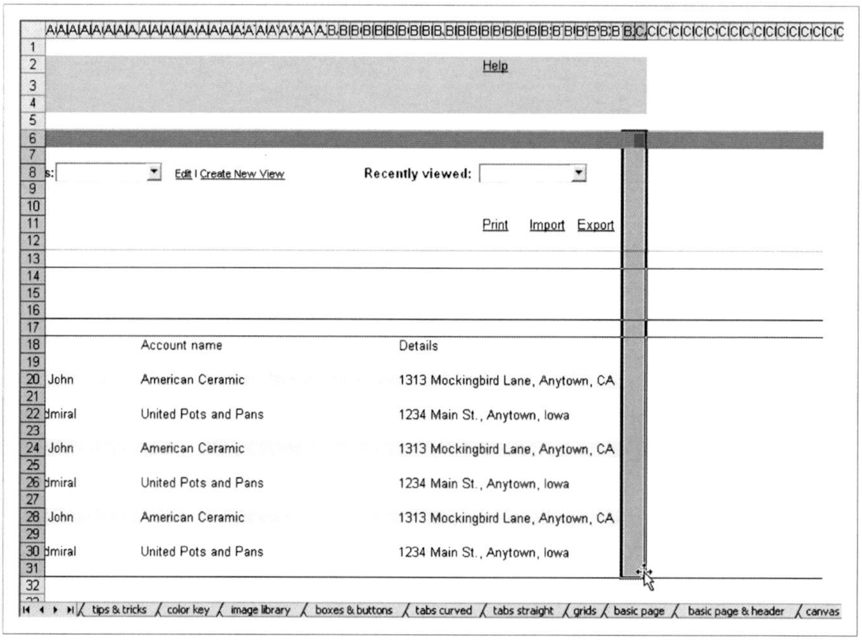

Figure 8.18.

Edge of table pasted into the correct position.

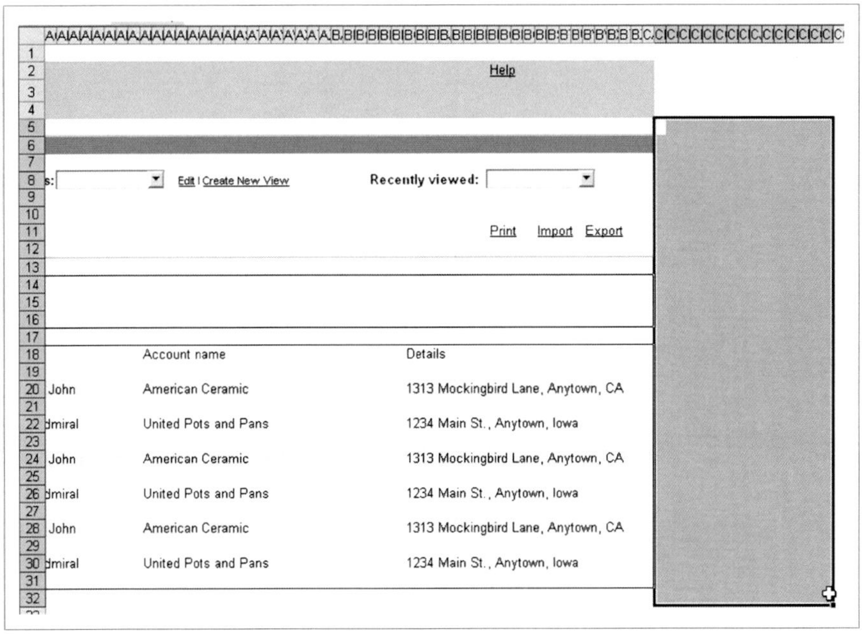

Figure 8.19.
Using duplicate to delete remaining unwanted table elements.

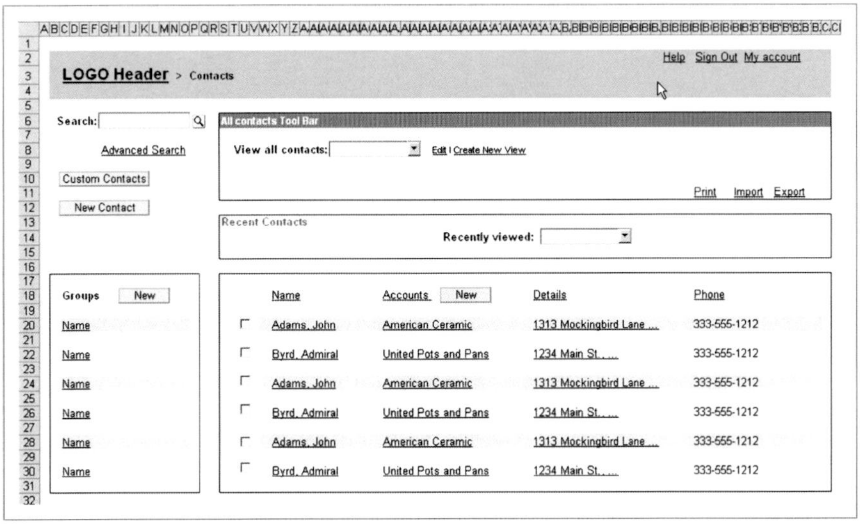

Figure 8.20.
Finished wireframe.

Iteration 4: Final Wireframe

Using the template, you have turned around this design iteration in record time, keeping the project on schedule and budget. Figures 8.21 and 8.22 show further iterations on the prototype, which are a closer representation of the team's intended design.

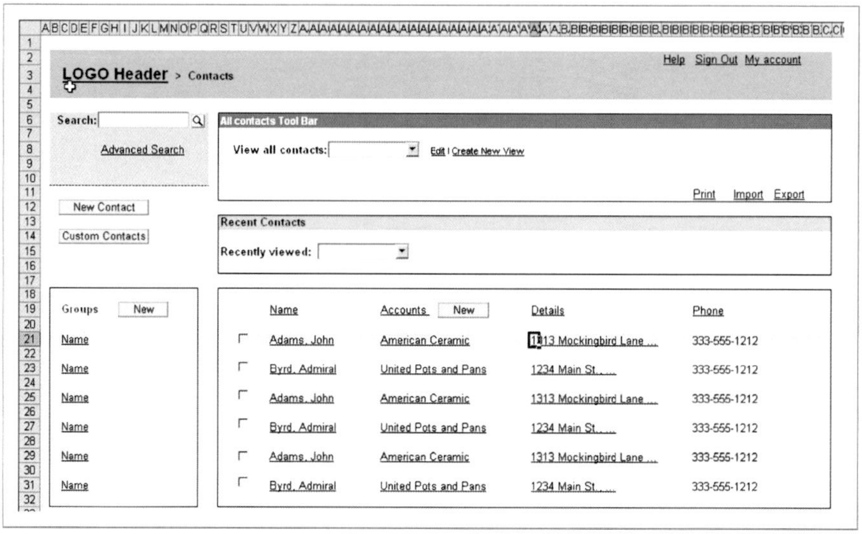

Figure 8.21.

Example iteration of a wireframe with some details.

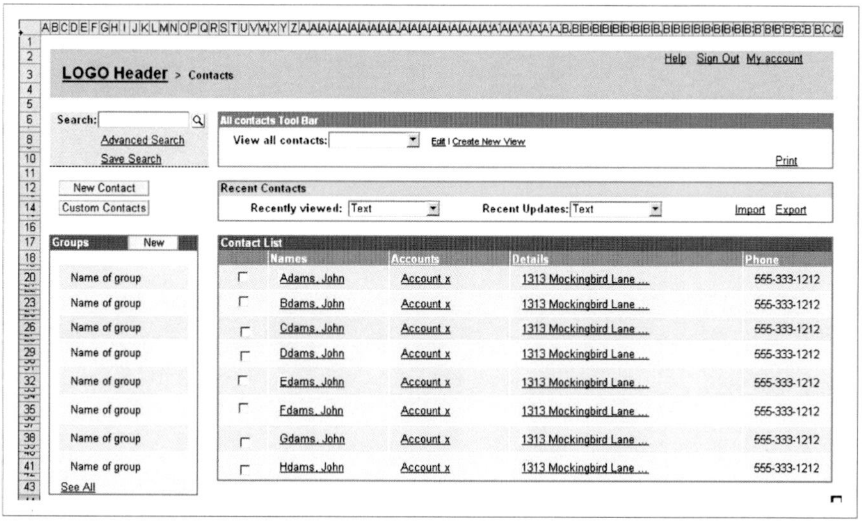

Figure 8.22.

Another example iteration of a wireframe with some details.

Conclusion

Now that you've pulled together your design requirements into a series of design iterations and have created a prototype representation of the final design, you're ready to move on to the next chapter. You will learn how to document your design, including using Excel prototypes as user interface design specifications, how to use the annotation features in Excel, and how to use other useful forms of documentation in the Excel prototyping environment.

References

[1] Jonathan Arnowitz, Michael Arent, and Nevin Berger, *Effective Prototyping for Software Makers*, San Francisco: Morgan Kaufmann, 2007.

[2] John S. Gero, "Design Prototypes: A Knowledge Representation Schema for Design," http://people.arch.usyd.edu.au/~john/publications/ger-prototypes/ger-aimag.html, referenced January 5, 2008.

[3] Thomas Erickson, "Notes on Design Practice: Stories and Prototypes as Catalysts for Communication," www.pliant.org/personal/Tom_Erickson/Stories.html, referenced January 5, 2008.

[4] Donald A. Norman, *The Design of Everyday Things*, New York, Basic Books, 2002.

CHAPTER 9

COMMUNICATING YOUR DESIGN IN EXCEL

In this chapter you will learn how to

- Communicate your design, including design specifications
- Add a ScreenTip (tooltip) to a content hyperlink
- Insert comments
- Add annotation areas

Introduction

If a picture can represent a thousand words, a prototype can elicit a thousand and one interpretations. Now that you have created a prototype of your design, you'll want to narrow the number of interpretations. To that end, you can add accompanying communications to your prototype. Prototypes rarely speak for themselves, and even when they do, they generally never tell the complete design story. Without good communications, other stakeholders can neither understand your design intent nor understand its context. Good communication should indicate what still needs to be further fleshed out or documented in your prototype.

After completing a prototype version but before you pass it on to others, establish clear, logical design communications based on

- Design objectives and rationale
- Requirements on which you based your design and applied to your prototype
- Design guidelines and specifications
- Task and navigation flow mappings
- Priority screens
- Design decisions and issues in the form of annotations

These communications help you reflect which objectives you have or have not addressed in your prototype. They can also be used to set audience expectations regarding your prototype. Creating clear communications and setting expectations, in turn, will help to avoid many of the inevitable opinion battles that often arise when presenting and rationalizing your design. Likewise, documenting your design rationale helps you remember why you made certain design decisions and helps you communicate that rationale to others.

Within Excel, you can communicate your design in these ways:

- Tooltips
- The built-in comment feature
- An annotation area within worksheets that contain your designs
- A separate worksheet devoted specifically to communicating your design

If you are creating a prototype for an internal group that already has a deep understanding of your design or if your changes are small in scope, you might need only minimal communications. On the other hand, if you are creating an entirely new interface or making significant changes to an existing design, you might want to choose a communication method that can support long and detailed descriptions of your ideas.

Table 9.1 will help you decide which of these communication techniques to use.

Table 9.1 Choosing a Communication Technique

How	When	Notes
Tooltips	To comment on a specific graphic or hyperlink	The disadvantages: ■ They get read only if a user knows to mouse over them. ■ They are not intuitive and must be communicated to the audience.
Inserted comments	To highlight a comment on a specific area or cells on a canvas	■ This has the added advantage of a red marker in a cell, which can be turned off. ■ However, the markers can distract from the visual design.
Annotation areas	To comment on an entire worksheet or area of a worksheet	■ This puts the comments off to the side, and using the view switch, you can hide/show the comments.

Separate worksheet in the Excel document	To separate the comments from the prototype	• This is the easiest way to capture copious notes without worrying about affecting the visual design of the prototype.
		• However, the disadvantage is that the user often has to flip back and forth between the comments worksheet and the prototype.
		• To make them discoverable, these comments should usually be the first worksheet in an Excel prototype document.

Adding a Tooltip to Excel Hyperlinks

As part of the hyperlinking function in Excel, you can add rollover tooltips (referred to as ScreenTips in Excel) to a hyperlink text or graphic. This method can be very helpful for including a succinct note about the hyperlink. However, there are a couple of drawbacks. First, you cannot add the notation to plain text—the text must be a hyperlink to have a ScreenTip. Second, there is no indication that the link includes a ScreenTip until you hover your cursor over the hyperlink text.

In some cases, you are prototyping an entire page with many hyperlinks; however, only a few hyperlinks have a tooltip. How can you tell the difference? You can also use your own variations on colors, underlining, bolding, and so on; just make sure your convention is adequately communicated to your audience.

In this exercise you will learn how to create tooltips in a prototype.

To Create a ScreenTip Annotation:

For example, you might want to create an annotation for the Advanced Search link, noting that this will be a pop-up link and not a link to another page. In this exercise and throughout this chapter you will continue using the same file you used in Chapter 8.

1. Right-click the table cell that includes the text **Advanced Search**.

2. When the pop-up contextual menu appears, click **Hyperlink** (Figure 9.1).

3. The **Insert Hyperlink** dialog box offers choices of what you can link to. In this case, link to the **Advanced Search** worksheet that has already been prepared in your workbook. In the input box at the top of the dialog, add the text that describes where the Advanced Search link goes (Figure 9.2).

4. In the upper-right corner of the dialog, click the **ScreenTip** button, which opens a dialog box with a text box for your notation (Figure 9.3).

5. Click **OK** for the ScreenTip and the **Insert Hyperlink** windows. The Advanced Search text has become a link. When you roll over it, the annotation you have written appears (Figure 9.4, page 172).

Figure 9.1.

Choosing Hyperlink.

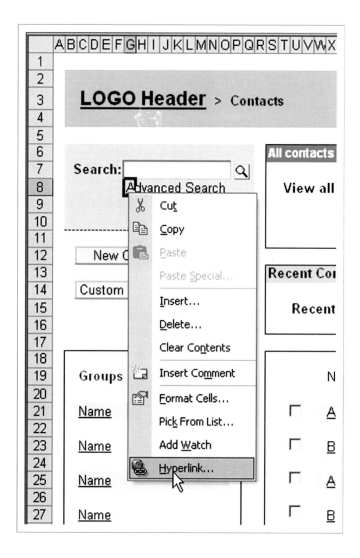

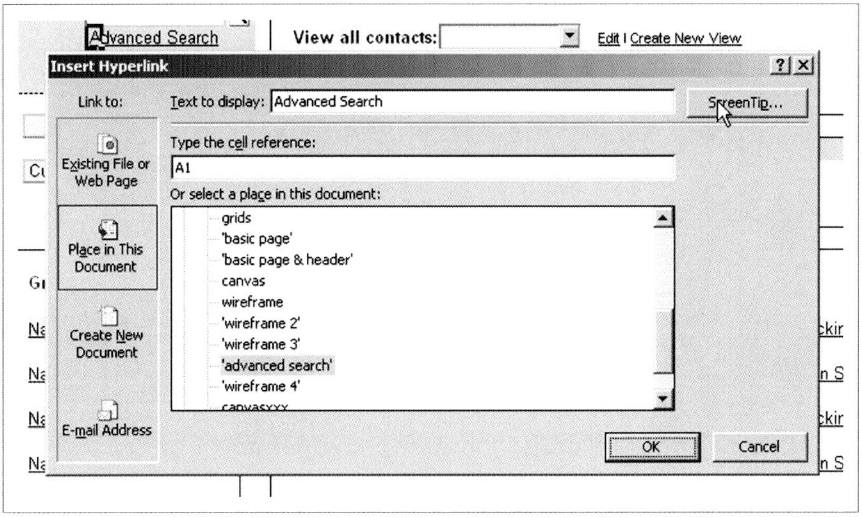

Figure 9.2.

Select ScreenTip in the Insert Hyperlink dialog box.

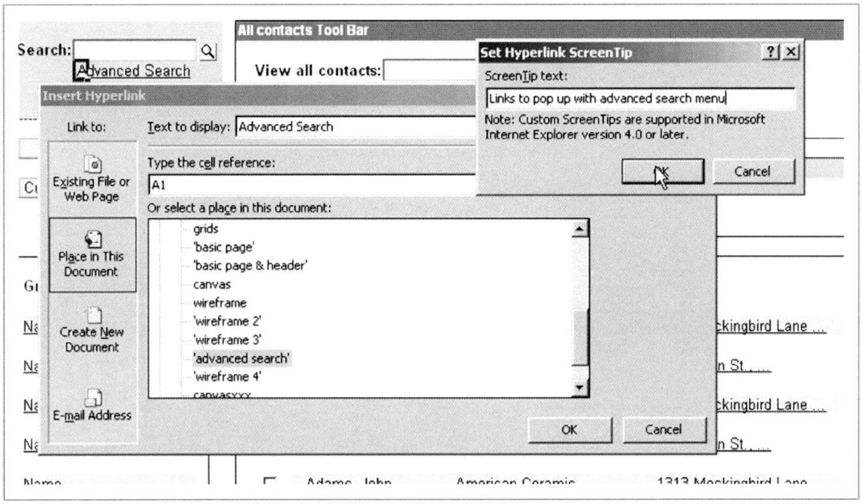

Figure 9.3.

Enter text for the ScreenTip.

For the tooltip to appear, you must roll over the first table cell that includes the hyperlink. If you want all the hyperlinked text to trigger the tooltip, you have to merge all the cells behind the hyperlink text.

Note

For an alternative way to make the hyperlink act on all the hyperlinked text, select all the cells that the text spans and then apply a hyperlink to the selected cells.

Figure 9.4.

Rolling over hyperlink to display tooltip.

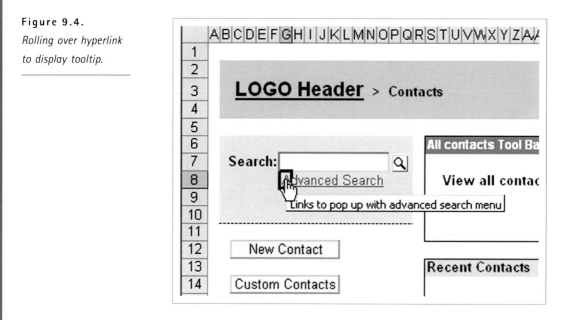

6. To merge the cells, select the cells behind the text, right-click, and select the **Format Cells** menu.

7. Click the **Alignment** tab and select **Merge Cells** (Figure 9.5).

8. Click **OK**.

All the cells behind the linked text will now display the text annotation on rollover (Figure 9.6).

Inserting Comments

Excel's commenting feature is an ideal way to make annotations on a specific area of a prototype that is not a hyperlink or graphical element. Excel's commenting is flexible to use and can be modified in many ways. By placing comments in table cells close to the features in your design, you can indicate what you are commenting on. The comments themselves can be modified by type, size, shape, color, or border style. The comment box can expand to accommodate relatively large amounts of text. Through the Reviewing toolbar, you can cycle through all your comments, show them all at once, or hide them.

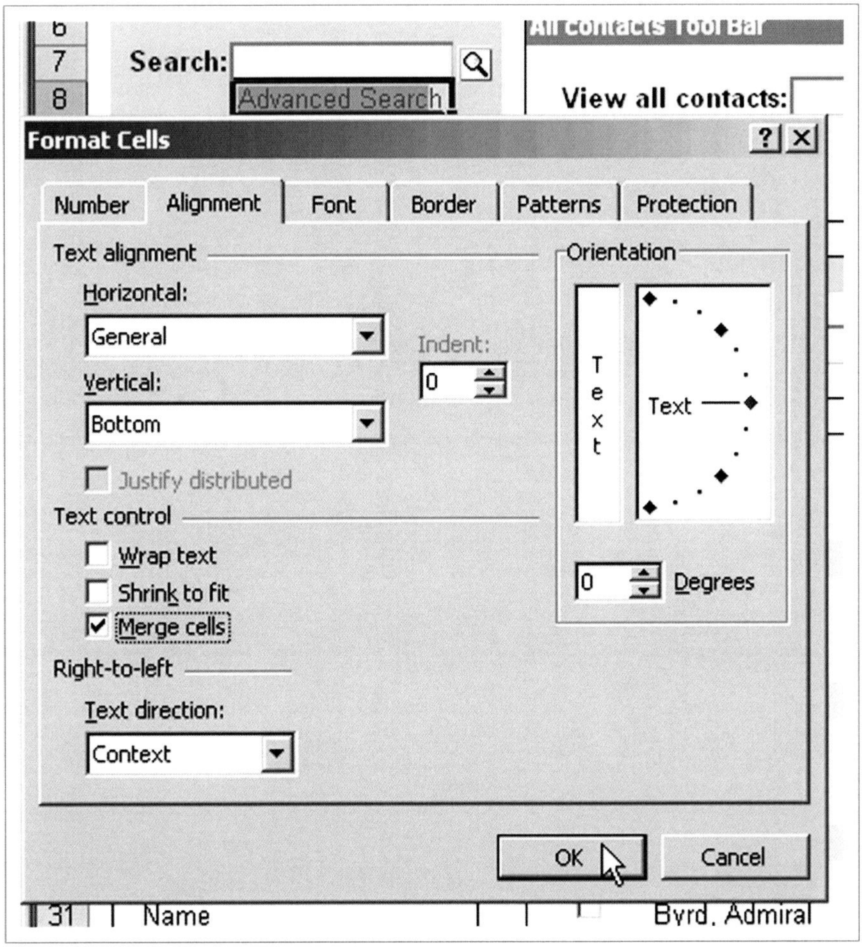

Figure 9.5.
Format Cells dialog box to merge cells.

Figure 9.6.
Tooltip appears over the entire hyperlinked text.

A red triangle in the upper-right corner of the table cell indicates a comment on a cell. Be careful—many comments on a worksheet can distract from your design. Another consideration in including comments is that all your comments will be isolated boxes scattered across your design. Though this helps in visually linking what the comments describe, it can be difficult to read them all at once or to copy them all to another design or requirements document.

To illustrate comments, we will use a case study using a New Contacts button in a design. This button is a new feature and will need a lengthy explanation.

In this exercise you will learn how to insert comments, customize the comments area, and use the reviewing menu to display the comments.

To Insert a Comment:

1. Right-click the corner of the contact button cell and select **Insert Comment** (Figure 9.7).
2. Right-click the red comment icon and the comment box opens. Here you can add text; in our example we added `This button is under technical feasibility review` by the engineering team (Figure 9.8).

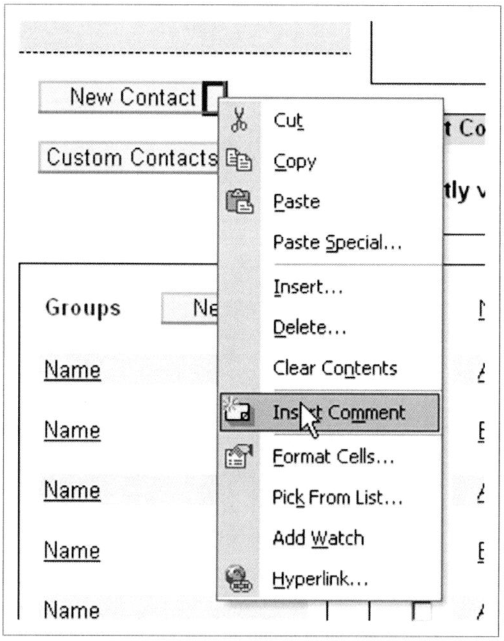

Figure 9.7.
Select cell to insert comment.

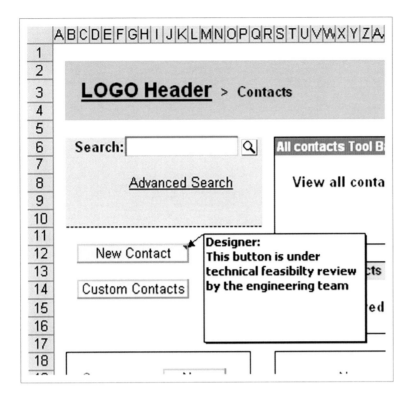

Figure 9.8.

Comment with text.

3. Right-click the open comment box and choose **Format Comment**.

4. To give the comment box the same style as all other technical comments in the prototype, in the **Format Comment** dialog box choose the **Colors and Lines** tab and give this comment box a blue background with an orange border (Figure 9.9, page 176).

The end result will have the style attributes defined in the dialog box and will look like Figure 9.10 (page 176).

After making several comments on the worksheet, you can manage them by opening the Reviewing toolbar. Use this toolbar to cycle through all the comments you've made, open them all up, or hide them.

In the Reviewing toolbar (Figure 9.11, page 177), you can

- Edit Comment: To edit comment text
- Previous Comment: To go from one comment to the previously viewed comment

Figure 9.9.
Customizing box border.

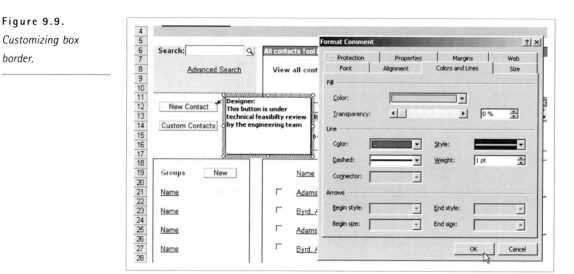

Figure 9.10.
Finished comment box.

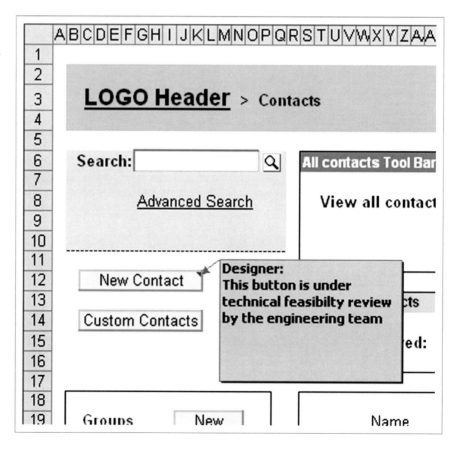

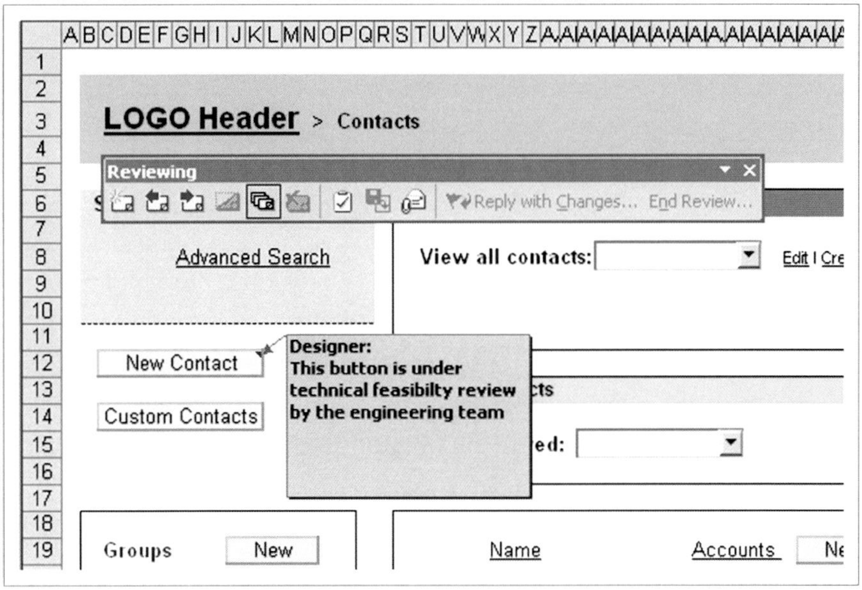

Figure 9.11.
Reviewing toolbar.

- Next Comment: To go from one comment to the next comment
- Show Comment/Hide Comment: To toggle the visibility of the comment in a selected cell
- Hide All Comments/Show All Comments: To toggle the visibility of all comments in a worksheet
- Delete Comments: To remove the comment from the currently selected cell

Creating Annotation Areas

You might want your annotations to appear on a worksheet without being hidden in a collapsible comment box or as hidden tooltip. By creating annotation areas, you can read the communications along with viewing the design.

First, you can make your own indicators, or graphical callout elements, that you position on the designs. These indicators act as references to your annotations.

- You can have all your annotations on a different worksheet within the workbook and link back and forth between the different worksheets.
- If your design is the full width of the application window, you can position a text box to enter your annotations off to one side so that they don't impose on your design and are either

- Only a short scroll away

- If you change the zoom to 75 percent, the annotations can be revealed and hidden by zooming back to 100 percent

- You can position the text box at the bottom of your design to keep annotations out of view. Making your indicators anchor links within the worksheet lets you link to the annotation for easy access.

- You can also link between Excel workbooks or other applications, such as Word. By using a word processing application, you can use more robust text tools to express your annotations if desired.

In this exercise you will learn how to annotate your prototype by creating areas on a worksheet with anchor links to annotations.

For this exercise we will create annotations in a separate worksheet. In anticipation of making annotations, you can create a series of indicators and place them in your image library worksheet in your Excel template. An indicator is an AutoShape with a numerical text reference.

To Create Annotation Areas:

1. From the Drawing toolbar, choose **AutoShapes** > **Basic Shapes** > **Rectangle**. Holding down the SHIFT key, create a small square.

2. Right-click the square and choose **Format AutoShape**. In the **Format Auto-Shape** dialog box, select an orange Fill Color, and set Fill Transparency to **50%** (Figure 9.12). Click **OK**.

We click Transparency so that annotations will not obscure any graphics that they are placed on top of.

3. Right-click the orange square, choose **Add Text**, and enter the number 1.

4. Repeat steps 1–3 to make five square indicators (Figure 9.13).

5. Select the first indicator and copy it.

6. Go to the **wireframe2** tab. Place the cursor above the groups box and paste the indicator (Figure 9.14, page 180).

7. Create a new worksheet and call it Annotations.

8. Use the rectangle **AutoShapes** tool, as you did in step 1, but this time click and drag a large area.

9. Add text: Annotation 1 (Figure 9.15, page 181).

10. Go to the **Wireframe2** worksheet. Select the Indicator, right-click, and choose **Hyperlink**.

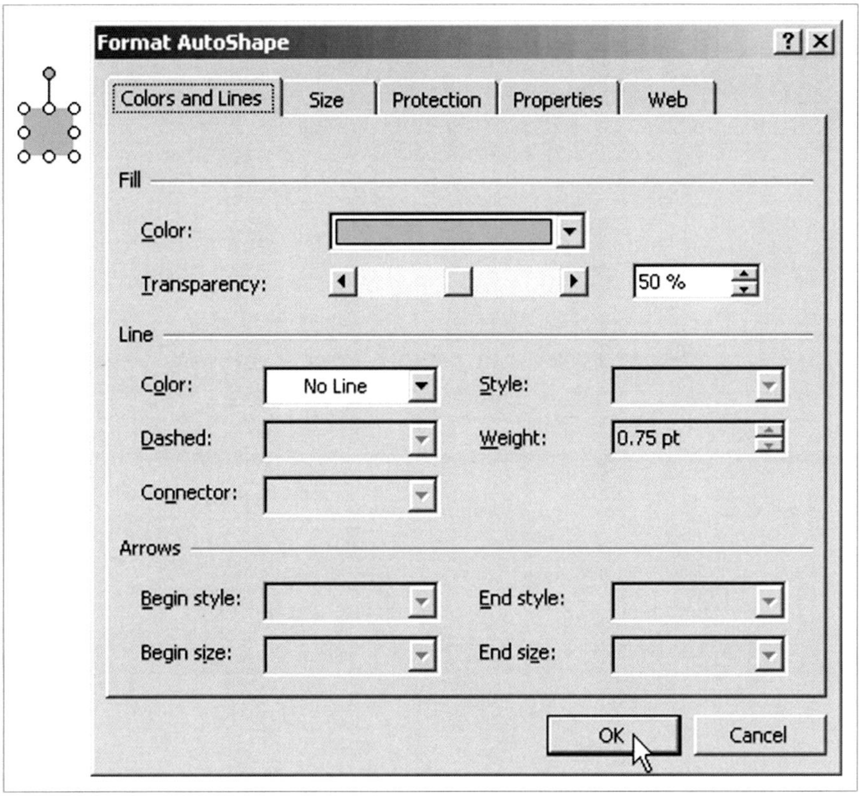

Figure 9.12.
Setting the color and transparency for the AutoShape.

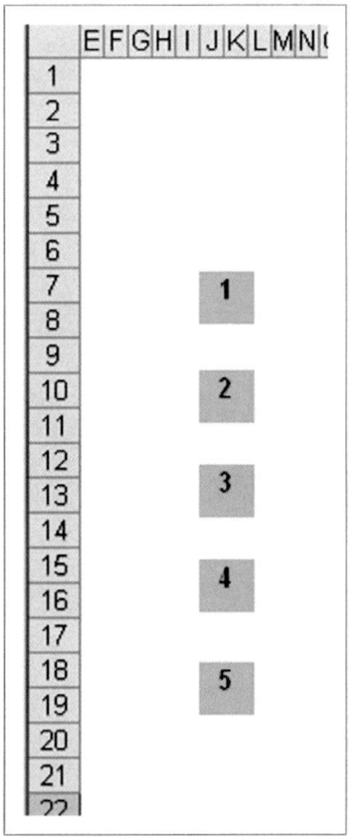

Figure 9.13.
Five orange square indicators.

Figure 9.14.

The pasted transparent indicator.

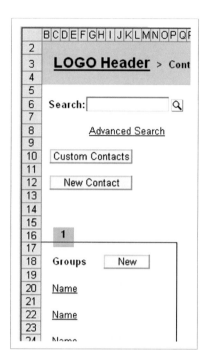

11. As you have in other procedures, choose **Place in This Document** and select **annotation** (Figure 9.16).

12. Click **OK**.

This will link the indicator to the annotation.

13. To create a link to return from the annotation back to the wireframe, go to the annotation worksheet.

14. Select cell **2J** and enter the text <Back.

15. Select the cells behind the text <Back, right-click, and choose **Hyperlink**.

16. In the **Insert Hyperlink** dialog box, link back to the **Wireframe** worksheet (Figure 9.17, page 182).

17. Click **OK**.

18. Repeat this process to annotate all necessary elements.

Your image will look something like Figure 9.18 (page 183).

This is where you will enter your annotations. Because the team might miss the annotation area, make your annotation indicators anchor links to the annotation area.

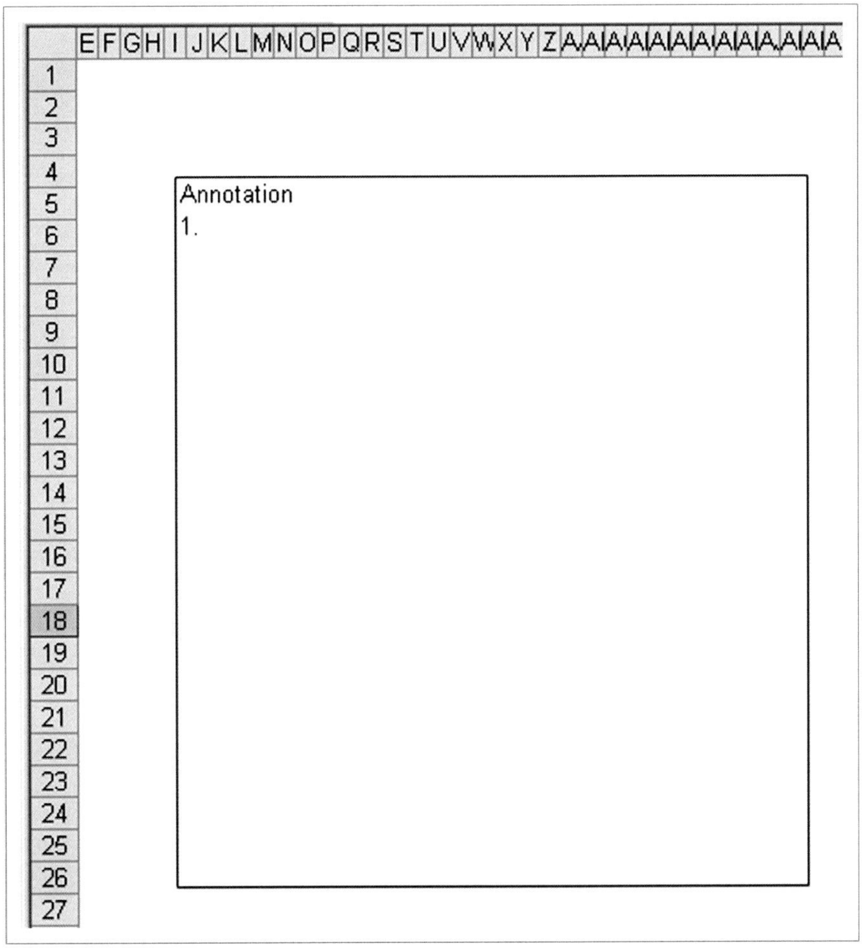

Figure 9.15.
Annotation worksheet.

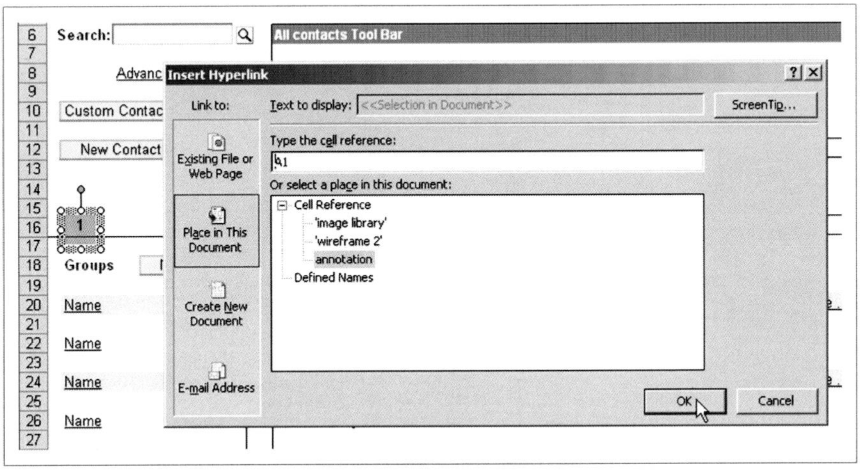

Figure 9.16.
Insert hyperlink dialog box.

Figure 9.17.

Insert Hyperlink to return to the wireframe.

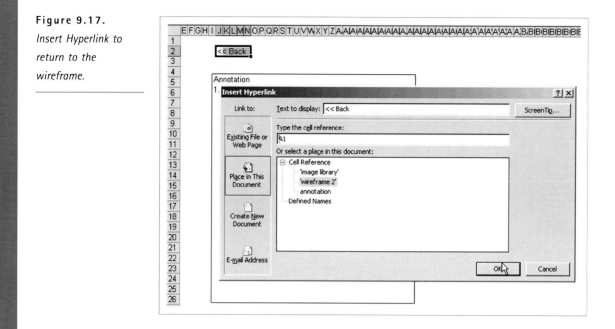

19. Right-click the annotation indicator and choose **Hyperlink**.

20. In the **Type the Cell Reference** text box, enter the cell reference cc1, which is the upper-right cell above your Annotation box.

21. To make it easy for your team to navigate from the annotation box back to your design, create a Return link above the box by using the default coordinates that will return a viewer to the original page orientation (Figure 9.19, page 184).

The annotation box could be to the right of the design, below the design, on a different page in this workbook, or in a different workbook altogether (Figure 9.20, page 184).

Another way to organize your page annotations is to create a prototype that is smaller in width so that you can have space to the left or right of the design for your annotations and other documentation. In this example (Figure 9.21, page 185), the column widths are narrower than usual and the type font is set to 8 points so that the resulting page is approximately 75 percent of the size of a full-scale page. The advantage to this method is that all the annotations are within the width of a full page, allowing for direct visual access to the annotation without having to click to another position on the worksheet or hyperlink to another document.

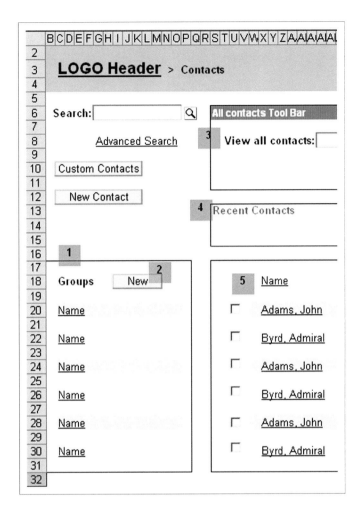

Figure 9.18.
The finished annotated wireframe.

Figure 9.19.

Add text to link back to the design.

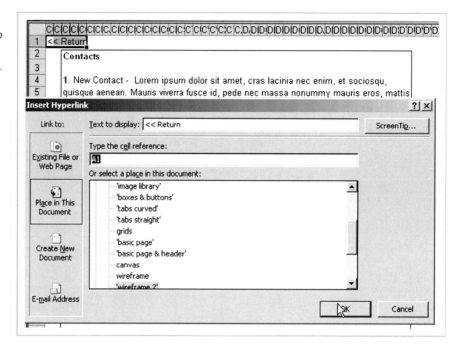

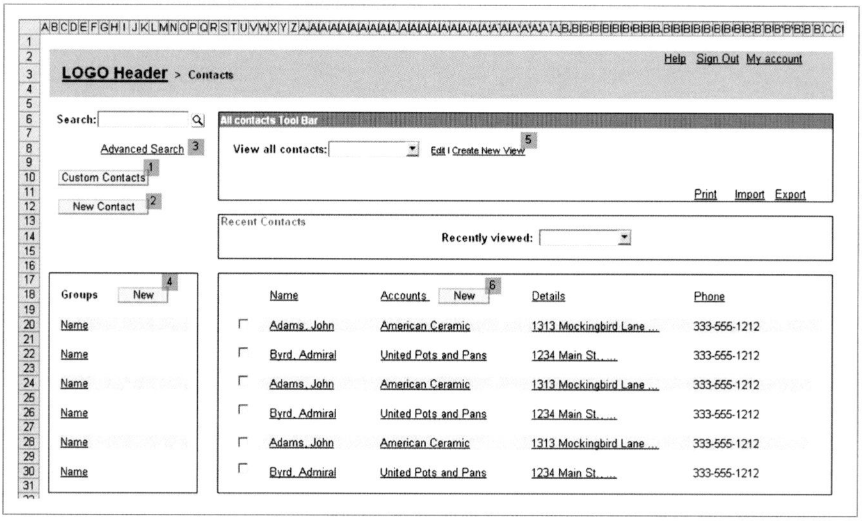

Figure 9.20.

Prototype page with annotation indicators.

Figure 9.21.

One page method with scaled-down design.

Conclusion

With your prototype finished, the documentation you have created throughout the prototyping process can become part of your final specification document. If you are using an application such as Microsoft Word that has a hyperlink text feature, you can link to your prototype, and conversely you can link from the prototype to your specification document. Or you can use your Excel prototype as a combined specification and design communication document.

References

[1]   Jonathan Arnowitz, Michael Arent, and Nevin Berger, *Effective Prototyping for Software Makers*, San Francisco: Morgan Kaufmann, 2007.

[2]   Dan Brown, *Communicating Design: Developing Web Site Documentation for Design and Planning*, Berkeley: New Riders Press, 2006.

CHAPTER 10

SHARING YOUR EXCEL PROTOTYPE

In this chapter you will learn how to

- Use your prototype for collaboration
- Mitigate the risks of implementing a finished prototype
- Avoid the risks in sharing your prototype
- Denote your prototype's interaction methods

Introduction

Your prototype is finished—now what? The way you share your prototypes with others and present them will determine the effectiveness of your designs and the impact they will have. Excel has many features that can help you effectively share your prototypes with other stakeholders. The process of sharing your design to achieve buy-in from the various stakeholders includes three important activities:

- *Collaboration*. Designing interactively with your colleagues, either in synchronous group interactive sessions or asynchronously, either ping-ponging prototype versions back and forth or synthesizing competing visions.
- *Presentation*. The way a prototype and accompanying explanations are communicated to the target audience.
- *Evaluation*. The assessment of the design embodied in your prototype by both internal and external stakeholders.

Using Your Prototype for Collaboration

Rarely is a prototype the product of a single person's effort. Often many people play roles in the design process. They all have some ownership of the iterations of prototypes that go into creating software. An early prototype might begin as a product manager's idea, but during the course of the design and implementation process, others will contribute their expertise and ideas. In today's world of global software creation, the people who participate in any prototyping activity might not even be on the same continent.

We have participated in many workshops in which we brainstormed on software designs by opening an Excel prototyping template and beginning to visualize ideas.

Someone will start with an idea for a design. We create the designs without spending time to make them look pixel-perfect, because Excel nearly automatically handles alignments and styles. The prototypes are clear enough for everyone to understand the ideas behind them. If some members of the design team are not available in the same physical space, we share the Excel files over the Internet by using meeting applications such as WebEx. Sometimes a participant tries to contribute an idea but cannot explain it adequately, either because English is not his first language or because he speaks a specialized domain language that not everyone understands. In such cases, we hand over the Excel file to that person, who can quickly show us in Excel what he is thinking. This way, when people are creating a real-time prototype, misunderstandings and mismatches in expectations are immediately identified.

Excel can be an even more powerful tool to help clarify competing visions and conceptual misunderstandings. When you create a prototype and distribute it to stakeholders, the feedback you receive will immediately show you whether you have hit the mark or not. With Excel, the advantage is that design team members can annotate or correct designs by directly changing the Excel files. This eliminates the dependency on a single gatekeeper prototyper or being limited to a prototyping tool that few participants know. Moreover, sharing Excel prototypes levels the playing field so everyone can contribute. People who are more visually oriented and less articulate in meetings are empowered to visualize their ideas.

Presenting Excel Prototypes

Excel can display a worksheet that is many screens deep by using a scroll bar. This can be a tremendous advantage if the content of your designs extends vertically below the visible area of the screen. Rather than showing designs at a reduced size or across multiple slides, as PowerPoint requires, you can present your designs in one screen scaled at 100 percent. Having a scroll bar also mimics how a user would see your design in a browser or perhaps as a client application. This single benefit can outweigh the other display features that come with a presentation application, such as PowerPoint.

Another form of collaboration is to have your prototype evaluated by internal stakeholders and objective external reviewers. Just as with other prototypes, Excel prototypes can be evaluated. For example, cognitive walkthroughs or interactive demos are among the methods that can be used in the different evaluation settings, such as usability testing, focus groups, and participatory design sessions. Whatever the evaluation or review techniques, it is important to avoid any potential risks with Excel prototypes.

Mitigating the Risks of Implementing a Finished Prototype

Why is sharing the results of a prototype the riskiest step in the prototyping process? What happens after you've finished your prototype can be unpredictable for four reasons:

- *Engineering can't implement the design.* If a prototype is designed without due consideration for the way it is to be implemented or without regard for adequate resources, the engineering team might go its own way with implementing—or *not* implementing—your design, creating tension between the design team and the engineering team.

- *Competing prototypes.* Multiple simultaneous prototypes within the context of a given design effort might offer differing and conflicting design directions. This happens when different prototypes are created by different parts of a larger software team, each unaware of what the other is doing. This is usually the result of either inadequate or no program management.

- *Outdated prototypes.* What happens when a prototype is no longer current? A prototype is generally created for a specific stage of the software creation process. Neither time nor requirements nor concept stand still during the software design and implementation stages. Watch for prototypes that degrade rapidly over a short period of time. An outdated prototype can compromise the outcome of a product design effort.

- *Misunderstanding and misinterpretation.* How is the audience of a prototype to know the primary intent of your design and how it should be interpreted? An audience can misinterpret the design intent of a prototype by not understanding its objectives, purpose, or design criteria. For example, a prototype meant to be merely proof of an innovative design concept can be confused with a finished design if the prototype's fidelity is too high and its intent is not clearly communicated.

How do you mitigate these risks by prototyping in Excel?

Engineering Can't (or Doesn't Want to) Implement Your Design

Your presentation should include a roadmap from the current design instantiation to the final design to be implemented. Be sure to share the Excel prototype with all your product stakeholders and go over the various design and requirements details with them before the presentation. The Excel prototype can either be shared during a meeting, where you can interactively work on it with your stakeholders, or distributed so that they can mark it up and return it to you.

Be sure that the design concepts of a prototype can be implemented by socializing your designs with the engineering team. What seemed to be possible in the beginning of a project might no longer be possible just weeks before code freeze—and definitely not possible during system testing. Again, solutions to issues found as a result of evaluation need to be reviewed carefully and signed off by the product stakeholders to assure they can be implemented.

Competing Prototypes

A simple process rule suggests that you never let any of the members of your product team prototype in isolation or diverge from the agreed-on product design plan. Assure that all prototyping activities are included in the project plan, even those by developers used for proof of concepts. These proof-of-concept prototypes can often undermine your design efforts by introducing conflicting design ideas that are orthogonal to the overall agreed-on design direction. In a presentation, everyone in development involved in prototyping should be present and actively participating. Include all stakeholders at your presentations and design reviews.

Outdated Prototypes

Archive outdated prototypes from project servers, project folders, and so on. Ensure that anyone who has seen the older versions of the prototype knows that a new one supersedes previous versions. Meet with stakeholders to inform them of and discuss the differences, and leave nothing to chance.

During a prototype presentation, provide a schedule of the future updates and other prototyping activities such as future validation testing, reiterations, and so on. Outline the types of changes that are anticipated. Early in the design process there could be conceptual changes, so developing to early conceptual prototypes is very risky. Later in the product design process, when no major changes are expected, developing to a more refined prototype is less risky—as long you allow for last-minute changes and refinements. Set everyone's expectations for the possibility of changes ahead.

After an evaluation takes place, the prototype is out of date. Planning of the evaluation activities must be clearly communicated to everyone. Published results should be made available to everyone and whenever possible integrated into the prototype.

You can integrate results into an Excel prototype in five ways:

- Insert an executive summary of the results in the first worksheet of the prototype.
- Include hyperlinks on the areas of the prototype using cell-based hyperlinks that take the user to the related evaluation results.
- Include text boxes to place the relevant results right over the prototype itself.
- On the old prototype, mark clearly that it is out of date, and then place links in the old prototype to the new designs in the new prototype. If the new prototype is not Excel and pinpointing the design is not possible, use a cell comment or hyperlink tooltip to explain where they can find the design in the new prototype.
- Make it a policy to place an expiration date in a prominent place on every prototype. For example, using Excel's text box feature, you can put an expiration date in the upper-left corner, which will not interfere with any cell-level-based designs or hyperlinks.

Misunderstanding and Misinterpretation

During a presentation, the moment can come when it seems that magic happens: Everything seems logical and intuitive. This is usually because someone is narrating a preconceived scenario to fit the design that was created. As long as the scenario is credible, the prototype comes across as effective and brilliant. But what can get lost in such a presentation is what, exactly, one is supposed to learn from the prototype. It might be impossible to distinguish what was temporarily added to support the flow of the scenario from what is the core, agreed-on design direction embodied in the prototype. To avoid any confusion, annotations can be created within Excel to communicate what has been and has not been tested.

Note

For more details about annotations, see Chapter 9.

Tips for Avoiding the Risks in Sharing Your Prototypes

The following tips are all designed to help you avoid the risks of sharing a prototype. Prototypes too often get bogged down in details that the product team never intended to demonstrate, but the details are nevertheless employed to help set context. One solution is to reduce the fidelity to mask these distracting details. Sometimes these details are essential to help an audience understand important aspects of a prototype and the conceptual design it represents. Some ways to control what you're trying to communicate with your prototype include

- Using a summary worksheet
- Setting the appropriate fidelity level
- Setting the appropriate visual emphasis
- Signaling how someone can interact with your prototype
- Tips to improve the visual appearance of the prototype

Using a Summary Worksheet

Setting expectations at the onset is essential. It helps to make sure that you adequately address the established requirements and the defined task flow, which are the focal points of the prototype. This can be done verbally in a meeting but can be quickly forgotten. It is much better to give the audience a short summary of these points. If you are distributing your prototype, you can include this summary as a kind of cover worksheet. In the downloadable files on our Effective Prototyping Website, we include a sample summary worksheet that you can copy and modify for your purposes. In addition to a summary, the key design requirements and task flow diagram can be included as worksheets that link to related screen design worksheets.

Setting the Appropriate Fidelity Level

Modulating degrees of fidelity within and across prototypes can be a powerful means of controlling what users focus on in your prototypes relative to what you are trying to portray and communicate. For example, one method for focusing the user on the right prototype characteristics is to reduce the fidelity of unimportant but contextually helpful characteristics. If you're displaying a wireframe to show a new visual design direction, one way of controlling what the viewer focuses on is to greek the text to prevent the viewer from getting immersed in the editorial content.

Tip

When you are copying text into an Excel prototype, it is important to use the Paste Special command and paste the values only. Using the values-only option, you assure that your prototype font styles are preserved. Otherwise, the copied font styles will be inserted into your prototype.

Setting the Appropriate Visual Emphasis

Another method for directing the user's attention where you want it is to deemphasize the parts of the design that don't require focus. This method involves toning down the unimportant areas of prototype screens by reducing their opacity; that is, modulating their translucency. For example, you're prototyping a new screen layout for a business application. Two elements in the prototype are two controversial data tables, which are not part of your design. You do not want the conversation to focus on these tables. To avoid that, you can lay a translucent shape over the table to preserve it as part of the larger context but diminish its potential for distraction.

To Create a Translucent Overlay:

For this exercise, deemphasize the table in the prototype screen design (Figure 10.1, page 194) by reducing its contrast relative to the background. Start by first laying a rectangle over the tables and then reducing its opacity so that the table elements are more subdued.

1. Choose the **rectangle AutoShape**; then draw a rectangle over the two tables that are to be overlaid (Figure 10.2, page 194).
2. While it's still highlighted, right-click the **rectangle AutoShape** and select **Format AutoShape** from the menu (Figure 10.3, page 195).

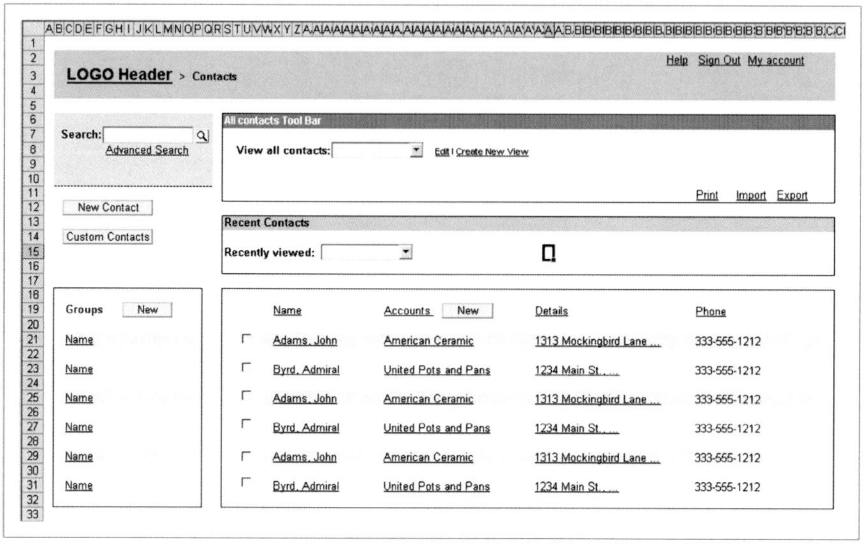

Figure 10.1.

The prototype design.

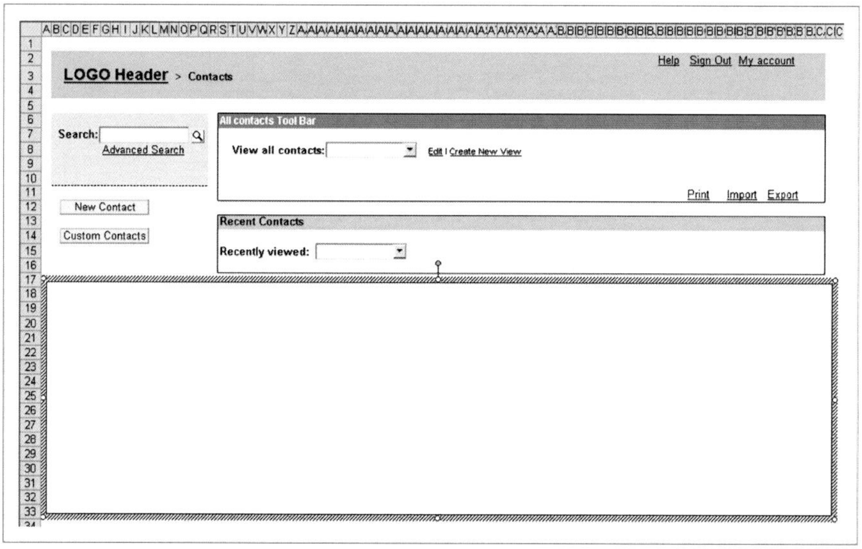

Figure 10.2.

A rectangle AutoShape laid over the designated tables.

3. In the **Format AutoShape** dialog box, specify the desired amount of translucency for the overlaid shape. In this case, enter **30%** transparency. To maximize the translucent effect and avoid visual confusion, choose the **Line Color, No Line** for the overlay, which eliminates the rectangle's unnecessary outline border (Figure 10.4).

With the overlay in place, the table portion of the screen is visually deemphasized while still sufficiently visible for reference (Figure 10.5, page 196).

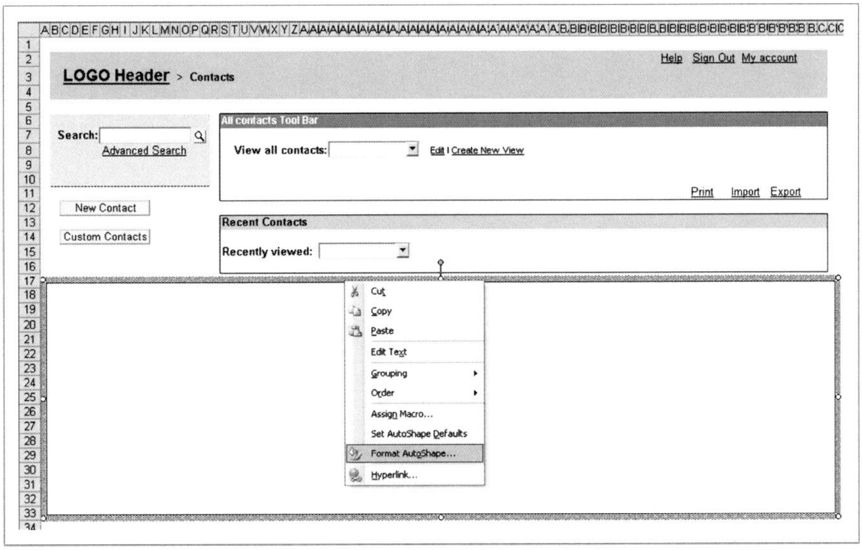

Figure 10.3.
Choosing Format AutoShape.

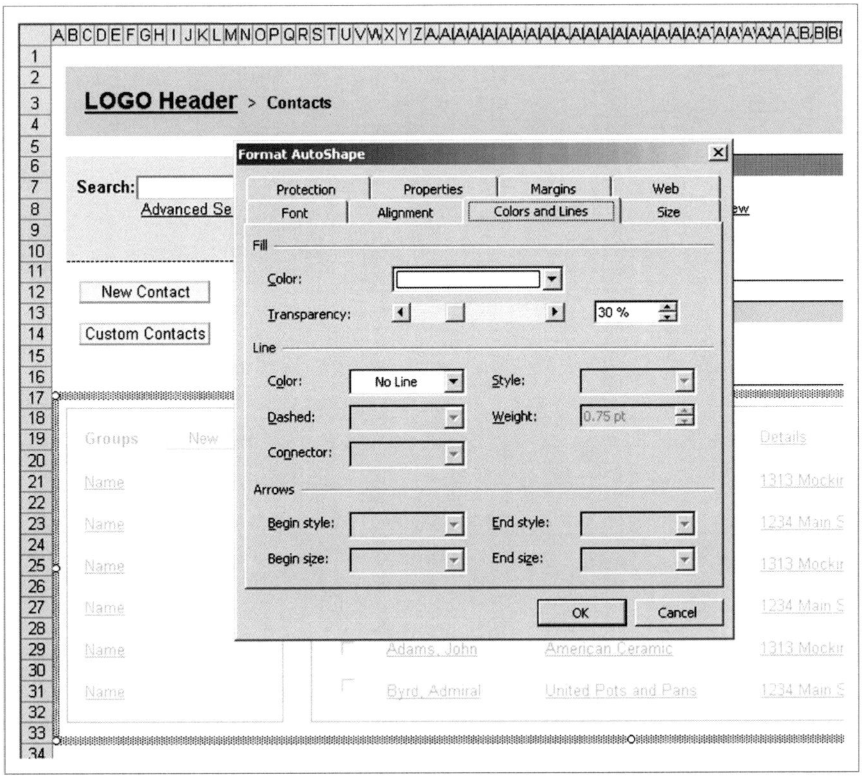

Figure 10.4.
Setting rectangle transparency to 30% and Line Color to No Line.

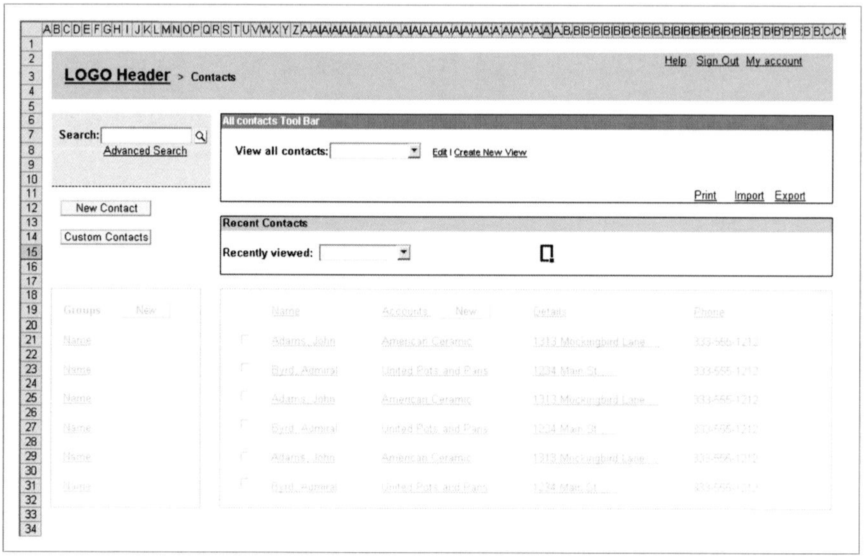

Figure 10.5.

Screen design with a translucent overlay applied to two tables.

Denoting Your Prototype's Interaction Methods

You can provide any of several interaction methods for your prototype:

- Creating simple click-through interaction
- Improving the appearance and presentation of your Excel prototypes

Creating a Simple Click-Through Interaction:

The tab bar at the bottom of the worksheet area affords simplified linear and non-linear click-through navigation of your prototype for presentations. As you're presenting your designs to an audience, they will inevitably have questions and discussions that require returning to earlier presented worksheets. To support this type of use, you can use a naming convention such as numbering that will make it easy for you to navigate among your prototype screens. You can also organize your tabs by color-coding them to help you quickly orient and reorient yourself.

To Name a Tab:

1. Right-click the **worksheet** tab.
2. Select **Rename** from the menu (Figure 10.6).
3. Type a new name into the selected tab.

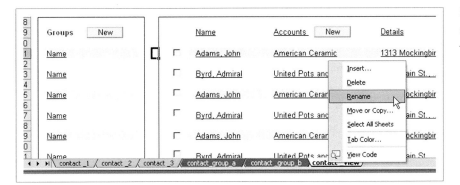

Figure 10.6.
Choosing Rename.

To Color a Tab:

1. Right-click the **worksheet** tab.
2. Select **Tab Color** (Figure 10.7).
3. Choose a color from the color palette (Figure 10.8).

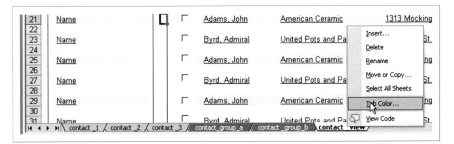

Figure 10.7.
Choosing Tab Color.

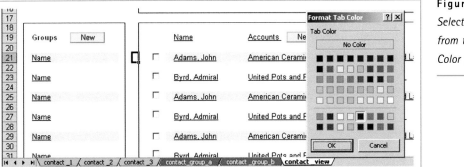

Figure 10.8.
Selecting a tab color from the Format Tab Color palette.

Tip

If you want to change the color of more than one tab at once, you can select multiple tabs by holding down the SHIFT key as you click each tab.

Now that you have renamed and recolored the tabs, you can now present your prototype screens by simply clicking through the tabs in the order that is appropriate for your presentation.

Identifying Which Links Work and Which Are Just Mocked Up

One recommendation for this type of presentation is to distinguish which links are functional from those that aren't by displaying the functional links in blue (with or without underlines) and the nonfunctional links in black with underlines (Figure 10.9). This is important to signal to the presenter or anyone else using this prototype which links are clickable and which are not (Figure 10.10).

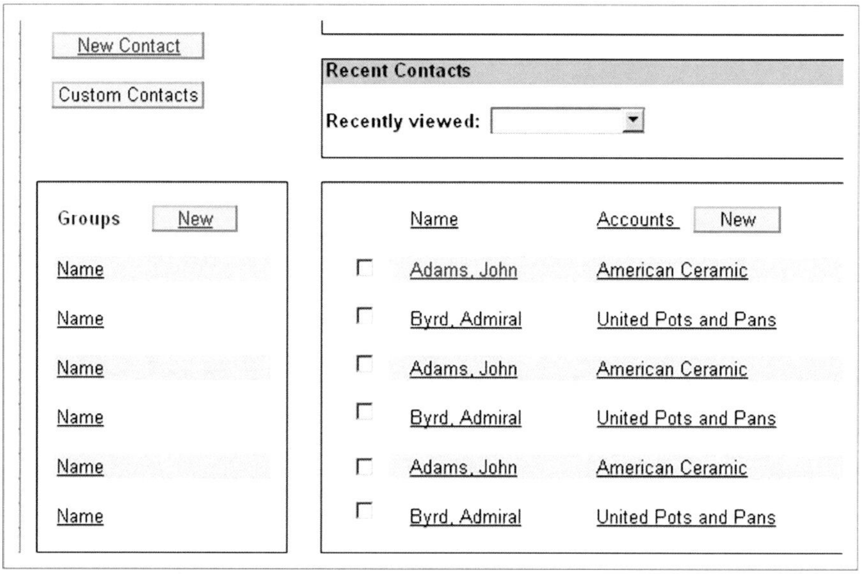

Figure 10.9.
Your design with hyperlinks for navigation.

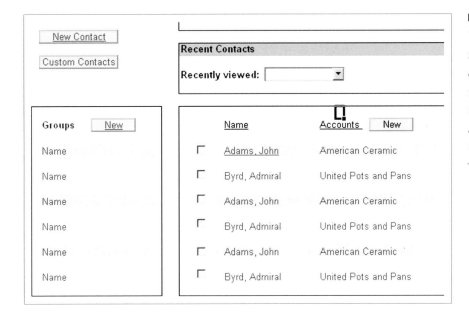

Figure 10.10.
Your design with functioning links in blue. It is difficult from this image to know which links have been implemented and which are for show.

Improving the Appearance and Presentation of Your Excel Prototypes

You can modify the Excel application user interface to achieve better visual presentations. To clear out some of the distracting visual screen clutter, start by closing any unneeded toolbars. From the **View > Tools** menu, deselect any toolbars that are not needed for your presentation (Figure 10.11, page 200).

Choosing **Tools > Options > View**, you can hide the row and column headers by deselecting that option in the **Options** dialog box (Figure 10.12, page 200).

Hiding the row and column headers allows your design to take full advantage of the worksheet width and removes extraneous visual elements that might detract from the presentation. In this dialog box you can also deselect the **Sheet tabs** setting that hides the tabs at the bottom of the worksheet. Although you might not want to hide the tabs if you plan to use them to navigate your presentation, you can still navigate from one worksheet tab to the next via **Ctrl-PgUp** and **Ctrl-PgDn** (Figure 10.13, page 201).

Figure 10.11.

Menu for removing toolbars from view.

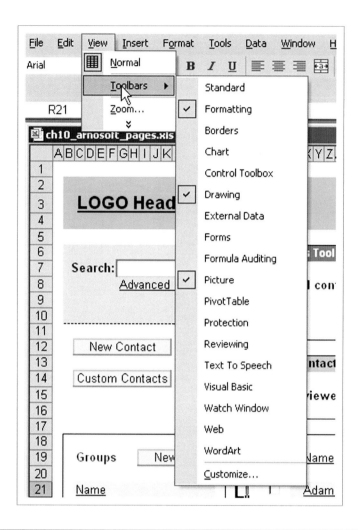

Figure 10.12.

Hiding the row and column headers by deselecting Row & column headers in the Options dialog box.

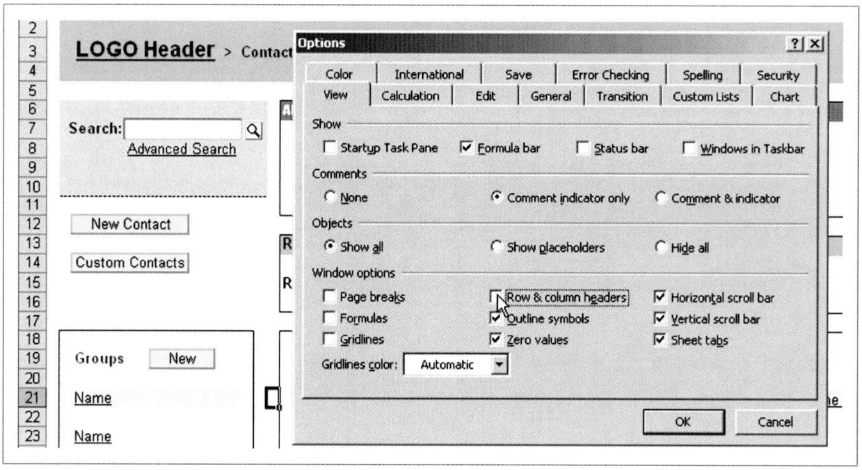

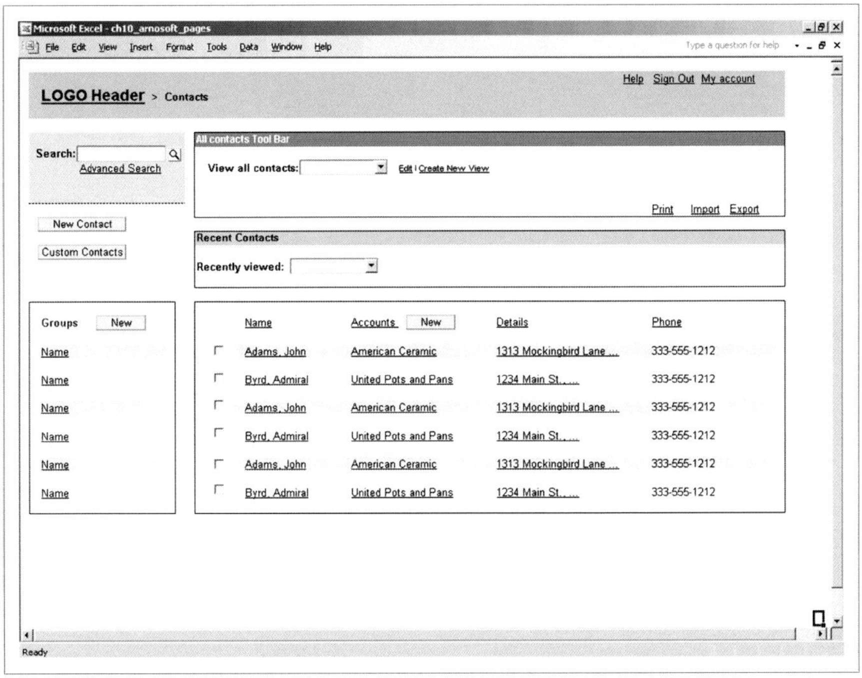

Figure 10.13.
Your design displayed with row and column headers and worksheet tabs hidden.

Tip

You can also quickly hide all toolbars and status bars by using Full Screen mode. Full Screen mode is initiated via VIEW > FULL SCREEN.

Another way to present your Excel prototype designs in a more streamlined and effective way is by saving the workbook as an HTML file and then using that as a presentation artifact. Saving as HTML

- Allows a browser user interface without the application user interface trappings of Excel.
- Affords a minimum of function bars that might distract from your presentation.
- Provides a convincing way to display your work to others, especially if your designs are meant to represent a Website or application.
- Allows you to show your designs virtually anywhere in the world by posting them on a Website and sending its URL to your stakeholders.

To save your prototype as HTML, in the **Save As** dialog box, select **Web Page** in the **Files of type** menu (Figures 10.14 and 10.15, page 202).

Figure 10.14.
In the Save As dialog box, selecting Web Page.

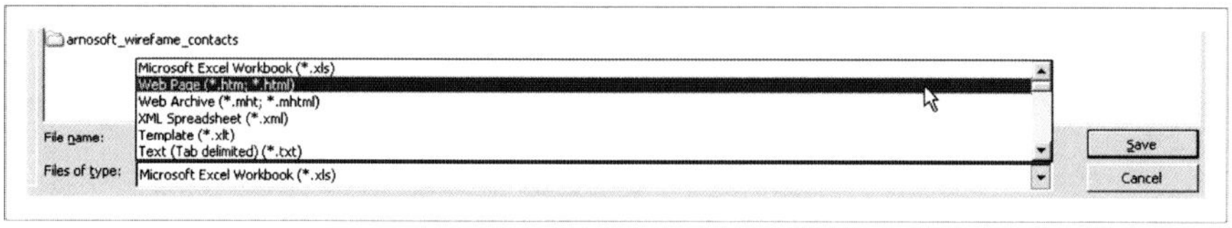

Figure 10.15.
Your prototype displayed as an HTML file in a browser.

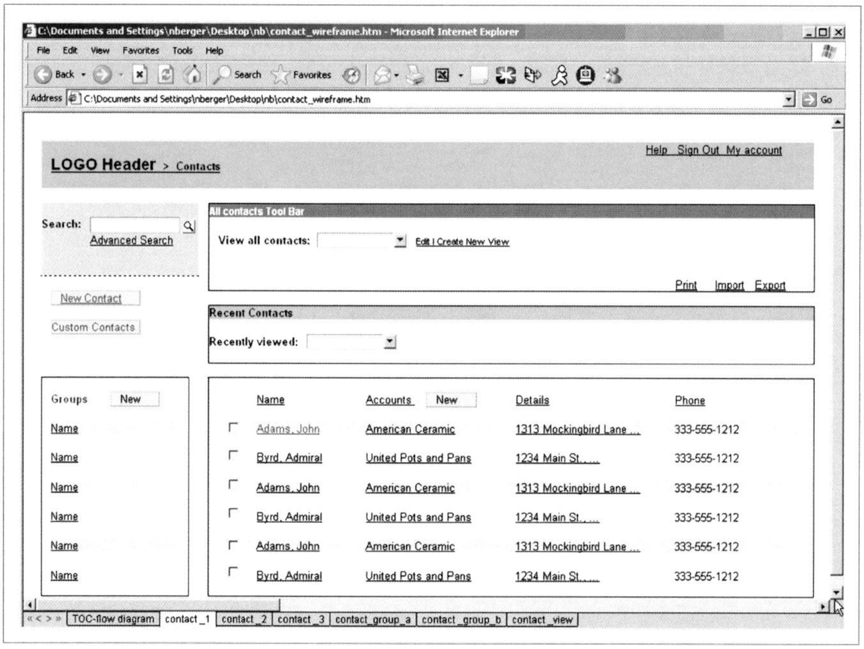

Note

Some Excel features do not translate directly into HTML. Centered or right-justified text reverts to left justified. Sometimes the positioning of graphics will be shifted slightly—enough to be annoying. If you have removed the tabs from the workbook, they will still show up at the bottom of the Web page with the names that you assigned them, but they will not maintain any colors you might have assigned to them.

Conclusion

Good preparation, thorough documentation, and thoughtful presentation and eval-uation can ensure buy-in from stakeholders for your design and can make your pro-totype useful throughout the design and development process. Selective use of presentation devices ensures an effective presentation of your prototype.

References

[1]   Jonathan Arnowitz, Michael Arent, and Nevin Berger, *Effective Prototyping for Software Makers*, San Francisco: Morgan Kaufmann, 2007.

APPENDIX A

USEFUL TECHNIQUES
WITH EXCEL

In this appendix you will learn to

- Eliminate background gridlines
- Set page attributes for the canvas
- Format table cells
- Use the drawing menu
- Create hyperlinks
- Save as HTML
- Insert and delete cells shortcuts
- Use drag-and-drop shortcuts
- Copy and paste
- Work with graphics

Introduction

This appendix includes a number of hints, gathered together here from the chapters in which they first appeared, which you might find useful while building prototypes in Excel.

As you discover new techniques and shortcuts in Excel, we invite you to share them by emailing them to tips@effectiveprototyping.com. We will post them on our site so that everyone can share in your discovery.

Creating the Canvas

To Turn Off the Display of Gridlines to Create a Blank Canvas:

- Select **Tools > Option > View** and clear the **Gridlines** checkbox, or
- Click the **Clear Grid** icon in the Forms toolbar.

Setting Page Attributes for Prototyping

To Select the Entire Worksheet:

- Click the top-left corner of the worksheet where the row and column headers meet. Keep this selected so the entire page will change at once.

To Ensure That Cell Contents Will Be Read as Text Only and to Prevent Accidental Reformatting:

- Right-click **Format cells > Numbers tab > Highlight Text**.

To Select a Default Color as a Background Color:

- Right-click **Format cells > Patterns**; then select a color.

To Select a Default Font Style:

- Right-click **Format cells > Font**; then select font and font styles.

To Specify a Background Texture:

- Under **Format** in the top menu, click **Sheet > Background**; then choose a picture to set as background.

Other than using a background as a texture for your designs as you would for a Web page, backgrounds can be very useful if you need to copy a design or use an existing design as a guide to get your proportions correct. Make a GIF of the whole page that you want as a background and then apply it as a background. After you have finished, you can remove it as the background, and you'll be left with all your elements in exact position.

You might want to use a full page as a background in your prototype. Remember that background images will tile and will repeat at the edges of your designs. To keep this from distracting from your designs, you can add white space at the right and bottom of the graphic before you make it a background. The background image will repeat but will not be within easy scrolling distance of your designs, hiding the fact that it is a repeating background.

To Apply a Special Background:

- Choose **Format > Sheet** and select **Background** (Figure A.1). You can browse for a file to use as a background.

Any image that you choose will become a tiled image.

The background color exists on a layer that is behind the grid, so anything that you input into a cell will be displayed on top of the color or texture (Figures A.2, A.3, and A.4, pages 208-209).

Another Way to Use a Background:

There might come a time when you want an image for a background and you don't want it repeated (tiled), but the image doesn't fill the entire worksheet. As shown in Figure A.4, the image of the cell phone is the background image over which you want to be able to prototype text. Create the background image with a large white field around it. Make the white area wider than the screen width you will be viewing, which would be either 1,024 or 1,230 pixels. The image will actually repeat, but because the image is larger than the visible area, it appears to be a single image. If you scroll to the right far enough, you will eventually see the image repeat. With the image as a background, it is not affected by anything you do in the table cell layer. Now you can easily add text or color table cells without fear of affecting the background image.

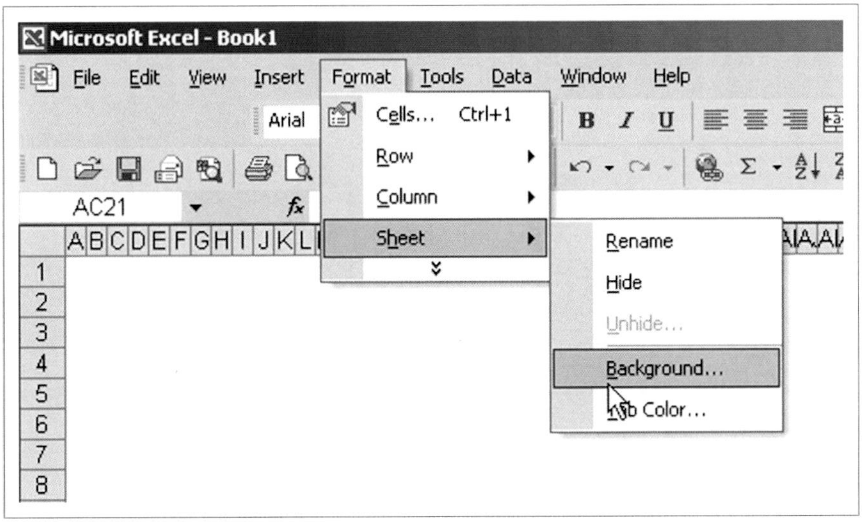

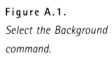

Figure A.1.
Select the Background command.

Figure A.2.

Example of text displayed on top of the background image.

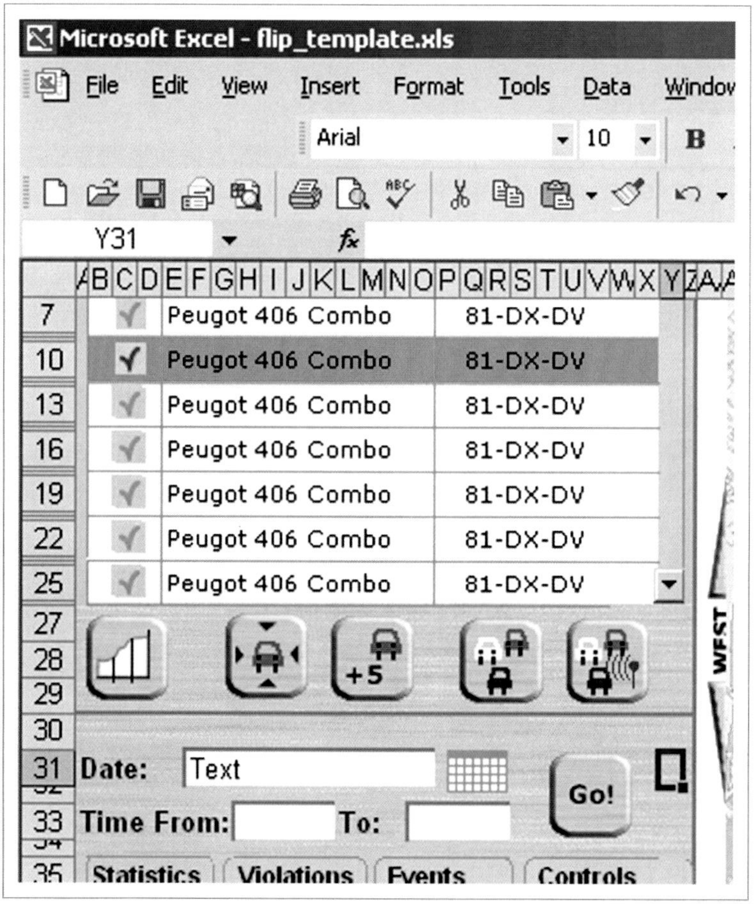

Figure A.3.

Example of text and graphics on top of the background image.

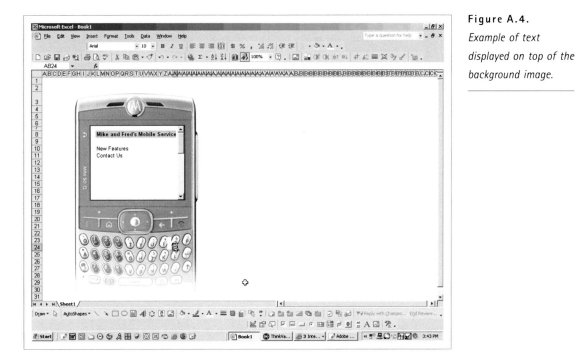

Figure A.4.

Example of text displayed on top of the background image.

To Change the Table Cell Orientation for Prototyping Rather than Making Spreadsheets:

1. Choose **Format > Row > Height**; then specify **13** (suggested size).
2. Choose **Format > Column > Width**; then specify **1** (suggested size).

Formatting Table Cells

To Specify How a Cell or Group of Cells Appears:

1. Select a table cell or group of cells.
2. Right-click and choose **Format Cells**.
3. From the **Format Cells** dialog box, select one or more of the following formats:
   - Number
   - Format Cell Alignment
     - *Vertical*. Aligns text at top of cell.
     - *Bottom*. Aligns text at bottom of row.
     - *Middle*. Aligns text in middle of row; good position for headers.
     - *Wrap Text*. Will wrap text within one cell or in multiple merged cells.
     - *Merge Cells*. Multiple cells act as one cell.

Note

If you want to copy and paste merged cells, the paste area needs to be same size as merged cells. If you want to delete cells that are merged, you will need to uncheck the merged option.

- *Font.* Sets font attributes for selected cell(s). Will override general settings. Good to use on prebuilt pages so that you can set the text in a header once and, when you copy and paste it, it will retain that font specification
- *Border.* Used to make cell outline borders. Choose a line style and color. Click edges of box to create borders. Using Borders to prebuild boxes and buttons will save time later.
- *Patterns (color).* Fills cells with colors.
  - See tips on Shapes to see a unique pattern effect for shapes.
  - To create customized colors, choose **Tools > Options > Color** (select a color in the palette) > **Modify**.
  - Choose from the color palette or click **Customize >** and use palette or RGB values.
  - To bring a palette into the workbook, go to **Tools > Options > Color** and in **Copy Colors From**: choose the open workbook that you want to copy the palette from. The palette will then update all the colors.

Note

The palette will exist in this workbook. If you copy a page to another workbook, it will use the host palette, or if you save a workbook page as a new workbook, it will use the standard palette.

Using the Drawing Menu

To Insert Shapes:

The AutoShapes menu is useful for creating basic shapes.

Connecters are very handy for creating flowcharts. The ends of connectors are sticky and will attach to shapes and move with them as you change your designs.

The Arrow tool in the Drawing toolbar is used to grab many pieces of art at once but will not grab table cells. However, you must click the arrow again to deselect it.

The Draw menu has many features, but the alignment feature is one of the most handy. Select multiple graphic objects; then choose the alignment style.

To Fill Shapes with Text:

- Right-click a shape and you see the option to Add Text.

If you have a content-heavy design, using text boxes allows you a lot of flexibility in where you position the text. You can make many types of text boxes in advance and keep them as a page in your workbook, making it a simple effort to copy and paste them where needed. Remember that you can eliminate the shape's outline or add color.

To Fill a Shape with a Pattern:

- Right-click a shape, then select **Format AutoShape**, and then click the box under **Colors and Lines > Fill Effects**.

In this dialog box you can fill the shape with blends of colors. You can create one- and two-color blends in different directions and degrees of transparency. This can provide interesting visual effects and easily dress up simple shapes.

To Group Shapes:

Select multiple shapes and then right-click to group them into one shape. If you need to change one of the shapes, you can use the **Ungroup** command. Excel has the ability to then regroup the original shapes again simply by selecting **Regroup**. This can be very handy if you are dealing with a complex number of shapes.

To Order Shapes:

Shapes that are on top of other shapes can be reordered by right-clicking them and then choosing **Order**. Order lets you send shapes or graphics forward or backward in dimensional relationship with each other. You will have to ungroup any grouped shapes to change their order.

Managing Worksheet Tabs

Multiple worksheet tabs can be selected by clicking them in succession as you hold down the **SHIFT** key. This tool can be very powerful if you need to make changes across multiple worksheets at once. As long as everything is positioned exactly the same way on all selected worksheets, changes you effect will happen across all the pages in the same manner.

Right-clicking a worksheet tab displays menu choices that let you copy, move, or save tabs as a new worksheets (see color tip). Worksheet tabs can also be renamed and deleted. Worksheet tabs can be renamed by double-clicking them and then typing over the existing tab name.

Worksheet tabs can also be moved simply by clicking and dragging them to a new position.

Hyperlinking

Text, shapes, and graphics can be made into hyperlinks linking to other workbooks, worksheets, or Websites. Select a text, shape, or graphic; right-click it; then choose **Hyperlink**. From the dialog box, choose from **Existing File** or **Webpage** or **Place in This Document**.

You can also link to a specific cell within a page. Highlight a cell in a worksheet, right-click, and choose **Hyperlink** in the dialog box. The resulting dialog box offers you the choice of where to link in the **Link to** menu. Choose **Place in This Document**. Type in the cell reference where you want the cell to link and click **OK**. The result is a hyperlink that, when clicked, will then position the destination table cell in the upper-left corner of the worksheet.

Hyperlinking can be used in many creative ways. It can mimic the navigation scheme of a coded Website or, by linking graphics, mimic interactive functionality, such as interactive buttons opening and closing a menu.

Saving a Workbook as HTML

A workbook can be saved as an HTML file. It will save all the necessary files needed to build a site using all the tabbed worksheets.

HTML prototypes are great if you want to have your prototypes displayed in a browser. It's easy to show your work to people who are remotely located by posting your HTML prototype to a Web server. It's also unnecessary to prototype files to other members of your team if they can access them online.

Note

In an HTML file, hyperlinks that have been set up will work, but unfortunately any drop-down boxes and certain cell features such as text flush left will not. In addition, if you have more than one worksheet, the tabs will show up at the bottom of the Web page, even if you have suppressed them in the workbook.

If you're using Internet Explorer (IE), you don't have to save your prototype as HTML. You can simply open up a file in IE and get a similar effect. However, the result will not look exactly like a Web page, since the Excel columns and rows will display.

Insert and Delete Cells Shortcuts

Windows and Macintosh operating systems now support multiple levels of undo and redo. These two simple features can be used in combination with Excel's insert and delete cell features to make precision sizing a breeze. You can use insert and delete cells to resize elements for alignment (Figure A.5, page 214), as shown in the following procedure.

1. Select a single column in the **All Contacts Toolbar** section, as shown in Figure A.6 (page 214).
2. Right-click the selected cells and choose **Insert** (Figure A.7, page 215).

Note

The Insert menu's Cells command can also be used.

3. In the **Insert** dialog box, select **Shift cells right** and click **OK** (Figure A.8, page 215).

The table is increased in size one column to the left. To continue to increase the size, you no longer need the Insert command. You can use **Ctrl-Y** to increase the size of the table until it matches the size of the Recent Contacts section (Figure A.9, page 216).

Figure A.5.

Unaligned elements to be aligned.

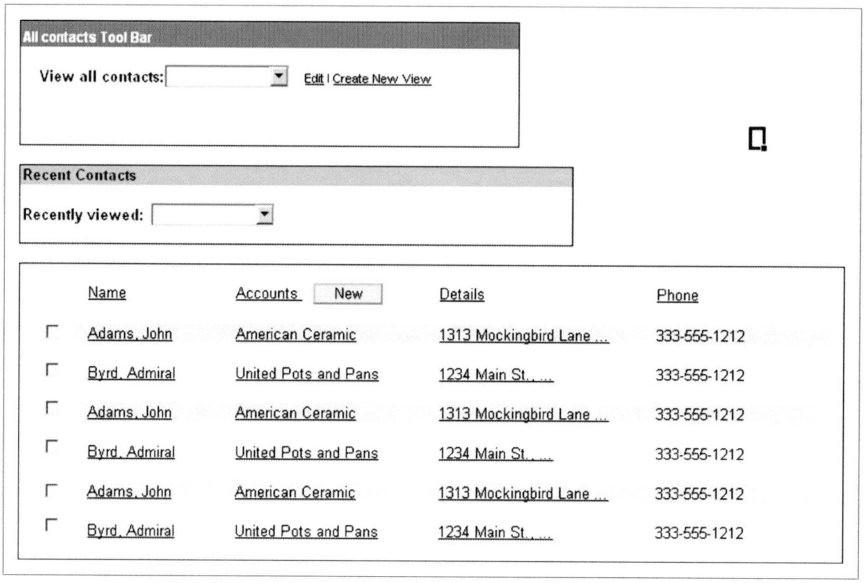

Figure A.6.

Selected a single column of cells in a UI element.

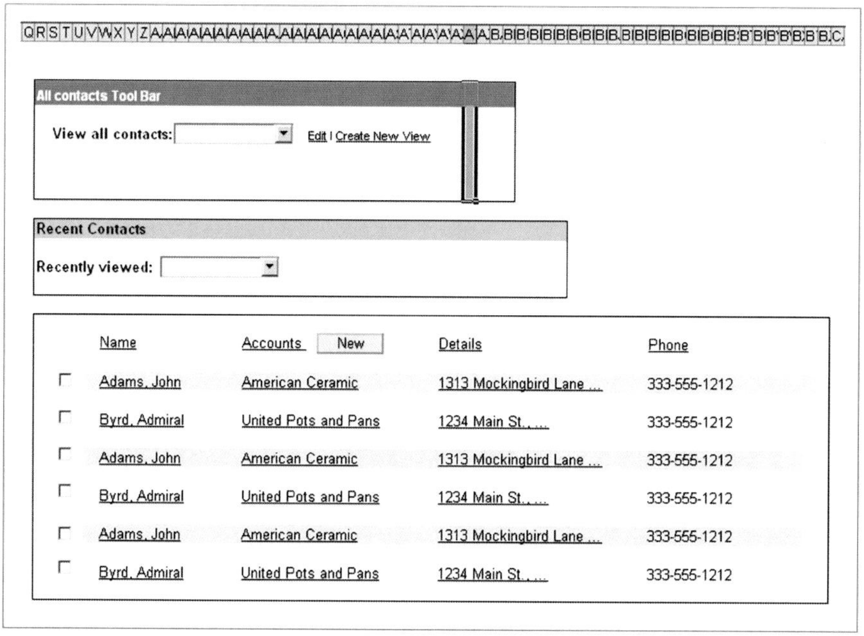

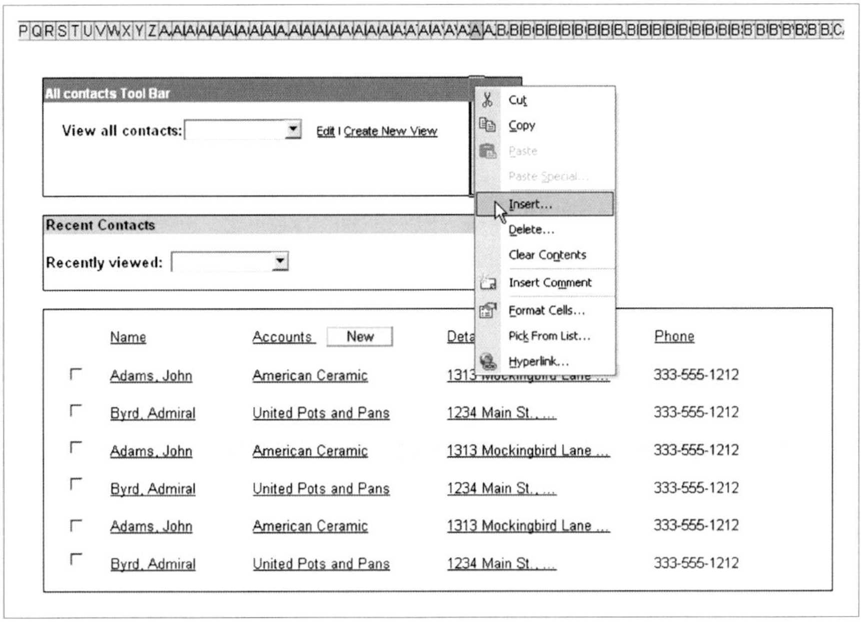

Figure A.7.
Right-click (context) menu.

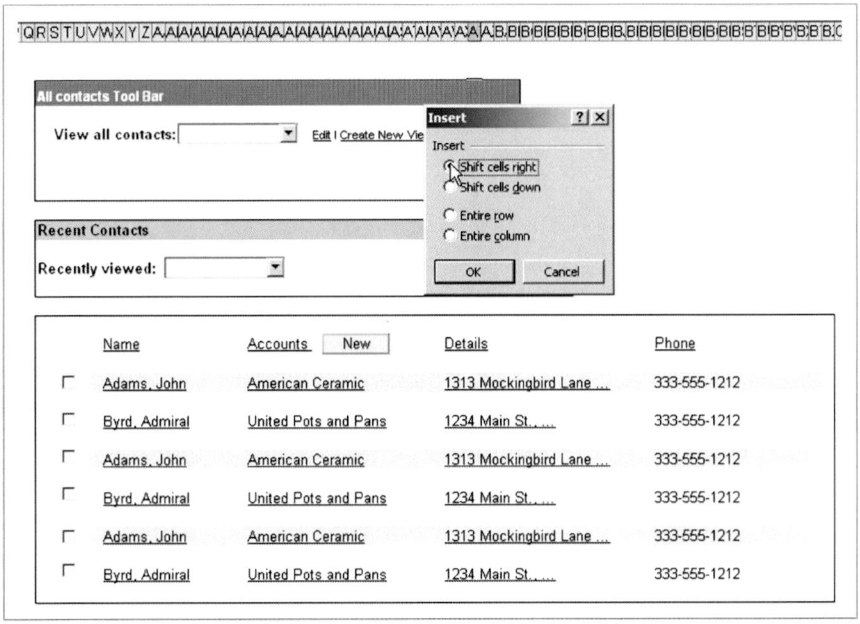

Figure A.8.
Selecting Shift cells right in the Insert dialog box.

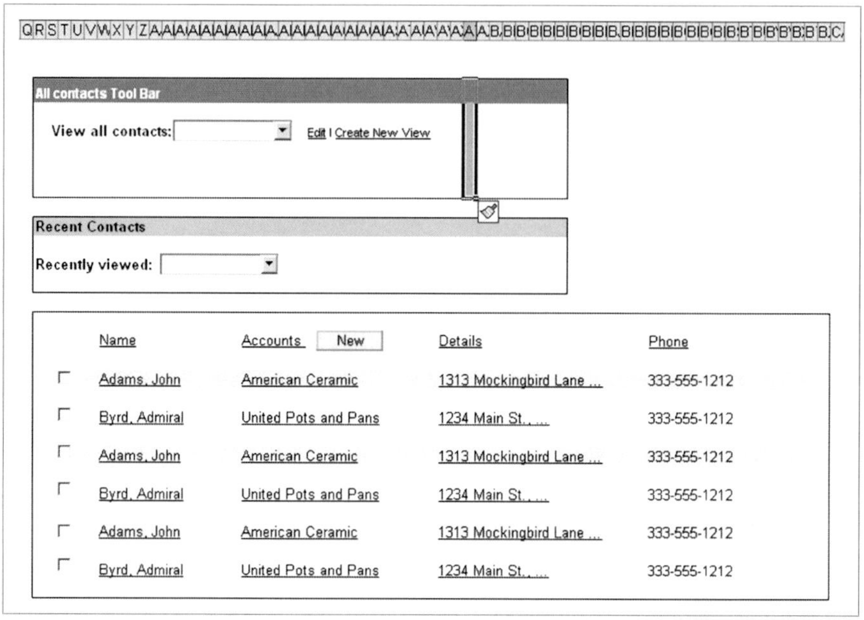

Figure A.9.

*Resulting alignment
from inserting cells
with no other
formatting required.*

Figure A.9.

Resulting alignment from inserting cells with no other formatting required.

If you make the table too big, use **CTRL-Z** (Undo) to make the table smaller.

If the table starts out too small, you can use the Delete cells command (and then shift cells left) to shrink the table size.

Drag-and-Drop Shortcuts

Excel's implementation of drag and drop takes the formatting of the source cells, allowing you to easily format patterns of styles on a canvas. For example, we can use drag and drop to easily match sizes among various elements in the prototype. Furthermore, Excel implemented drag-fill, a way of dragging a selected series of cells and then dragging them up or down, which causes a series of numbers or patterns of numbers to be filled in based on the cells you have selected. How drag and fill works in general can be found in the Excel help file, but suffice it to say that it is a small handle you will find in the lower-right corner of any selection. However, just because it is in the lower-right corner does not mean you can drag only to the right or down; drag and fill works in any direction. This spreadsheet functionality also works with cell formatting, making the creation of regular formatted areas uniquely simple in Excel.

To Align Elements on a Page:

1. Select the last three columns of cells in both the **All Contacts Toolbar** and the **Recent Contacts** sections, as pictured in Figure A.10.

2. Drag the selected cells horizontally to the edge of alignment with the outer edge of the table (Figure A.11, page 218). Be careful not to drag a cell row above or below. (If you do, simply redrag it and drop it back into place.)

3. Select the row of cells with the formatted header and footer in both the **All Contacts Toolbar** and the **Recent Contacts** sections, as pictured in Figure A.12 (page 218).

4. Click the special drag-fill selector at the bottom of the selection and drag across to fill in the gap (Figure A.13, page 219).

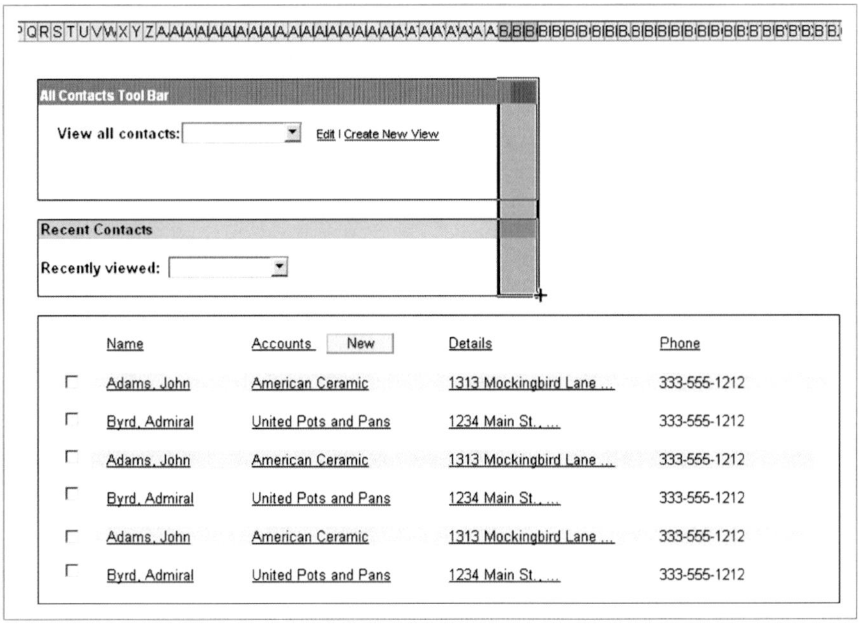

Figure A.10.

Select two or three columns from the end of the UI items you want to resize.

Figure A.11.

Drag the selected cells to where you want to resize your UI element.

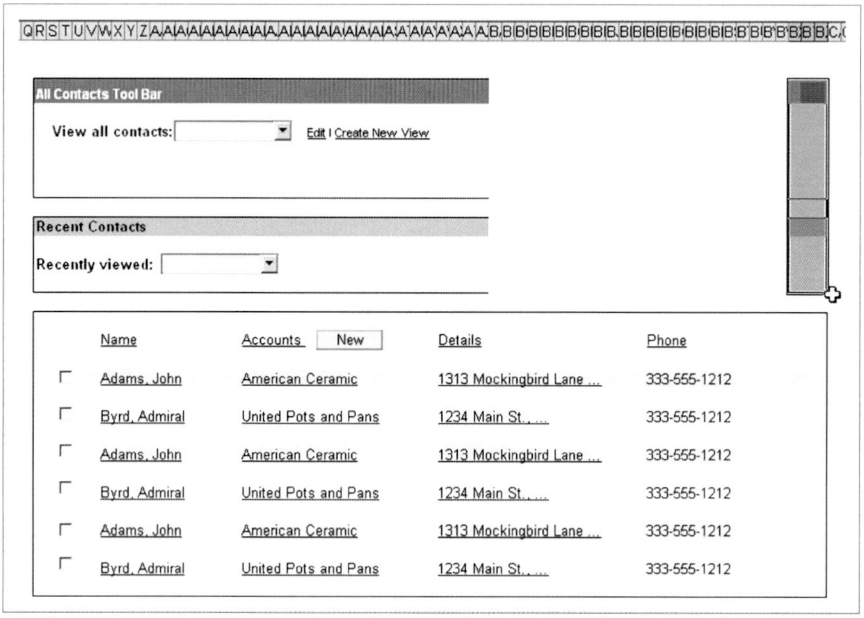

Figure A.12.

Select a column of the formatting you want to fill and then perform a drag-fill to fill in the cells with your selected formatting.

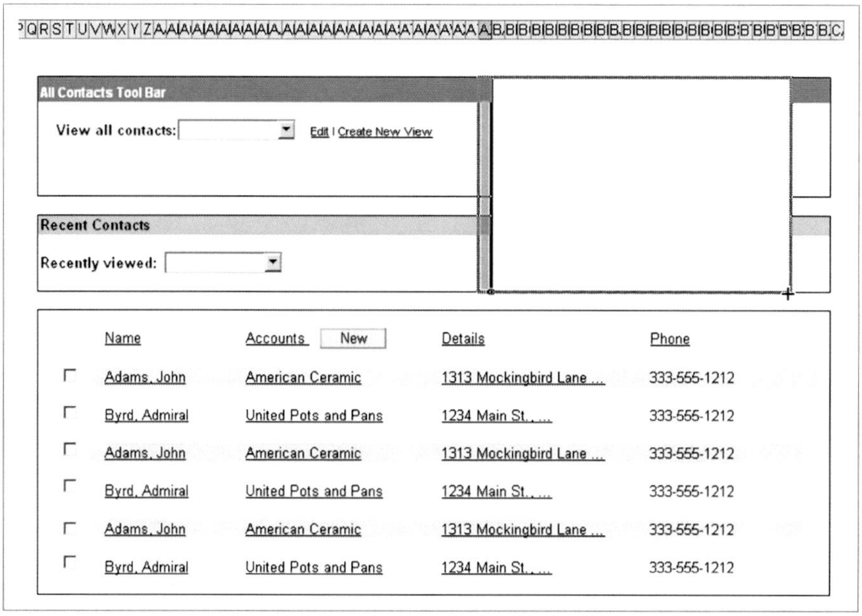

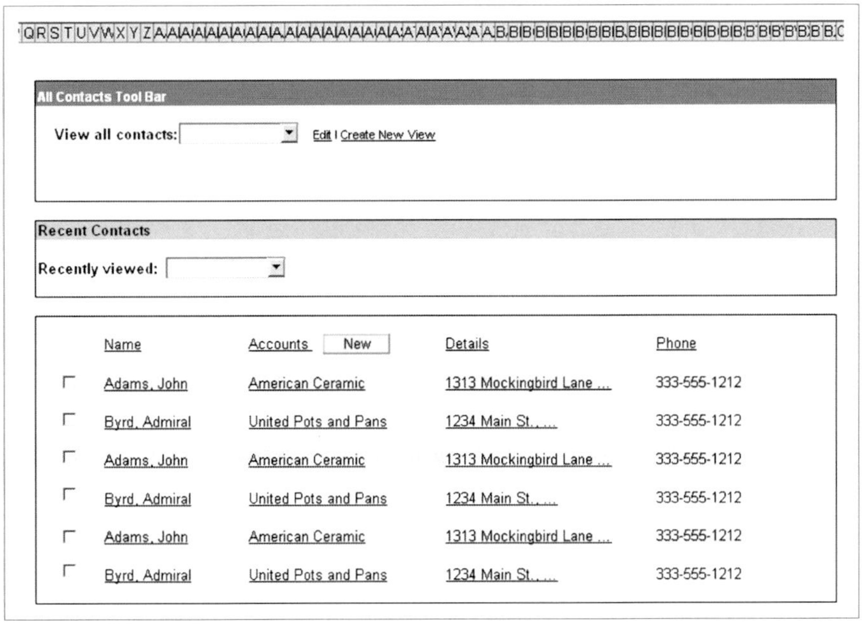

Figure A.13.
All the formatting is carried over and the size of all the elements is now equal.

Drag-Fill Shortcuts

Excel's implementation of drag-fill shortcuts helps with the formatting of the source cells, allowing you to easily duplicate the format patterns of styles on a canvas. For example, we can use drag-fill to easily fill in areas on a prototype worksheet, as shown in the following procedure. Furthermore, Excel-implemented drag-fill is a way of dragging a selected series of cells and then dragging them up or down; this causes a series of numbers or patterns of numbers to be filled in based on the cells you have selected. How drag-fill works in general can be found in the Excel help file, but suffice it to say, it begins with the small handle you will find in the lower-right corner of any selection. However, just because it is in the lower-right corner does not mean you can drag only to the right or down; drag and fill works in any direction. This spreadsheet functionality also works with cell formatting, making the creation of regular formatted areas uniquely simple in Excel.

To Apply Drag-Fill:

1. Select the last three columns of cells in both the **All Contacts Toolbar** and the **Recent Contacts** sections, as pictured Figure A.14, (page 220).
2. Drag the selected cells horizontally to the edge of alignment with the outer edge of the table (Figure A.15, page 220). Be careful not to drag a cell row above or below. (If you do, simply redrag it and drop it back into place.)

Figure A.14.

Select two or three columns from the end of the UI items you want to resize.

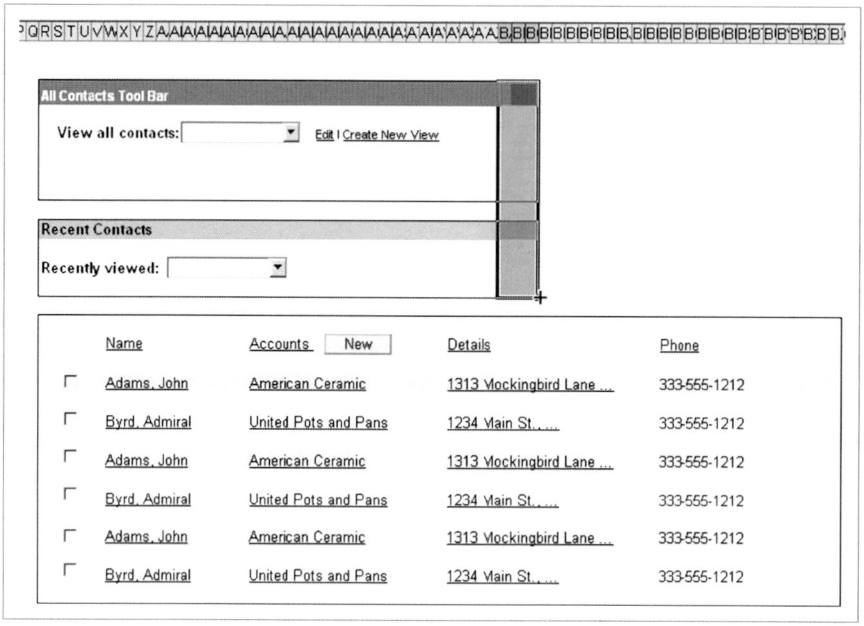

Figure A.15.

Drag the selected cells to where you want to resize your UI element.

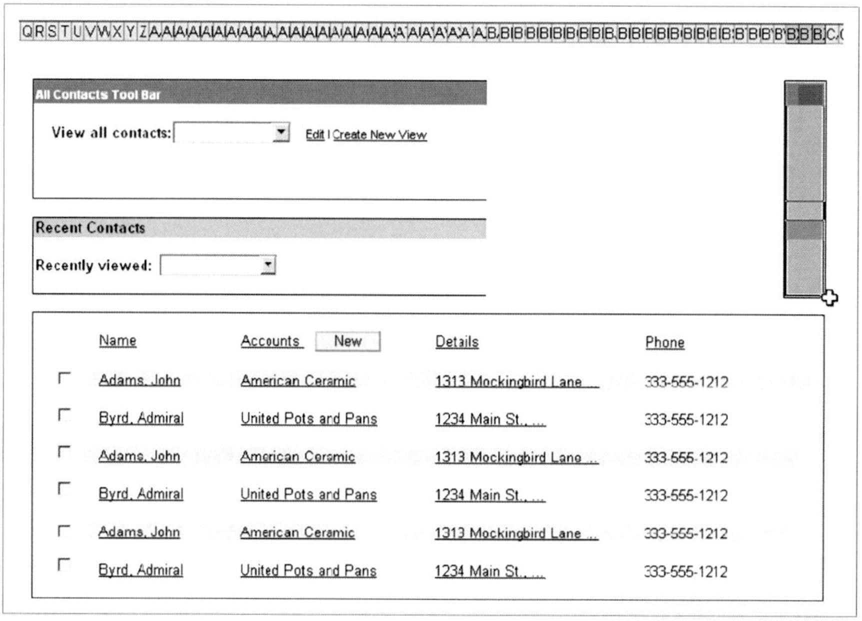

3. Select the row of cells with the formatted header and footer in both the **All Contacts Toolbar** and the **Recent Contacts** sections, as pictured in Figure A.16.

4. Click the special drag-fill selector at the bottom of the selection and drag across to fill in the gap (Figure A.17, page 222).

Drag–Fill Patterns:

Drag-fill also works with patterns. After creating a pattern, you can then select the pattern you created. Then drag over a larger area and Excel will re-create that pattern in the area that you have dragged. For example, you need to create a table in which every five cells has a vertical border. All you need to do is create the first column of the table. Select this first column pattern; then use the drag-fill to repeat this pattern along the length of a longer selection. Your pattern will repeat automatically.

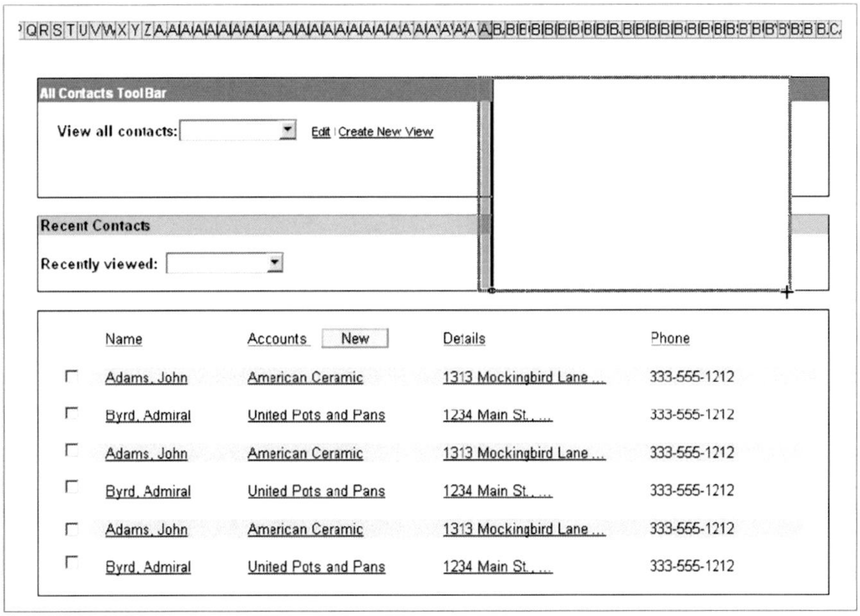

Figure A.16.

Select a column of the formatting you want to fill and then perform a drag-fill to fill in the cells with your selected formatting.

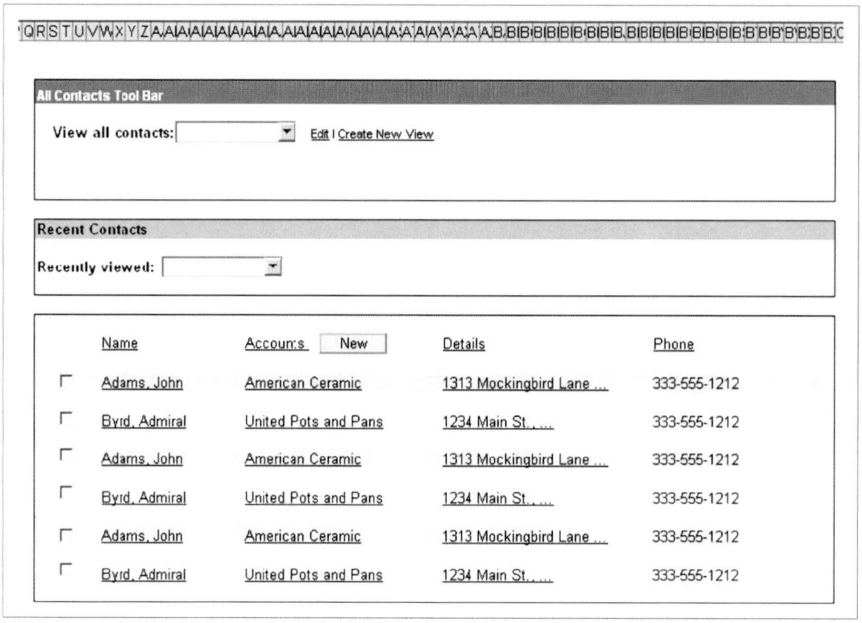

Figure A.17.

All the formatting is carried over and the size of all the elements is now equal.

Copy and Paste: Building Prototype Screens Quickly

The effective use of Excel's copy-and-paste functionality is crucial to the success of rapid prototyping. Though copy and paste might seem to be one of the simplest features to use because it is so familiar and is virtually ubiquitous, its simplicity is what makes it so powerful. Remember that behind the canvas worksheet is a grid of table cells. Pasting into those cells enables pasting with pinpoint accuracy.

These two factors, simplicity and accuracy, directly affect the way you use the template for prototyping. First, you are making all your template worksheets and prototype screens from the same canvas template worksheet. All these worksheets have the same grid dimensions and predefined attributes. The widgets, buttons, and other features you create are all made up of differently styled table cells on the same background grid. So, anything that you copy from one worksheet can easily be pasted into another. All the relationships between the various widgets and worksheets will be the same so they can easily be copied and pasted from worksheet to worksheet. When using copy and paste, you can choose the exact sized widget or tab configuration that you need, and copy it from that template worksheet into the prototype design you are working on.

Copy and paste, as implemented in Excel, includes some special characteristics that you can use to your advantage as you build your prototype. You can use copy and paste in the conventional manner: Select the cells that you want to copy; then choose **Copy** under the Edit menu (or press **Ctrl-C** on the keyboard) to copy the cells. Then paste it into a new selected area—but the selected area must be exactly the same size in exactly the same configuration that you copied from. That can be a challenge when you are moving from one template worksheet to another.

But Excel has an alternative method of pasting: You can choose to paste into a single cell rather than into a group of cells. When you are pasting into a single cell, everything that you copied is pasted in, starting from the target cell to the right and below. Your copied cells are pasted over any existing cells. When copied, the attributes of the pasted cells overwrite any preexisting styles. You can take whatever you have made on one worksheet and paste it into another worksheet. You can copy and paste small elements, such as buttons, to parts of designs or complete prototype screens.

Copying and pasting becomes so convenient that many times it is easier to simply copy and paste something from somewhere else on a worksheet than go through the process of choosing a color or border color to create a new page or element.

Working with Graphics in Excel

The tools and techniques for working with graphics are virtually the same among Microsoft applications, so we are not going to go into depth describing how to work with them. However, we have some tips that might save you time and effort.

Selecting Object Mode:

In the **Drawing** toolbar, which you might usually have open, note the **Select Objects** (arrow) on the left (Figure A.18, page 224). This turns the cursor into an object selector and will not select a cell in the spreadsheet grid. When clicked, the cursor changes to an arrow/crossbar icon. In this mode, the cursor selects only graphics. Use this mode when you are working with a complex design that mixes text, patterns, and graphics and you want to select only the graphics. You have to click **Select Objects** again to be released from that mode.

Figure A.18.
Clicking the graphics arrow.

Draw ▾ ⬚ AutoShapes ▾ ＼ ⬚ ◯ ▦ ◢ ⟳ ▣ ▨

Draw Menu

The Draw menu offers ways to keep your graphics organized. The selections are

- *Order.* This has four options that allows you to move graphics spatially forward or backward in relationship to each other. This feature can be very helpful if you're trying to construct a more complex graphic, such as a dialog box, which we will cover later in the advanced Excel section.
- *Snap.* Allows you to align a graphic to the grid or shape by using snap.
- *Align or Distribute.* Provides several choices for positioning multiple graphics.
- *Rotate or Flip.* Allows you to alter the orientation of a graphic.

Formatting Toolbar

Excel also includes handy tools in the **Formatting** toolbar that allow you to manipulate graphics (Figure A.19).

- *Color.* Allows you to adjust some color attributes, change your graphic to grayscale or black and white, or wash out the colors.
- *Contrast.* There are two tools that allow you to change the contrast of an image; one will increase contrast, whereas the other will lower the contrast.
- *Brightness.* Two tools that allow you to change the brightness of an image; one will increase brightness, whereas the other will decrease the brightness.
- *Crop.* Allows you to crop the size of a graphic. The only problem with this tool is it keeps the original graphic in memory in case you want to expand your crop back to its original size. This can cause problems with file size if you are cropping many large graphics to smaller sizes. After you crop a lot of large graphics, your template could become too large. Albeit, there is a solution. In the Compress Pictures features in the same toolbar (see below), you can select a graphic and delete the cropped areas. This adds an extra step to the process but makes it easier if you don't have access to a graphics application to do your cropping.

Figure A.19.
Formatting toolbar.

- *Rotate Left.* Allows you to rotate a selected graphic to the left at a 45-degree angle. You can also rotate a selected graphic by clicking on the green anchor. With this method you can move the graphic at any increment you wish.

- *Line Style.* Allows you to create a border with a black line for your selected graphic.

- *Compress Pictures.* Allows you to change the compression of a selected graphic in case you imported a graphic that is too large to use. You can also delete unwanted cropped areas of a graphic.

- *Format Picture.* This feature encompasses most of the features we have already mentioned while giving you even more control over each feature. When you click on the icon, a dialog box appears that offers many formatting choices.

- *Color and lines.* Allows you to fill Excel shapes with a color and adjust the transparency of the color. This function also allows you to add a border to any graphic and arrows to any lines drawn in Excel.

- *Size.* In this dialog box you can adjust the size of a graphic and rotate it.

- *Scale.* Allows you to scale an image size or return it to its original size.

- *Picture.* You can crop your image; alter the color, brightness, and contrast; compress and reset your graphic back to its original settings.

- *Set Transparent color.* Allows you to set the transparency level of a graphic color. What that means is, if you have a graphic with a particular color that you wish was invisible, you can click on that color and manipulate its transparency. This works best on colors that are made up of only one color. The tool can select only one color at a time. So if you are selecting a color that is made up of many colors, such as the blue in a sky, you will not be able to select all the colors in the sky at one time.

APPENDIX B

NEVIN DISCOVERS EXCEL
AS A RAPID PROTOTYPING TOOL

First Exposure

My first exposure to Excel as a software prototyping tool came while I was working at PeopleSoft as a senior interaction designer in the Financial Applications User Experience group. I was assigned to a project that was already well into the early stages of application design. The project team gave me some printouts of prototype screens representing the current state of the design so that I could review them and get up to speed with the design. The paper prototypes that I was given were clean and accurate, although their representation of the interface was a bit rough around the edges. Given that this was the early stage of the design process, the prototypes fulfilled their purpose and clearly described the interface.

While reviewing the screen printouts, I was curious about the tool that was used to build them, so I asked for the original files. Much to my surprise, Mark Miller, a lead engineer on the team, sent me an Excel file. This caught me off guard because I had always thought of Excel as the preferred program of accountants and managers working on budgets and analyses. Up to then I had never used Excel much and, unfortunately, had no time to learn more due to the accelerated development schedule for this project. I was left to review the paper printouts of the prototypes Mark made, penciling in design recommendations to the team. I did notice that no matter how quickly I sent the changes in, Mark created new corrected prototypes. I have always prided myself on being able to quickly turn around changes, so I was impressed with the agility and speed with which Mark updated these prototypes. I made a mental note to find out more about prototyping in Excel when I had the chance.

The early iterative design phase of the project was nearing its end and most of the pages had been sketched out. It then became my job to convert them to Dreamweaver as was PeopleSoft process at the time. I gathered up the latest printouts of the prototypes and spent about two weeks rebuilding them in Dreamweaver. PeopleSoft had created Dreamweaver design templates, which made the process relatively painless. When I had finished, I sent them to Mark for review. I received a very courteous note that thanked me for the attractive prototypes. But apparently in the time that it had taken me to build them, many of the concepts had been evolved by the developers and my prototypes were obsolete. I groaned, thinking about how much work it was going take to update them in addition to maintaining the Dreamweaver files going forward. I compared my prototypes with the newest

Excel prototypes and realized that there was no benefit in continuing with Dreamweaver. I then decided to abandon my Dreamweaver efforts and fall back to proofing the Excel prototypes that were still being updated on a daily basis.

My First Attempts with Excel

Soon after my involvement with the project ended, I decided to find out more about using Excel for prototyping. Mark gave me a 15-minute explanation on how he used Excel. As he explained the concept to me, I immediately saw how really quick and simple it was. A light bulb flashed on in my head and I had one of those "Got it!" epiphanies. I returned to my office with visions of Excel prototypes dancing in my head and quickly got to work.

After experimenting with Excel and making my own prototypes, I quickly realized that it was the simplest of Excel's rich feature set that made it so compelling for rapid prototyping. To build a prototype did not involve complicated Excel features such as coding or writing macros. Most of what I was doing was simple copying, pasting, coloring table cells, creating borders, and typing in text. It became apparent that what makes Excel an excellent spreadsheet application also helps make it a great prototyping application. The grid of rows and columns could be modified for prototyping purposes, making alignment of graphics and text a snap. Excel could easily handle imported graphics and allowed the ability to create simple graphics with its built-in set of tools. The tabbed worksheets could contain a large number of pages, allowing me to keep all my designs and design elements for a project in one file. The hypertext feature could be used to link the different pages together. Within a single Excel file I had the all the screen designs I created for my prototypes, all linked together to allow simulation of interactivity and navigation. Once I completed my prototype, I could then send the file or allow access to it anywhere in the world for viewing, collaboration, and design feedback.

A Test Case

I decided to build a test case of the Excel prototyping environment by creating a template based on the PeopleSoft interface. I was trying to spread my ideas by showing the template to various groups within PeopleSoft. There had been interest from developers who were already experts in Excel and saw it as an easy way to visualize their design ideas without having to use HTML (which they hated) and Microsoft Paint (which they found difficult to use). Some members of the user experience group quickly saw the value in this new approach and adapted it to their own work. However, many were skittish about opening to this new tool simply because it was Excel.

I had been perfecting my skills with the new Excel template I had evolved when I was drafted into a "dream team." It was a project that was, on one hand, very exciting because of the innovation and challenges associated with it, but at the same time it was ominous, because of the very, very tight deadline. The project directive came from on high, so it would have a great degree of visibility leaving little room for error. Early in the project I was called into a meeting where some early ideas needed prototyping on a quick turnaround basis. It was late Thursday afternoon, and the developers were on the hot seat. The prototypes needed to be delivered by the following Monday. There was general moaning and groaning because a weekend would be lost to work, and it seemed that even a full weekend would not allow enough time to complete the prototypes. It was then that I offered the idea of using the Excel template as a means to get the job done on time.

There was interest in what I had to offer, so a one-hour meeting was set up for 8:00 the next morning. I was all ready to give my usual one-hour demonstration to the team. Many doubted that I could help them, but since the boss was there, they showed up. I was about halfway through the demonstration when the meeting seemed to start breaking up. But before anyone left, they asked where they could get hold of the template.

The VP of engineering stayed and we talked. She explained that the meeting broke up earlier than expected because the team didn't need further explanation. They also had that "Got it!" experience and were ready to start using the Excel prototyping environment right away. Soon afterward I was assigned to another project. The VP of engineering made sure to stop by and thank me, letting me know that with the Excel tool, they were easily able to meet their deadline.

APPENDIX C

GLOSSARY

affordance A visual clue to the function of a user interface object.

assumption An unvalidated requirement.

audience A group of stakeholders intended to view or interact with a prototype. Audiences fall roughly into two categories: internal and external to the software creation and development team.

canvas An empty Excel worksheet page that has been prepared for prototyping.

characteristics Traits that define or characterize a prototype. Until recently, high and low fidelity, in addition to rapid, have been the primary traits of focus. Eight high-level prototyping characteristics are defined in Chapter 3 of *Effective Prototyping for Software Makers*: Fidelity (high-low per prototype content); Audience: internal/external; stage: early/midterm/late; Speed: rapid/diligent; Longevity: short/medium/long; Expression: conceptual/experiential; Fidelity: low/medium/high; Style: narrative/interactive; and Medium: physical/digital.

color key A color palette or graphical representation of the way colors are used within a prototype or design.

content The elements that make up a prototype, such as blocks of text, branding elements, icons, graphics, interaction controls, and so on.

design guidelines A set of design rules that inform the design and layout of screens. They do not guarantee a good design but rather provide guidance to achieve best-practice designs.

Dreamweaver An application that is used to create HTML-based user interfaces.

fidelity Prototyping characteristic: A degree of prototype detail and finish that conceptually represents real system user interface elements—graphics, text content, interactivity, functionality, and performance. Fidelity ranges from very low to very high. Each stage of prototyping contains design elements that can be represented by a mix of fidelities.

greeked text (greeking)   Latin text used to mock up the visual layout of editorial content in advance of the actual editorial content.

longevity   Prototyping characteristic: The life expectancy of a prototype, characterized as short, medium, or long.

mock up   A general term for any prototype.

MS Excel   Microsoft Excel, a spreadsheet application that can also be used for prototyping.

MS Office   Microsoft Office, a word processing application.

narrative   A story or sequence of events that describes how a user might interact with a software application or service.

product manager   A person who manages the conception, planning, deliverables, and production of a given product within a company.

prototype   A model used to represent a software and/or hardware idea for the purpose of exploring design concepts and determining their efficacy. Relative to various design objectives, prototypes can be rendered with varying degrees of completeness.

prototyper   Anyone who creates prototypes.

prototyping   Act of planning, conceptualizing, creating, and building prototypes.

rapid prototyping   A type of prototype conceived and built in a very short time frame.

requirement   A comprehensive description of the intended purpose and environment for software under development that fully describes what the software will do and how it will be expected to behave and perform. There are four fundamental requirement types: business/marketing, functional, technical, and usability. [1]

scenario   The description of a user activity or task in the form of a narrative presentation.

site map   A site map is a visual or textually organized model of a Website's content that allows users to navigate through the site to find the information they are looking for. [2]

storyboard   A narrative prototype, usually created in the early stages of the soft-ware-making process, to articulate business and marketing requirements in the form of a usage scenario or story.

template   A prepared set of Excel worksheets that are built from Excel canvas worksheets. Each template worksheet contains different reusable elements or groups of elements for a given prototype design.

thumbnails   Miniature versions of pages, graphics, or pictures used to make it eas-ier to visually scan and recognize them.

widget   A graphical user interface (GUI) element with which a user interacts.

wireframe   A GUI mockup, usually created in the beginning phases of the design process. It is often a sketch representation of a design concept with moderate to minimal detailing of the GUI elements.

workbook   A collection of Excel prototyping worksheets.

worksheet   A prototyping work area in Excel indicated by a tab.

References

[1] SearchSoftwareQuality.com Definitions, http://searchsoftwarequality.techtarget.com/sDefinition/0,,sid92_gci1243658,00.html, June 1, 2008.

[2] SearchSoftwareQuality.com Definitions, http://searchsoa.techtarget.com/sDefinition/0,,sid26_gci541375,00.html, June 1, 2008.

INDEX

A

Add Text, 32, 111, 102, 134, 178
Affordance, definition, 231
Alignment tab, 44, 47, 111, 172
All Contacts Toolbar, 213, 217, 219, 221
Annotation area
  communications needs, 167
  creation, 177–184
  disadvantages, 168
  hyperlinks, 180–182
  uses, 168
Assumption, definition, 231
Audience, definition, 231
AutoShapes tool, 102, 125–126, 128–130,
    140, 178, 193, 210

B

Background
  special background application, 207
  texture specification, 206
  tiling prevention, 207, 209
Basic page worksheet template, 155
Basic Shapes, 111, 125–126, 128–130, 178
Bolding, text, 25
Border tab, 29, 57, 59, 67, 210
Boxes and buttons worksheet
  creation in template, 56–63

iteration of prototype, 155, 159
  tab, 25, 27
BRD, *see* Business requirements
    document
Brightness, Formatting toolbar, 224
Business requirements document
    (BRD), 123
Buttons, *see* Boxes and buttons
    worksheet

C

Canvas
  creation for prototyping
    gridline hiding, 40–41
    overview, 39
    preparation, 39
    row and column dimension setting,
      42–43
  definition, 231
  storyboard prototyping, 97
  worksheet tab, 22–23
Case studies, prototyping with Excel, 5–6,
    94, 122–123
Cell
  color selection, 45, 49
  insertion and deletion, 213–215
  width setting, 42
Cell Reference, 145
Center Text, 61, 69